Counseling Persons of African Descent

MULTICULTURAL ASPECTS OF COUNSELING SERIES

VOLUMES IN THIS SERIES

1. **Increasing Multicultural Understanding (2nd edition):** A Comprehensive Model by Don C. Locke
2. **Preventing Prejudice:** A Guide for Counselors and Educators by Joseph G. Ponterotto and Paul B. Pedersen
3. **Improving Intercultural Interactions:** Modules for Cross-Cultural Training Programs edited by Richard W. Brislin and Tomoko Yoshida
4. **Assessing and Treating Culturally Diverse Clients (2nd edition):** A Practical Guide by Freddy A. Paniagua
5. **Overcoming Unintentional Racism in Counseling and Therapy:** A Practitioner's Guide to Intentional Intervention by Charles R. Ridley
6. **Multicultural Counseling With Teenage Fathers:** A Practical Guide by Mark S. Kiselica
7. **Multicultural Counseling Competencies:** Assessment, Education and Training, and Supervision edited by Donald B. Pope-Davis and Hardin L. K. Coleman
8. **Improving Intercultural Interactions:** Modules for Cross-Cultural Training Programs, Volume 2 edited by Kenneth Cushner and Richard W. Brislin
9. **Understanding Cultural Identity in Intervention and Assessment** by Richard H. Dana
10. **Psychological Testing of American Minorities (2nd edition)** by Ronald J. Samuda
11. **Multicultural Counseling Competencies: Individual and Organizational Development** by Derald Wing Sue et al.
12. **Counseling Multiracial Families** by Bea Wehrly, Kelley R. Kenney, and Mark E. Kenney
13. **Integrating Spirituality Into Multicultural Counseling** by Mary A. Fukuyama and Todd D. Sevig
14. **Counseling With Native American Indians and Alaska Natives:** Strategies for Helping Professionals by Roger D. Herring
15. **Diagnosis in a Multicultural Context:** A Casebook for Mental Health Professionals by Freddy A. Paniagua
16. **Psychotherapy and Counseling With Asian American Clients:** A Practical Guide by George K. Hong and MaryAnna Domokos-Cheng Ham
17. **Counseling Latinos and La Familia:** A Guide for Practitioners by Azara L. Santiago-Rivera, Patricia Arredondo and Maritza Gallardo-Cooper
18. **Counseling Persons of African Descent:** Raising the Bar of Practitioner Competence edited by Thomas A. Parham

Counseling Persons of African Descent

Raising the Bar of Practitioner Competence

Thomas A. Parham
University of California, Irvine

SAGE Publications
International Educational and Professional Publisher
Thousand Oaks ▪ London ▪ New Delhi

For information:

Sage Publications, Inc.
2455 Teller Road
Thousand Oaks, California 91320
E-mail: order@sagepub.com

Sage Publications Ltd.
6 Bonhill Street
London EC2A 4PU
United Kingdom

Sage Publications India Pvt. Ltd.
M-32 Market
Greater Kailash I
New Delhi 110 048 India

Printed in the United States of America

Library of Congress Cataloging-in-Publication Data

Main Entry Under Title:
Counseling persons of African descent: Raising the bar of practitioner excellence / edited by Thomas A. Parham.
p. cm. — (Multicultural aspects of counseling series; v. 18)
Includes bibliographical references and index.
ISBN 0-8039-5345-3
ISBN 0-8039-5346-1 (pbk.)
1. Mental health counseling. 2. African Americans—Counseling of. I. Parham, T. M. Jim (Thomas M. Jim) II. Series.
RC451.5.N4 C685 2002
616.89′14′08996073—dc21

2002000289

02 03 04 05 06 07 10 9 8 7 6 5 4 3 2 1

Acquiring Editors: Nancy Hale/Margaret Seawell
Editorial Assistant: Vonessa Vondera
Production Editor: Denise Santoyo
Copy Editor: Amy Kazilsky
Typesetter: Siva Math Setters, Chennai, India
Indexer: Teri Greenberg

Dedication

In the spirit of our African brothers and sisters, on whose shoulders we stand, we offer a drink and pour libations to the:

Creator—The source of all knowledge, truth, goodness, and everything that exists on the planet and in the Universe. We are thankful for all of the ways we have been blessed in our lives.

Ancestors—Whose names may not be known, but whose sacrifices will never be forgotten. We honor their sacrifices and struggles.

Elders—To Imhotep and Ptah Hotep; Hatshepsut and Nefertiti; Ramses and Amenhotep IV (Akhenaton); Malcolm X and Martin Luther King, Jr.; Sojourner Truth and Harriet Tubman; Nat Turner and Denmark Vessey; Marcus Garvey and Elijah Mohammed; Rosa Parks and Fannie Lou Hamer, all of whom taught lessons in strength, perseverance, struggle, tenacity, and community empowerment. To Robert L., Robert G., Na'im Akbar, Wade Nobles, Linda James Myers, A.J. and Nancy Boyd Franklin, Marimba Ani, William Cross, and Asa Hilliard for profoundly affecting my consciousness and blessing me with a friendship that endures and life lessons that continue to teach and inspire.

Children—The hope of any people is in the children. We who now occupy the adult corridors of the world hope to help create for you a future bright with possibilities.

Finally, this text is dedicated to my:

Mentors—To Joseph White, who saw in me genius and promise I couldn't see in myself and gave me a vision of hope, a road map of my future, and support that has been and continues to be unwaivering. To Horace Mitchell: who taught me about professionalism, conscious manhood, and reinforced the value of friendship. And to Janet Helms, who refined my skills, sharpened my intellect, and like a "Queen Mother," held me close until I was ready to sprout wings and fly.

Contents

Series Editor's Introduction

The literature on multicultural counseling has now gone beyond the level of supportive rhetoric and moved toward "raising the bar" of measured competence. Professor Thomas Parham has done an excellent job of showing us how that can be done with African American populations. This is not an easy job. Some of the more simplistic attempts to achieve measured competence have resulted in lists of rules that might "keep you out of trouble" but that do not reflect the deeper emotional and affective levels of multicultural counseling competence. The truth is, many majority counselors are "frightened" by their African American and minority clients and are perhaps primarily interested in protecting themselves as much as protecting the client.

For those counselors who don't care about doing the right thing, nothing will help; for those conscientious counselors who do care, even though they may be unintentionally making mistakes, this book will provide a valuable resource. It does, however, depend on the reader's intentional caring attitude in the first place. This book will provide specific strategies and techniques to put that caring attitude into practice beyond vague and general statements of support. It is important to understand that Thomas's primary objective is to empower those caring counselors, increase their success, and multiply their job satisfaction. This book is directed toward making the job of caring counselors easier and not more difficult.

Although this book is about African American culture, it has a generic application for the reader to generalize the ideas presented to other cultural groups and to the reader's own professional self-awareness. The book represents a kind of journey for Thomas, visiting different sad as well as happy places in his life and professional context. The reader benefits vicariously from his journey through an enriched text. The result has been an African-centered worldview that will help readers discover their own sometimes similar, and sometimes different, worldview. Reading this book will be a journey for the reader just as writing the book has been a journey for Thomas.

Thomas recruited excellent authors to write chapters in this book, leading the way with his own introductory chapter. Cheryl Grills does an excellent job of identifying the indigenous and unique features of African-centered psychology in specific rather than general terms. Thomas and William Parham build a conceptual framework on those basic assumptions followed by a chapter by Thomas Parham on how to measure those conceptual features. Ezemenari Obasi applies the conceptual framework to the notion of the "self" and how a reconceptualized notion of self is essential to personal or professional competence. Cheryl Grills continues to build the conceptual framework combining the notions of self and consciousness in a new "Akan Model." Thomas describes other models that can be built on the African-centered perspective for use in counseling. Michael Connor ties this conceptual framework in with the role of the family, and particularly the role of African American fathers, for successful counseling. Finally, Thomas Parham ends the book with a discussion of this new level of competence for counseling, synthesizing the different conceptual models of the previous chapters.

The *Multicultural Aspects of Counseling* book series has become like a multivolume encyclopedia on multicultural counseling and each new volume in that series builds on the comprehensive coverage of the series as a whole. Thomas's book is consistent with the practical and applied focus of the *MAC* book series. The books in this series seek to go beyond the obvious aspects of multicultural counseling and struggle with basic underlying assumptions that shape the field and the practice of counseling. The *MAC* series is attempting to fill in the gaps in the multicultural counseling literature and this book does an excellent job of contributing to that process.

Paul B. Pedersen
University of Hawaii

Preface

There is a popular rhythm and blues song that counts down the 6 months, 8 days, and 12 hours since one lover has been away from another. That cadence begins to capture the sentiment behind the writing of this text. Although the appreciation of this expression requires a contextual shift from romantic relationships to one of intellectual enterprise, the story about the process dynamics and the journey to the completion of this book are no less interesting.

This project began almost eight years ago with an invitation from two colleagues, Dr. Paul Pedersen and Dr. Joe Ponterotto, to contribute to a series of books proposed by Sage Publications titled *Multicultural Aspects of Counseling*. Subsequently, my brother and I submitted a proposal to Sage outlining our intent to produce a book that would deal with the specific mental health issues related to people of African descent. This text was not intended to be a resource that would be relegated to virtual obscurity within a few years because of its irrelevance. Rather, we set out to produce a text that would break new ground and explore new territory in defining and treating mental health issues for African American people.

At that time, the profession seemed to be struggling less with the notion of being culturally sensitive with African American populations and more with trying to develop and understand specific strategies and techniques that clinicians and others could use to effectively intervene with the African American clients they were serving. With that in mind, we set out to produce the text you now see.

Along the way, we experienced a bit of a struggle between two competing forces. On one side was interest, excitement, anticipation, and the ability to produce the text proposed to Sage. On the other side were forces intent on reminding us that in spite of our excitement about the possibilities of producing this text, life happens. As editors for this text, it was our responsibility to keep the projects moving and the contributors focused on completing their tasks. The first drafts of the early chapters of the book began to take shape and the project began to take on real form and substance. Unfortunately, our trip down the road of this academic endeavor intersected at the corner of conflict avenue. Time became shorter and schedule demands increased. Invitations to trainings, consultations, and speaking engagements around the country began to eat away at the time otherwise allocated for writing.

Beyond the professional endeavors, personal circumstance also began to dominate our life space. In the span of approximately four and a half years, my (Thomas) mother-in-law passed away, I required extensive spinal surgery and recovery, my wife developed breast cancer requiring surgery and treatment, and my mother developed an illness that she ultimately succumbed to some seven months later. Subsequent to my mother's passing, my brother Bill's daughter, Khalia, was diagnosed with Type I diabetes and his father-in-law passed away following an extended bout with cancer. Subsequently, he reduced his role on this project to that of contributor. Indeed, life happens along the road to dreams and aspirations.

There is a piece of African wisdom I have stylized over time and I'm fond of quoting, one which says that *life at its best is a creative synthesis of opposites in fruitful harmony*. Although this pearl of wisdom has several interpretations, one of those suggests that disappointment and setback oftentimes breed opportunity and possibility. Throughout my academic life, I have been trained, nurtured, and mentored by some of the best minds in this country. The contributors to this text and I have all been blessed to acquire an extensive array of knowledge and information that could be used in effectively treating African American clients. However, something wasn't quite right. Perhaps the extensive life circumstance that so dominated my intellectual, emotional, behavioral, and spiritual space was a way for the ancestors to subtly, and not so subtly, suggest that the time for producing this text was not quite right. Yet, when I thought about backing out of the project, Drs. Ponterotto and Pedersen were there with an empathic ear, supportive questions, and a reaffirming voice that said you are the one that must complete this project. To them, I am very grateful.

In retrospect, it is true that the years it has taken to produce this project have also allowed me to gain much deeper and richer insights into the treatment of African American people. Of particular note are my travels to Africa, where I had an opportunity to witness firsthand how African-centered principles were and are implemented by African people in different generations. In the summer of 1999, I was blessed to travel to Kemet (Egypt) with brother Asa Hilliard, a renowned scholar, teacher, author, and Kemetologist. There, I was not only exposed to the genius of African people, but I was also able, for the first time in my life, to center my intellectual theories and constructs in time, space, and people who were themselves testaments to the correctness of an African-centered ideology. Accordingly, this text has been influenced by my studies in ancient Kemetic civilizations and culture, and readers of this text will find that information appropriately integrated.

In the summer of 2000, I was blessed to travel with my colleagues in the Association of Black Psychologists to Ghana, in West Africa. Beyond the emotional elation we felt at being home for the first time in nearly 400 years and visiting the slave dungeons of Elmina and Cape Coast, it was an eye-opening experience about how the culture of African descent people is manifest on the continent of Africa itself. Travels to other lands (e.g., Japan, France, Switzerland, England, Canada) experienced by other authors have provided an additional perspective of African descent people within the context of other cultures. As such, readers will find that information incorporated into the text in meaningful ways. Clearly, we are different people as a result of our travels, life experiences, and academic pursuits, and it is my belief that you, the reader, will be better served by this intellectual endeavor because of the richness of those experiences.

And so, what have I learned in our newfound discoveries? Clearly, an African-centered worldview provides the conceptual pillars around which we build our beliefs, perceptions, intuitions, about the nature of reality. The African-centered worldview is bolstered by and built on several fundamental principles and assumptions:

- There is a spiritual essence that permeates everything that exists on the planet.
- Everything in the world is interconnected and in concert with the principle of consubstantiation (elements of the universe are of the same substance).
- The collective is the most salient element of existence.
- Self-knowledge is the key to mental health (Parham, White, & Ajamu, 1999).

Thus, the culture of African descent people, which provides for them a design for living and a pattern for interpreting reality, is based on these principles.

In consolidating the ancient and historical African worldviews, we have also come to understand that where African descent people are concerned, we have learned that:

- There is a rhythm and order to life that demands, or at least requires, alignment with those forces within the universe.
- Each of us is a seed of divinely inspired possibility that when nurtured in its proper context can and will grow into the fullest expression of all we are supposed to become.

- We all must discover our destiny or passion in life and align our consciousness with it (*ori-ire*). The alignment produces a healthy, ordered integration of the various aspects of the self.
- The spirit, energy, and life force in each of us is also comprised of a self-healing power. Thus, when one's spirit, cognitions, feelings, and behaviors are misaligned or out of balance, we have the capacity to restore healing and comfort to our lives (Fu-Kiau, 1991).
- Therapists and counselors are really *healers* who serve as a conduit through which spiritual energy flows. Thus, healing and the restoration of balance and harmony occur *through* healers, not because of them. Healers participate with clients in confronting their mental, physical, emotional, behavioral, and spiritual debilitations.
- There is a spiritual essence that permeates everything that exists on the planet. Human authenticity, then, is having a sense of one's origin (cultural essence) and the indisputable and irrevocable connection to that which brought you into existence: the spirit of God (Nobles, 1986).
- The psyche of African descent people is comprised of several interrelated parts or dimensions. These include a soul, a personal self, a tribal self, a social self, and a physical self.
- The task of a healer is to heal thyself, know thyself, remember the past, access the spirit, and confront the *maafa*.
- The nature of African people is essentially *divine*. This divinity is not so much in elevation to God-like omnipotence, but rather, is reflected in the desire to be God-like in aspiration (i.e., *maat*).
- Despite how oppressive the nature of reality can be, African people have always been able to generate and sustain some movement and momentum represented by struggle and a quest for liberation. Therapeutically, then, we come to understand that as clients avail themselves of the counseling process, it represents their struggle against those forces that contaminate their lives. In having their say about the psychic and spiritual abrasions they have suffered, they tell us that they refuse to give misery the final word in their life circumstances. As my brother, Cornel West, reminds us, "We should never allow misery to have the last word."
- Disorder occurs when one's sense of self loses harmony with one's healing power or energy, the global unit's social body, and the consciousness (collective) of one's people.

And so, this text is as much about perseverance through adversity as anything else. It represents the best of our thinking to date about this discipline we call African psychology and its related manifestations. Chapter 1 begins to summarize issues in counseling African Americans and talks about the current state of affairs. Here, information focuses on the need and rationale for an African-centered worldview in the treatment of African people as well as a mental health profile of clients of African descent.

Chapter 2 introduces the reader to the basic principles of an African-centered psychological perspective. Chapter 3 discusses the necessity for new conceptual paradigms. Here the authors argue that attempts to effectively treat African American clients cannot be successful if these attempts rely solely on seasoning traditional Eurocentric theories and constructs with the cultural flavor of an African worldview. Rather, if theories are the road maps that guide our therapeutic interventions, then those theories must be supported by a new set of constructs and principles that are anchored in a reality specific to African descent people.

Chapters 4, 5, and 6 provide the reader with more conceptual depths into the personality dynamics of African descent people. These chapters are less concerned with finding consensus or agreement about the one theory or set of principles and constructs that captures African American personality and cultural realities. Rather, they expand the notion of within-group variability by exposing the reader to different models and conceptual systems used to understand the personality dynamics of Black people. In this regard, you will find some exciting possibilities as you explore the ancient Kemetic worldview as well as a more historical African worldview that are anchored in the tribal Akan and Yoruba systems of belief.

Chapter 7 attempts to provide a specific model that can be used to guide the therapeutic work of clinicians. In suggesting that the two most important questions in therapy are "what" and "how," this chapter attempts to walk the reader through what needs to happen in therapy and what specific techniques can be used to accomplish that therapeutic goal. In a similar fashion, Chapter 8 continues with specific intervention strategies but focuses the intervention on a population that has been underserved in the context of mental health service delivery. That population is African American fathers.

Chapter 9 begins to summarize the text with an invitation to "raise the bar." Raising the bar recognizes that the typical standards of psychological reform, despite how progressive they may seem, represent a low-bar approach to effective intervention. The knowledge contained in the first eight chapters should allow students and professionals alike to not only redefine notions of competence but raise the bar of what passes for appropriate therapeutic intervention with African American people.

Without question, the field of African psychology has taken center stage with cultural diversity initiatives. The amount of information that is now available is helping to redefine notions of mental health, mental illness, appropriate assessment, and culturally congruent therapeutic intervention. The road to becoming more culturally competent with African American people is not an easy one. It is not possible to read one book or attend one workshop and consider yourself sufficiently informed to be labeled an expert. Rather, real competence requires mastery, and mastery requires time. It requires time to read, time to study, and time to experience the reality of a new conceptual worldview. The journey to greater levels of expertise is an exciting one. I hope that this contribution, in some small way, will make your travels down that road a little easier, while simultaneously "raising the bar" of what passes for competence.

Thomas A. Parham, Ph.D.

Foreword

The practice of therapy and healing does not begin in a vacuum. Like all human activities, it begins in a specific context. A "one-size-fits-all" approach to the provision of mental health services is more likely to harm than heal. Years ago, Fanon sounded an alert about political and ethnocentric professional practice, "The unilaterally decreed normative value of European culture deserves our careful attention" (Fanon, 1965).

I am highly honored to have the opportunity to write this foreword. I have the highest respect for the authors and have had the opportunity to work closely with some of them. The work that they have done here is indeed seminal. They wade into the difficult territory of clarification of ideas, assumptions, models, and practices and a construction of a valid foundation for professional practice in psychology, psychiatry, and related services.

All of the behavioral sciences, in their current form, were born and developed during the global phenomena of slavery, colonization, and White supremacy ideology. The ubiquities of these forces, over the course of nearly four centuries, have left their mark on everything: ideology, theory, values, and practices in behavioral sciences including psychology. There is a robust body of literature documenting the existence of these insults and the consequences of this hegemony, a confounding of politics, science, and professional practice (Gould, 1981; Guthrie, 1976; Hilliard, 1997; Kamin, 1974; Smith, 2001).

A central part of this confounding of politics, science, and professional practice is a misunderstanding and politically inspired misuse of human culture, especially its varied manifestations throughout the world. Fanon's alert sprang from his understanding of the struggle in Algeria to be a healer, a professional in the ugly theater of French colonial domination. This domination forged the dehumanization of Africans as its primary strategy, the crushing of souls and spirits. The only way for this strategy to have worked was to base it on academic legitimation.

This book is about rescue. It is about resistance. It is truth telling about the African cultural and political experience. Above all, it is about healing, about making whole.

Within its pages, we see the struggle of the authors to break out of the conceptual incarceration learned from systems that were and still are rooted in hegemonic ideologies, philosophies, and theories that were designed to elevate Europeans at the expense of dominated populations. The authors seek to modify and to create new philosophical, theoretical, and practical tools, tools that depoliticize professional practice as much as is possible and that advance the healing arena based on cultural truth.

The authors are correct—the central issue is one of competence of professionals when dealing with people of African ancestry. Any approach to healing for African people must, of necessity, begin with *who* rather than *what* Africans are. In Western psychology, there is virtually no understanding of who Africans are. Even a cursory view of psychological literature reveals the abysmal ignorance of African historical and cultural reality, on the African continent or in its connected diaspora, including the United States.

A brief glance at the bibliographies in mainstream psychological texts and other literature will show two very distinct deficiencies. One is the absence of valid and relevant cultural material on African people. In part this is due to the Western ideological commitment to individualism in which personality but not culture is of interest. For Western- or European-centered psychology, the African as a member of an ethnic group does not exist. An alternative reason is that those who use the field to dominate Africans and others actually must calculate to destroy African culture, not to acknowledge or to affirm it.

The second deficiency in European-centered psychology is the absence of an awareness of the important work by psychologists and psychiatrists of African descent who have gone far beyond their standard training to develop and to include culturally salient materials pertaining to people of African ancestry. They have also constructed powerful paradigms, definitions, and assumptions that differ fundamentally from European psychology. They have created approaches that have resulted in powerful professional services.

At the outset, the central issue before us is *the existence of African people as a people.* It is an issue of *ethnicity and cultural identities*. The primary hegemonic strategy under slavery, colonization, and White supremacy ideology was the *reduction of a cultural people to their finite "racial," social class, or oppressed condition*. Thus, they became, "the

Black," "the poor," "the oppressed," or the "minority." Of course, their derivatives are "the disadvantaged," "the inner-city," "the at-risk," and so forth. Although each of these may have meaning, *the reduction of African essence to them is a scientific error of major proportion*, stripping heritage, ethnic bonds, worldview from our understanding of who African people are (Hilliard, 1997).

It is essential that we call attention to the record here of the extensive and well documented White supremacy uses of science and behavioral science in particular. Those uses continue to the present time (Herrenstein & Murray, 1994). It is for that reason that we must articulate the hegemonic influences on the discipline, studying them as *ever-present intervening variables* in professional practice and in the social environments that we study.

However, that is far from sufficient. Yes, we must articulate White supremacy ideology and behavior and we must articulate White supremacy psychology and psychotherapy. But this is still not enough. We must articulate the realities of African life in the past and in the present, on the African continent and in the diaspora. We cannot fall victim to false glorification of and nonempirical rhetoric about African people anywhere. We must rely on the enormous empirical record. To be ignorant of the vital record of African culture, or to ignore it, is a *scientific error*, not merely an "inequity" or "fairness" issue.

In understanding the African cultural reality, we display our understanding that *there is no normative population anywhere in the world.* Certainly, Western European behavior is not normative, nor is European American behavior normative, except for Europeans. All human behaviors are rooted in a context that has evolved out of their own unique experiences. For professionals, there can be no attack on or minimization of the culture of any group, including European culture. Any attack by Africans is on European *hegemony* over African culture and African people, not on European culture nor European-centered thinking. It is just that the thinking and culture hold no authority over Africans. The *bias* issue is the small one. The ignorance issue is the big one.

On the African side, clarification about identity and its behavioral meaning as a cultural reality is critical. We must recognize that people of African ancestry have choices. At the core of the choices is the question "To be African or not to be."

Many people of African ancestry, whether they use the name African or not, have been and continue to be African in behavior, maintaining cultural connections to traditions. Other Africans have, sometimes quite consciously, chosen alternatives to their own historical identity, and have made their commitment to resocialize or "integrate" themselves into other cultural contexts. Some even choose to reject any conscious association with African people at all, occasionally even becoming what Dr. Naim Akbar has called "Anti-Self" along with "Alien Self." Still others exhibit identity confusion. Some simply choose not to choose. Those alternatives are simply the realities of the adjustment of people of African ancestry to their contemporary conditions. No choices can or should be forced. They simply must be recognized as the realities that they are.

These are the things that those who reduce African people to their pigment, their "race," or "racial identity" overlook or ignore. These are things that deal with *who* the person is. Ultimately, this is the question of the humanity and worldview of people of African ancestry. After all, it was the attack on African humanity and the worldview of the African that was at the core of the hegemonic strategy of European exploiters.

Within the text, Dr. Parham quotes Fanon, who says that the identity question contains a response to three queries: " Who am I? Am I who I say I am? Am I all that I ought to be?" European-centered psychology responds to these questions only on the individual "personality" level. Currently, they are almost totally incapable of helping people of African ancestry to answer these questions. European-centered Europeans and European-centered Africans cannot accept these as valid questions.

The rescue attempted here is to seek better options in defining what is healthy and what is healing. This will be a long-term struggle. This book is a very strong beginning. It provides documentation, description, and interpretation of things that are almost totally outside of mainstream Western psychology, such as an African worldview, value system, and understanding about what it means to be human. It combines the insights of students of culture, students of African descent, both on the continent and in the diaspora. In some cases, this is work that is rooted in innovative clinical uses of our cultural traditions in therapy, nurturing, and teaching, on the African continent and in the diaspora.

This is cutting edge work, putting the pieces back together again. This is work that goes far beyond justifiable criticism of European hegemony and worldview. It is work that offers something essential to people of African ancestry, and even something essential to anyone in the world.

Even though there is much more to be done—more criticism, more documentation of African cultural reality, more validation of therapeutic approaches, more creative application of our understandings of culture—this book can, and I predict will, serve very important heuristic functions. The views provided here do indeed open fresh possibilities and allow open-minded psychologists, both African and others, to see possibilities for becoming more competent, more culturally salient, and in doing so, to have a model that applies to other cultural and ethnic groups as well.

If there is universalism, it will occur at the level of cultural deep structure, not at the surface. Particular manifestations of humanity are just that. Only arrogance and hegemonic intent can explain the blind application of particular experiences of humanity as if they were valid global models. This work is a major contribution to breaking the back of that fantasy.

We all have much to learn. I am impressed by the way the authors of this book have attempted to synthesize a wide range of diverse ideas, even diverse ideas within the African community. I am impressed by their critical, honest, and open examination of their own ideas. One thing must be emphasized and that is that for those authors who I know very well, and I suspect for all of them, the views expressed in this text are not merely abstract and theoretical. They actually are manifest in the day-to-day personal and professional lives of the authors. They have made transcontinental cultural connections, academically, in their therapeutic work and in their service and lives in their communities. They have been involved in African and African American communities, in healing activities that go far beyond the therapists' office, to such things as rites of passages, and assisting organizations to become more conscious and more effective and salient to their communities. In that sense, what is on paper here is a reflection of a reality of success and commitment by the authors.

Yes, T. Parham, W. Parham, Connor, Grills, Obasi, and Ajei give us models of how to put the family back together again, and to restore health to the broken body. They offer the leadership *to make us whole.*

—*Asa G. Hilliard III Nana Baffour Amankwatia II*

References

Fanon, F. (1965). *A dying colonialism*. New York: Evergreen.

Gould, S. J. (1981). *The mismeasure of man*. New York: W.W. Norton.

Guthrie, R.G. (1976). *Even the rat was white.* New York: Harper and Row.

Herrenstein, R. J., & Murray, C. (1994). *The bell curve: Intelligence and class structure in American life*. New York: Free Press.

Hilliard, A. G. (1997). *SBA: The reawakening of the African mind.* Gainesville, FL: Makare Publishing.

Kamin, L. (1974). *The science and politics of IQ*. New York: John Wiley and Sons.

Smith, L. T. (2001). *Decolonizing methodologies: Research and indigenous peoples*. New York: Zed Books Ltd.

Healing is therapeutic, but not all therapy is healing.

—Thomas Parham

1

Counseling African Americans

The Current State of Affairs

Thomas A. Parham

"Life at its best is a creative synthesis of opposites in fruitful harmony."

—African proverb

The anticipation of receiving one's doctorate degree or professional license to practice psychology is great indeed, for it signals the arrival at the door of professional competence. Once the degree or certification has been awarded and the threshold crossed, numerous opportunities await. As professionals, we seek to showcase and demonstrate the skills and knowledge learned through years of study, and counseling and clinical training gained in the graduate institutions of psychology, counseling, education, social work, psychiatry, or some related mental health field. Usually, this work is carried out in the mental health centers, hospitals, counseling centers, and academic departments in communities throughout the United States.

Yet, the paradox of our position as professional psychologists, psychiatrists, social workers, and counselors is that although we have amassed a number of classes and applied counseling hours, in many ways we are less prepared to provide services to certain populations. Franklin (1975) was clear that training that was restricted to Eurocentric psychological paradigms and worldviews would potentially render the African American clinician—young, gifted, and Black—with inappropriate professional preparation. The question of professional authenticity is one that is not restricted to African American mental health services providers alone. Indeed, service providers, irrespective of race and gender, need to similarly question their levels of competence for providing psychological interventions to populations they are not specifically trained to serve.

The invitation to question one's level of competence for providing mental health services has also been extended beyond early career practitioners to practitioners (irrespective of race and gender) presumed to possess advanced levels of counseling and clinical skills (Parham, 2001). For those who ask why, you have only to peruse the following case study and then review the mental health practices of the past three and a half decades for the answer.

This text is designed to address the more pragmatic aspects of our work with African American clients. Accordingly, we begin with a case presentation that is intended to stimulate your thinking. After you review it, we invite you to answer just the "general questions." Afterward, review the "culturally specific" questions and try to discern the areas of convergence and divergence in your thinking.

Case Study

Roland (a pseudonym) is a 29-year-old African American male (self-identified) residing in a medium-sized urban area. He has been encouraged by his wife to seek treatment because they are concerned about his recent behavior: He is constantly on edge, frequently agitated and angry, and otherwise moody. He has also begun to spend more time away from home, involving himself in assorted activities (working out, etc.). This pattern has persisted for approximately two months and seems to coincide with a change in Roland's job three months ago when he was assigned a new supervisor. Roland has been with this company for four and a half years.

His new supervisor (a 44-year-old White male) exhibits a management style characterized by little encouragement, praise, or support. Instead, Roland receives constant critique, autocratic directives, and feels he is being constantly watched. Even though his work performance has been rated as "good" and he has been a steady performer, he now believes he is being targeted and unfairly treated because of his race.

In addition, Roland has also begun to doubt his own sense of competence and worth, despite believing he does a reasonably good job. He is oriented times four and looking for help to resolve some of his emotional distress. Roland has no previous psychiatric history and denies the use of any substances (alcohol or drugs).

General Questions

Roland is assigned to you for short-term therapy where you agree to treat him. Assume that you employ a cognitive-behavioral orientation in his treatment.

1. What is the etiology of his distress?
2. What is the target of your intervention?
3. What is your role as a therapist?
4. What assumptions do you make about how and why change will occur?

Culturally Specific Questions

1. What theoretical assumptions are made that may run counter to his cultural worldview?
2. What factors (variables) may inhibit or facilitate the process of therapy?
3. What do you know about the cultural manifestations of psychological symptoms and how might that change your diagnostic conclusions or treatment strategy?
4. What is the standard of normality for African American people and how might it be used to assist this client in achieving some sense of healing?

Having now reflected on these questions and case study, let us now turn our attention to how the mental health system has historically treated people like Roland.

Historical Overview

Over the past several decades, there has been increasing attention in the literature on providing psychological services to culturally different populations (LaFromboise & Rowe, 1983; Leong, 1986; Padilla, 1980; Padilla & DeSnyder, 1985; Pedersen, 1985, 1988; Ponterotto, 1986; Sue, D. W., 1981; Sue, D. W., & Zane, 1987; Sue, S., 1988; Westwood & Ishyman, 1990; Wrenn, 1962, 1985). Until the mid-1960s, the professions of psychology and counseling demonstrated little interest in the status of culturally different people. However, by the mid-1970s, these fields began to recognize the unique counseling and therapy needs of ethnic minority populations (Atkinson, Morton, & Sue, 1989). Before this time, it was commonly believed that work involving ethnic minorities was only validated if a comparison to Whites was included (Peoples & Dell, 1975; Webster & Fretz, 1978). And so, much of the earlier research conducted by ethnic scholars themselves was focused on a critique of traditional counseling theories and approaches (Atkinson, 1983, 1985; Atkinson, Morten, & Sue, 1979; Block, 1980; Brislin, 1981; Casas, 1985; Dillard, 1985; Ibrahim & Kahn, 1987; Ivey, 1987; Sue, 1981, 1988).

A quick examination of the literature reveals a multitude of topics and several general themes that minority scholars used to echo their concerns about issues of culturally different people in a therapy context. Among these topics were questions about the appropriate mix of cross-ethnic counseling (Vontress, 1971); testing of minority children (Williams, 1972; Williams & Mitchell, 1980); the need for more systemic approaches in counseling practices (Gunnings & Simpkin, 1972); the counselor preference of minority students (Banks, Berenson, & Carkhuff, 1967; Jackson & Kirshner, 1973; Harrison, 1975; Parham & Helms, 1981); and the help-seeking behaviors and underuse of psychological services by culturally different people (Acosta, 1980; Sue, 1981). Vontress (1971), for example, raised questions about the appropriateness of White counselors providing therapeutic services to Black clients. Essentially, he argued that the culture and ethnic differences between service providers and their clients made establishing healthy relationships extremely difficult.

Williams (1972) called attention to the issues of testing African American children, highlighting the detrimental effects such practice had on Black children's self-image, school performance, long-term labeling, and career aspirations. Not only were the testing instruments seen as (and subsequently proven to be) biased, they were also not valid or reliable standards for assessing the IQ or personality constructs they purported to measure. Similarly, Williams and Mitchell (1980) raised concerns about the fairness of the entire testing practice and enterprise, commenting that educational institutions as well as corporate test producers share responsibility for the harm caused to Black children.

Gunnings and Simpkin (1972) appropriately recognized that specific therapeutic interventions could and should not be confined to individual or intrapsychic domains. Rather, they argued that social, political, and economic factors that negatively affected the lives of Black clients must also become the focus of more systemically oriented counseling practices. In echoing a similar theme years later, Atkinson, Morten, and Sue (1989) claimed that counselors might be insensitive if they employed strict intrapsychic views to client's problems when working with culturally diverse groups. In correctly noting that traditional models stress that client problems are located within the clients themselves, they recognize that too often the target of clinical therapeutic interventions were directed internally. In actuality, what counselors and psychologists should be exploring, according to these writers, was the possibility that client concerns or problems were not intrapsychic at all, but rather related to their victimization by an oppressive society. Consequently, counselors might need to affect the client's environment in a way that helps the client master whatever difficulty he or she is confronting. In addition to the recommendation for modified approaches to service delivery, the profession also struggled with the question of who best to provide services to culturally specific populations. In that regard, preferences expressed by the client for a particular service provider have also been a topic of discussion in literature.

Parham and Helms (1981) sought to enhance the utility of the counselor preference debate by using racial identity attitudes rather than simply racial designation (Banks, Berenson, & Carkhuff, 1967; Harrison, 1975) as variables to predict client preferences for demographic profiles of the service providers. Also, Acosta (1980) and Sue (1981) focused on the fact that despite the number of culturally different clients that benefit from therapy, a high percentage of them who participated in therapy self-terminated treatment after the initial session. One could conclude that clients generally, and ethnic clients in particular, were being underserved and that they underused psychological and counseling services in communities across the country.

The general themes that seem to emanate from this body of research focus on two main issues: (a) calling attention to the need for more culturally diverse perspectives in counseling and (b) reacting to racist and stereotypic notions and practices perpetuated by practitioners and researchers in the counseling and psychology fields. Although each of these general themes were necessary to underscore the importance of addressing issues affecting culturally different people, one limitation of such a broad focus in research was the tendency to overgeneralize. As a result, many scholars are now calling for much more cultural specificity in theoretical constructs, research strategies, and treatment modalities (Boyd-Franklin, 1989; Nobles, 1986; Parham, 1989). It is important, therefore, that we move beyond the confines of generic multicultural counseling philosophy and begin to explore, as many of our predecessors did, more culturally specific models and techniques. This text is devoted, then, to the discussion of specific therapeutic models, paradigms, and techniques that are appropriate for use with an African American population.

Assessment of Personal and Collective Debilitations

The counseling and psychological literature has now begun to demand (Sanchez-Hucles, 2000; Sue & Sue, 1999) and expect (Lee, 1997; Pedersen, 1999) service providers to be more culturally sensitive when treating African Americans in general. Although these expectations seem reasonable, they become less cogent in the absence of some understanding about what disorders clinicians should be treating. It is therefore appropriate to discuss issues of mental health and mental illness among the African American population.

Historically, African descent people have been characterized as a population plagued with higher rates of mental illness when compared to their White counterparts (Adebimpe, 1981). However, more than a decade before this work by Adebimpe, many of these same conclusions were supported by studies whose methodologies were seriously flawed, questionable, or both (Fisher, 1969). Kardiner and Ovesey (1951), for example, reported that the social context in which American Black people found themselves created pervasive personality traits characterized by a "mark of oppression." Similarly, St. Clair (1951) and Rosen and Frank (1962) not only implied that Blacks were hypersensitive to racial issues, but also concluded that Black clients were psychologically warped and difficult cases to treat (Banks, 1980). That such conclusions could be reached without more definitive study is interesting, to say the least. Yet, when one considers Fisher's (1969) critique of this body of literature, it is easy to understand how flawed the research was.

Fisher essentially argued that (a) mental illness rates were based on incidents and prevalence data and (b) that incidents and prevalence data were obtained from state-supported versus private-funded psychiatric facilities. He believed that these factors helped skew the data because of the overrepresentation of African Americans and other poor people in state mental health facilities. When these factors were coupled with the higher likelihood of misdiagnosis and misclassification of African descent people by primarily White clinicians, obvious biases began to emerge.

More contemporary literature continues to document the potential for and actual incidents of misdiagnosis of African American clients (Akbar, 1981; Block, 1980; Kambon, 1992; Parham, White, & Ajamu, 1999). Yet, if we are to gain some insight into mental health and mental illness issues, we must rely on some data to inform our thinking.

In 1981, Eton, Regier, Locke, and Taub conducted one of the largest surveys of national mental health trends for the National Institute of Mental Health (NIMH). This report studied five catchment areas across the country, including Los Angeles, California; Durham, North Carolina; St. Louis, Missouri; Baltimore, Maryland; and New Haven, Connecticut. Data from that survey have been analyzed by several authors (Snowden, 1999; Zhang & Snowden, 1999) and reported in the most recent literature. These data provided one of the best pictures of mental illness rates among African Americans as well as other ethnic groups.

In reporting on the relationship between ethnicity and mental disorders, Zhang and Snowden (1999) found that African Americans were less likely than Whites to have major depressive episodes, major depression, dysthymia, obsessive-compulsive disorder, drug and alcohol use or dependence, antisocial personality, and anorexia nervosa. Conversely, they found African Americans to have higher incidences of phobias and somatization complaints when compared to their other ethnic counterparts. Zhang and Snowden further found no significant differences between African Americans and Asians, Hispanics, and Whites in incidences of manic, bipolar, schizophrenia, and schizophreniform disorders.

A report from the Office of the Surgeon General of the United States (U. S. Department of Health and Human Services, 2001) offers a similar, but slightly contradictory, analysis of mental health trends and African Americans. Their data suggest that mental illness rates may be slightly higher in African Americans than in other groups. Furthermore, they suggest that African Americans may be underrepresented in outpatient services but overrepresented in accessing hospital emergency rooms for mental health concerns.

Despite the thoroughness of the report, it too, like much of the literature, suffers from one or two questionable assumptions. One of these is that progress in the areas of brain research and biological bases of behavior is the most promising aspect of modern psychological research. I, however, would argue that although promising, that focus helps to reinforce the perspective that the etiology of mental disorders rests with individuals rather than social pathology and people's reactions to it.

The report does, however, make several broad generalizations that I wish to support. First, we know more about treating mental illness than how to prevent it. Second, the mental health field is plagued by disparities in access to treatment. Finally, poverty and socioeconomic class are related to mental illness in a significant way. In addition to these assertions, it is also essential to recognize that despite progress in mental health treatment, we know so very little about treating African Americans in a culturally specific context; that the field is plagued not simply by disparities in access, but also disparities in treatment methods and modalities; and that poverty alone is not the only social pathology related to mental illness.

Although the mental health-mental illness profile of African Americans is an important picture to assess, equally important is how African Americans are treated once they access the mental health system. Data from national studies indicate that African Americans continue to receive differential treatment when compared to their White counterparts and that treatment differences can be attributed to factors such as race and income. Melfi, Croghan, and Hanna (1997) found that when treated for depression, for example, African American Medicare recipients were more likely to receive older tricyclic antidepressants and less psychotherapy. Conversely, they found that White, privately insured patients received a newer selective serotonin reuptake inhibitors (SSRIs) and higher rates of psychotherapy in their treatment for depression.

Cultural Debilitations

Despite the remarkably comprehensive data sets used to develop the mental health–mental illness profiles listed above, problems still remain.

Classification of African descent people using terms and constructs developed for and used by a European American oriented profession assumes a universality that may not be accurate. Most, if not all, of the conditions or diagnostic labels used to classify mental disorders come from diagnostic nosologies (e.g., DSM-IV or theoretical orientations) that have not been normed or influenced by cultural standards that differ from those of White populations. Even the latest attempt to infuse some cultural information into the DSM-IV diagnostic system is, at best, substandard. Obviously, this raises the question of whether African descent people can be appropriately and accurately classified and diagnosed using these systems (Atwell & Azibo, 1991; White, 1972; White & Parham, 1990). Given the track record of psychology and psychiatry to misdiagnose Black clients (Thomas & Sillen, 1972), these concerns are more than justified.

Although misdiagnosis and misclassification are serious issues, they represent only one dimension of a two-sided dilemma. Diagnostic nosologies developed by and for primarily White people have the added burden of potentially missing some debilitations particular to Black people. Take, for example, the following scenarios:

- An African American male or female finds it difficult to develop a meaningful relationship with another African American partner unless that partner's phenotypical features (i.e., skin color, hair texture, facial features) mirror those of their White counterparts.
- An African American male or female has no vision for his or her future, believing instead that financial subsidies from federal, state, or local government entities are the only sources of survival.
- An African American police officer tries to distance himself or herself from the African American cultural group by constantly demonstrating for White counterparts that he or she can be tougher and more aggressive toward African American residents, and especially suspects, than White partners can be.
- An African American school child refuses to excel in school because doing so, in his or her mind, is synonymous with being White. Thus, achievement rates fall well below capability.
- An African American business executive or other white-collar professional believes his or her sense of self is enhanced because of the acquisition of a nice house, cars, clothes, and career position. Conversely, a recently laid-off, African American, blue-collar worker believes he or she is of little benefit to the family given the lack of financial means.

Each of these scenarios represents some level of psychological debilitation. If we examine the larger African American community, we could even create a frequency distribution in which some segment of that community (i.e., percentage) is represented by one or more of the scenarios listed above. These premises, on which current diagnostic nosologies are based and in which current and past psychological training programs are rooted, raise the distinct possibility that an ethnic minority (African American) might be misdiagnosed, underdiagnosed, or overdiagnosed. In all likelihood, the diagnostic nosologies (whether theoretical orientations or classification systems like the DSM-IV) currently in use would be unable to account for these conditions. Why? I suspect that the reason relates to Eurocentric psychological worldviews that see the etiology of client distress as an intrapsychic phenomenon. The other reason reflects how culturally sterile traditional psychology is in its understanding of the culture of African descent people. There is little, if any, room to recognize that there may be social, cultural, and environmental factors (e.g., oppression and discrimination) that instigate the debilitations listed above.

Summary

The practice of providing psychological and counseling services to African American populations has been a challenge. Historically, African descent people have a history with a mental health system in which they have been underserved, misdiagnosed, inappropriately classified, and treated with differential methods when compared to their White counterparts.

The newfound cultural sensitivity of the past decade has inspired many counselors and clinicians to review their former practices and commit to enhancing their knowledge and skills. Unfortunately, much of what has evolved into "more sensitive" contemporary approaches has been encapsulized into a generic multicultural framework (Sue, Arredondo, & McDavis, 1992; Sue, Ivey, & Pedersen, 1996).

Although efforts at multicultural counseling have vastly improved over what historically existed in the profession, they are, nonetheless, limited in their utility because they lack the cultural specificity necessary to more effectively intervene with the African American population. This book, then, is committed to offering a contribution toward that cultural specificity in which African models and methods guide our thinking, research, and practice.

2

African-Centered Psychology

Basic Principles

Cheryl Grills

There exists in us a unifying link that rationalism cannot explain, that quantitative, equational logic cannot grasp. This link enables us to see an object as a single image observed from different angles; to isolate at will different sounds heard simultaneously; to taste, that is, to coordinate flavor and odor; and to comprehend corporeality through touch. This is in no way a reasoned coordination, but a phenomenon of intelligence that resides in the synthesizing milieu, in other words, a faculty for canceling sensorial specifications.

—Schwaller de Lubicz, 1998

Introduction

This chapter essentially builds on Chapter 1 by introducing the Western-trained practitioner to a different paradigm: a different way of thinking and a different set of tools for discourse, understanding, and intervening in human behavior that is more consistent with an African ethos and reality. What is offered here is not a compilation of new African-centered techniques. That would be putting the proverbial cart before the horse. Instead, an alternative conceptualization of human behavior must be understood first, before viable treatment strategies can be meaningfully applied.

To truly embrace an African-centered approach, clinicians must be willing to make a shift in the lens through which the world is seen, how reality is defined, and how human behavior is understood. As we know from cross-cultural psychology, "cultural differences are not primarily differences in behavior, but rather in the meanings attached and attributed to the same behaviors" (Landrine, 1992). What will be presented here is an African-centered understanding of the self and notions of consciousness. The intent is to equip the practitioner with some conceptual tools by which the frame of reference can be shifted from a Western perspective to an African understanding. This is the first step in adopting a truly African-centered approach wherein the strategies applied can have more depth for therapist and client. It would be an insult to traditional African therapeutic practice to assume that one could teach or learn its praxis within the confines of a book or book chapter. One can, however, present an overview of the fundamental theoretical tenets and glean an appreciation for important distinctions in worldview.

Western psychology (self-appointed as the universal authority on human behavior) is defined as the *scientific* study of behavior and mental processes. Behavior refers to observable actions such as moving, talking, and the measurable activities of cells (Coon, 2001; Nairne, 2000). Mental processes include thoughts, ideas, and complex reasoning processes (Lefton, 1997). Because the "mind" is intangible, definitions of psychology typically refrain from examination of such intangible features in favor of objective mental processes. When the mind is examined, it is usually done so only with reference to the measurable activities of subjective experience: sensations, thoughts, and emotions. In addition, the study of consciousness has waxed and waned as a valid pursuit in psychology (Lefton, 1997). With the emergence of cognitive psychology in the 1960s and 1970s—investigating thought, perception, and memory—consciousness again became a viable topic. Seen as a process on a continuum, Western psychology defines consciousness as a general state of being aware of and responsive to events in the environment, including one's own mental processes. Western psychology, then, relying on reason (rationality), experience (empiricism), and other aspects of science (objective methods and precise procedures), draws conclusions, makes predictions and generalizations about human behavior, and socializes clients in the treatment process to relate to their own phenomenology within this framework. This represents an important divergence from psychology's own origins.

During its formative years, Western psychology presupposed the existence of the mind and defined consciousness as its primary focus of study (Lindskoog, 1998). As it searched for a *legitimate* identity among the sciences, the mind became redefined as secondary—if not rejected altogether. As a result, the study of the mind, consciousness, agency, and personhood became systematically excluded from the purview of psychological inquiry. In other words, "First, psychology lost its soul and then it lost its mind" (Jung, 1916).

Western psychology's definition of psychology and human consciousness does not permit the type of synthesis referred to above by Schwaller de Lubicz. Western science defers to a *reductionist* mentality. Everything in the universe is brought into the frame of our senses. The type of synthesis that recognizes the primacy not of the material thing but the essence and function of the thing requires a different type of mental processing or synthesis. This type of synthesis, however, is central in African[1] phenomenology and psychology. Human consciousness, a central feature of African-centered psychology, is not defined within the narrow band of Western phenomenology. This distinction has important implications for the resulting theories of human behavior, expressions of human behavior, and prescriptions for maintaining and restoring adaptive human functioning. Psychology, Western and African, is replete with theories of human behavior. Tried and tested to varying degrees, these interrelated ideas and facts put forward to explain and predict behavior and mental processes are used to shape praxis in their respective fields. What we often fail to realize is that the theoretical enterprise, including as it appears in psychology, is religious at its core (Dooyeweerd, 1953). Theory tends to reflect the most deeply held values of the theorist and the theorizing community. Theorizing with integrity, then, recognizes the impact of these values on the resulting theoretical constructs and consistently expresses them throughout the theorizing process (Lindskoog, 1998). The heart of this discussion will be establishing the integrity of African psychology's theories of human behavior and praxis through a presentation of its values, beliefs, philosophy, and assumptions.

Basic Principles in African-Centered Psychology

Subsequent chapters will outline the basic tenets of the African-centered perspective articulated by African-centered scholars over the past few decades. At this juncture, we seek to penetrate the deep structure meaning of the African-centered perspective drawing from the reservoir of diasporan African thinkers. The African-centered perspective presented here is not restricted to a specific African ethnocultural group, but rather reflects a basic historical continuity, historical consciousness, and cultural unity (Diop, 1962; Obenga, 1997; Sundermeier, 1998). As an expression of African culture, African-centered psychology offers a deeper understanding of things African, African culture and cultural adaptations, and what it means to be African. In fact, it has been argued that matters that fall within the purview of psychology are among the most critical of tasks facing today's African-centered scholars (Obenga, 1997).

> The yeoman's task for the present and forthcoming generations of African scholars is to penetrate the depths of African history and culture in an attempt to not only understand and describe, but to analyze how African people explain themselves. The explanations that human beings provide of themselves are inextricably linked to the concept of culture. (Obenga, 1997, p. 31)

In the African worldview, the person and community adopt a teleological orientation (attention to purpose) to existence and are equipped with "patterns for interpreting reality" and a "general design for living" (Nobles, 1986). This teleological orientation informs the African mind that everything in the world has been designed by God to be of service to man. There is a resulting purposiveness to nature. An animal's behavior, for example, may be best described by its goal (food seeking), whereas a chess player's activity can be understood by its purpose—to win. As it discerns its purpose and the purpose of things around it, the African mind is informed in the world in ways that are not limited to cognition, the conscious mind, and intellect. African-centered psychology provides a framework for understanding this orientation to existence. Psychotherapeutic work with an African American client may require the therapist to understand the cultural thrust that contributes to the client's greater emphasis on (a) consciously or unconsciously being African in their orientation to life, (b) the spiritual basis of life, (c) an inclusive metaphysical epistemology, and (d) how or what one "feels" in relation to people, places, or things. Each of these is defined below beginning with a definition of African-centered psychology.

African-Centered Psychology: A Basic Definition

African-centered psychology is concerned with defining African psychological experiences from an African perspective, a perspective that reflects an African orientation to the meaning of life, the world, and relationships with others and one's self. Emerging out of the deliberations of the African Psychology Institute and members attending the Western Regional Retreat facilitated by Thomas Parham, the association of Black Psychologists defines African-centered psychology as

> the dynamic manifestation of the unifying African principles, values and traditions. It is the self-conscious "centering" of psychological analysis and applications in African reality, culture and epistemology. African-Centered Psychology examines the process that allows for the illumination and liberation of the spirit. Relying on the principles of harmony within the universe as a natural order of existence, African-Centered Psychology recognizes: the Spirit that permeates everything that is; the notion that everything in the universe is interconnected; the value that the collective is the most salient element of existence; and the idea that communal self-knowledge is the key to mental health. (Parham, White, & Ajamu, 1999, p. 95)

African-centered psychology is ultimately concerned with understanding the systems of meaning of human beingness, the features of human functioning, and the restoration of normal/natural order to human development. As such, it is used to resolve personal and social problems and to promote optimal functioning.

The essential features of African-centered psychology as presented in this definition address matters related to

1. *Self-definition.* For too long, Africans in the diaspora have been other-defined, other-defended, and other-reliant under the wake of European enslavement and colonialism. As Ani (1980) aptly notes, "We, as Black people, have been told that we are not African for so long and with such social scientific 'expertise' that we have great difficulty believing otherwise." This paradigm calls for re-Africanization of psychology for African descended people, a conscious centering of perspective, analysis, theory, and praxis in an African frame of reference.

2. *Spirit.* Spirit is as important as the physical manifestation of the self. Spirit refers to that incorporeal, animating principle and energy that reflects the essence and sustenance of all matter.

3. *Nature.* Nature (consisting of all elements contained within the natural environment) provides rules for living peacefully in society and provides a window to the inner workings of the person. The processes in nature provide lessons on human functioning, the rhythms of life, and natural order of things.

4. *Metaphysical interconnectedness.* There is a metaphysical component to the person that requires certain social and natural obligations that are accompanied by rituals (rhythms in life). We, as human beings, do not exist alone in the universe, but are always interacting with and under the influence of other forces (Dukor, 1993).

5. *Communal order and self-knowledge.* We come to know ourselves through our relationships with others. In the African world, there is no I without a we. In fact, in several African languages, there is no equivalent for the English term "I." Indeed, "To be human is to belong to the whole community" (Mbiti, 1990). Individuals exist because of the community and the community is responsible for the conduct of its individual members (Kamalu, 1998). In this African schema, the corporate or collective reality predominates.

The resulting African-centered paradigm contains distinctly African values and ways of accessing knowledge, defining reality, governing and interpreting behavior and social relations, and designing environments to sustain healthy, adaptive development and functioning. Its origins can be traced "to that point in time [pre-colonial Africa] when Blacks of Africa produced an *organized system* of knowledge (philosophy, definitions, concepts, models, procedures, and practice) concerning the nature of the social universe from the perspective of African cosmology" (Azibo, 1996).

To the extent that culture provides a general design for living and a pattern for interpreting reality (Nobles, 1986), African-centered interventions grounded in their own theories of the self, consciousness, illness, health, and wellness must be able to explain how African Americans construct their design for living and describe the patterns they use to interpret reality (Parham, White & Ajamu, 1999).

In the African centered framework, the life experiences, history, and traditions of people of African ancestry are at the center of analysis. In other words, the challenge is to examine or analyze phenomena with a "lens" consistent with an African understanding of reality, values, logic, methods of knowing, and historical experiences. Ani (1994) describes this as an *utamawazo* or worldview. The African-centered *utamawazo* provides a lens through which to see the world and a map by which to navigate and negotiate life on life's terms. Some of the major components of world-view are

1. *Ontology*. An orientation to reality with a belief about what the essential nature of reality is
2. *Axiology*. A value orientation—defining the relationship of humans to nature
3. *Cosmology*. The structure of reality and a definition of the relationship to the divine
4. *Epistemology*. A system of truths and a method for revealing or understanding truth or generating knowledge
5. *Praxis*. A system of human conduct.

According to Diop's Two Cradle Theory (Wobogo, 1976), among the cornerstones of the African worldview are ancestor veneration, social collectivity, and the spiritual basis of existence.

- *Ancestor veneration*. In Africa, ancestors are deified, viewed as part of the cosmogony and influence daily living. As such, they are venerated (respected, celebrated, admired, emulated), but not worshipped.
- *Social collectivity*. Wealth and resources are distributed by need; class stratification is influenced by clan grouping; therefore, lines are less rigid. "We" is most important.
- *Spiritual basis of existence*. The universe is essentially spiritually manifested in matter, leading to a view of oneness with the universe and subjectivity in epistemology. Truth, derived through this epistemology, is revealed through the language of symbols, nature, the cosmos, and the human being. Phenomena in nature become forms of speech allowing nature to reveal the esoteric (immanent meaning that is implied, but may be inexpressible in words) and exoteric (manifest, material, functional aspect of an object or

principle). According to the ancients, "*Learning* is establishing, by means of the senses, the reality of what one believes; *believing* is having the conviction about the reality of that which cannot be demonstrated; but *truth* is the congruity of what one believes or learns—believes and learns—with that which is." (Schwaller de Lubicz, 1998, p. 40)

Spiritness

In the African cultural worldview, the essential ingredient and essence of everything, including humans, is spirit. To have spirit is to be imbued with life, a mind and soul, energy, force, passion, allegiances, and a guardian presence. It is the condition of *being* spirit, not merely practicing spirituality. The human being not only has spirit, he or she *is* spirit. In the African worldview, spirit has both real and symbolic meaning. It represents the divine spark which gives human beings their "(be)ingness; the essence of which becoming is an ongoing expression" (Nobles, 1998). Spirit refers to that incorporeal, animating principle and energy that reflects the essence and sustenance of all matter. What, then, are some of the essential features of spirit and spiritness?

- Spirit is the basis of existence.
- Spirit exists before, after, and beyond material existence.
- The source of spirit and one's spiritness is the divine.
- Spirit is the energy, force, or power in and circumjacent to people, places, and things. It should not be understood as simply something invisible. "It is not defined in contrast to the body, like the supernatural in contrast to the natural; it is not idea in contrast to matter" (Sundermeier, 1998). Spirit or spiritness is both in and with nature and the corporeal.
- Spirit is both the inner essence and outer envelope of human beingness (Nobles, 1998). This "centrifugal self" (Taylor, 1963) experiences reality through spiritness and is limitless.
- Spirit is encountered through your own spirit. When a Mende walks through the bush and sees an object such as a stone that "catches his attention," he will want to pick it up and take it home. It could be that the spirit of the stone has something special to say to him. Why else did the stone "catch" his eye (Little, 1963)? Through his own spirit, something was discerned about the significance of this stone. In Western thought, we would simply relegate this to coincidence, but African thought broadens the options for interpretation of such an event. African American clients may do the same in relation to encounters with events, people, and places. Do we provide them with an environment conducive to the full spectrum of attributions possible for any given phenomena, or do we socialize them into a narrow band of "acceptable, rational, cognitively defensible" forms of interpretation?

To understand the importance of spirit and the subtle ways in which it may manifest itself in a client's presentation, consider an interview conducted on "The Today Show" with singer Natalie Cole (Cole, 2000). As Cole reflected on her years of drug abuse and addiction, she commented on the miracle of her survival, stating that it was clear to her that "something else" had intervened to keep her alive and out of harm's way. Like the story in the "Footprints" poem, she was convinced that some divine force had "carried her" when she was most vulnerable and unable to carry herself. Belief in a divine force capable of guiding and protecting the individual, the family, and community is, in fact, a very old African belief directly related to African ontological theories of reality and human behavior. Therapists who validate and reinforce this belief system provide an excellent opportunity for client empowerment.

African Inclusive Epistemology

Epistemology refers to the method of knowing or coming to an understanding of reality, of what is real (Kambon, 1999). This understanding reflects the particular racial-cultural perspective and experience of a group and will differ from culture to culture. An African epistemology emphasizes an affective-cognitive synthesis as a way of knowing reality. This reality does not limit itself to the five senses or methods dependent on Aristotelian logic as the only means for securing information and understanding.

In contrast to Western epistemology, within the African schema of knowledge acquisition knowing includes and extends beyond linear reasoning. It includes and extends beyond the boundaries of space and time. The senses, cognition, and tangible verification or control are not the only pathways to knowledge. The spiritual basis of all there is to know makes African epistemology accept realities that Western epistemology shuns as a way of knowing. In the pursuit of knowledge, the African willingness to engage and include that which is empirically, tangibly verifiable and that which is not makes this an inclusive epistemology. Within the venue of European American clinical praxis, therapist and client are socialized to remain within the confines of linear reasoning and materialist explanations of knowledge acquisition. In clinical practice, to what extent do we negate the existence and experience of an inclusive epistemology? To what extent do clients silence their internal experience of pretersentient knowledge (knowledge that is derived without the agency of the sensory system), linear reasoning, and unverifiable intuitive data? What validity is given to intuition as a real and legitimate source of information? As Bergson (1946) notes, "Intuition is the direct vision of the spirit by the spirit. Intuition, therefore, means, first of all, an immediate consciousness, a vision barely distinguishable from the object, a knowledge that is consciousness and even coincidence." This definition of intuition compliments the African-centered paradigm of the centrality and function of spirit in human functioning and consciousness. Within the African-centered model, an inclusive epistemology is not only germane to understanding all knowledge production, it is an integral part of praxis.

The European American fascination with the obvious elements of the tangible object shuts the door to an identification of what is less than evident among the things we observe (Schwaller de Lubicz, 1998). Among African descended people, the material world is not taken as the end of it all. Their inclusive epistemology is concerned not only with intangible, spiritually imparted knowledge. There is also attention given to the esoteric (the inner meaning; the implied but inexpressible in words) aspects of any given tangible stimulus or phenomena. A cerebral approach to knowledge leaves parts isolated from each other whereas the esoteric approach aims for synthesis and an appreciation for the simultaneity of complements ("When we look to the front, we feel that there is a behind. We cannot look in one direction without opposing to it a complementary pole, and although this pole is not sensorially observed, the awareness of it exists within us" [Schwaller de Lubicz , 1998]). What emerges in this framework is a richer source of knowledge and understanding. Schwaller de Lubicz offers an insightful analogy.

> The West looks upon the world from the exoteric side, that is it objectively observes the forms of the body, and its investigation is nothing but an anatomical analysis of quantities.... Western thought never "enters into" a body, does not see it from its living interior outward, from the perspective of its growth and the functional characteristic of its life. For example, the Westerner will look at the form of a tree—the form of its trunk, the form of its bark, the form of its branches, the form of its leaves—and finally, he will study this object *through what is revealed to him by his senses*, which is a cerebral, quantitative view. On the other hand, Hindu and pharonic *symbolique* show that the foliage of a tree, for example, is considered as the respiratory function, the lung of the plant. Then, under the general form of a leaf, foliage will serve as a symbol for respiration in general; the trunk around which the serpent is entwined will show the rising spiral of the life flux around the spinal column. The whole *symbolique* of traditional thought indicates the character of this thinking: the object that strikes our senses exoterically is the consequence of vital functions, that is, *we transform cerebrally into corporeal forms that which is in reality an interrelation of momentary specificities*. (p. 40)

The implications of this method of knowing can be essential to understanding the African American client who may have retained and actively uses this inclusive metaphysical epistemology. Some African American clients come to know what they know about themselves, others, and situations in ways that extend beyond rational-logical cognitive processes of reasoning and beyond the mechanics of the five senses. In a number of settings, I have found African Americans share the powerful experience of dreams, intuition, clairvoyance, déjà vu, and other such mental phenomena that fall beyond the typical purview of psychotherapy discourse. To what extent are these given legitimacy and used in the treatment process as the client explores concerns, issues, and strategies for resolution of their problems? To what extent do we, in fact, undermine this process when clients tell us they have a "feeling" about something or someone but cannot provide a rational explanation consistent with Western theories of cognition? How often, then, do we "train" clients to think in Western models of what is defined to be healthy cognitions and ways of knowing? Are we, as clinicians, actually imposing a European American perspective on African Americans at the expense of their indigenous construction of epistemology? "Western [trained] clinicians must incessantly ask themselves these cross-cultural questions: Are my therapeutic goals mere proselytization? Does my effect on this family, [community]—on this culture—differ significantly from that of colonialism" (Landrine, 1992)?

Finch (1998) discusses African ways of knowing or epistemology in relationship to the "fifth dimension" within which the universe is perceived through spirit. Finch states:

> We are not dealing here just with symbolic material arising from deep within the Jungian "collective unconsciousness." The *Pale Fox* (Griaule and Dieterlen, 1986) shows us that highly complex empirical information has come into the possession of a people lying almost entirely outside modern techno scientific culture. Since the Dogon do not possess the methodologies or apparatus of modern science, we are driven to conclude that there must be other "pathways" for acquiring such data, veritably, other ways of "knowing." (p. 260)

This perspective exemplifies an important position in African concepts of consciousness, that there are other ways of knowing (and realms of consciousness) that do not rely on the basic senses, logic, or reason. African traditional priests-healers use a multitude of strategies (divination, rhythm and sound, the drum, speech, ritual, manipulation of electromagnetic and vibratory energy) to increase their ability to tap into this fifth dimension of preterrational methods of perceiving reality. Preterrational thought is defined as consciousness that operates beyond mere rational methods (Ayoade, 1979). In the preterrational process, the mind can look simultaneously at the future, present, and the past and possibly influence all. In African psychology, it is believed that human beings are able to access this fifth dimension in daily life through the agency of components of the self known as *sunsum* by the Akan, *ori* by the Yoruba, *chi* by the Igbo, and so on.

The Affective Sensorium—Source of Information and Illumination

In ancient African thought, we knew that the rational mind was constrictive. It narrows what we experience or observe into an image. In contrast, Schwaller de Lubicz (1998) argues that emotion dilates; it expands our awareness and knowledge of things. The ancient Kemites believed that "the emotional sense (*and not the emotion which is a result*) is a radiating substance" (Schwaller de Lubicz). Emotion has the capacity to generate information and levels of insight that exceed cognitive and linguistic analysis and expression. Within the African schema, the affective sensorium, often misunderstood in Western psychology due to the limited role assigned to emotions, becomes a major conduit of information and illumination. This dilating emotional intelligence can "open our eyes" to a vastly different way of thinking and acting that no longer excludes direct knowing and needs no physical or descriptive intermediary. Herein resides the mechanism labeled as the Western concept of intuition and telepathy. This medium can be cultivated to the point of enabling the receipt of information and communication of thought without the usual verbal and nonverbal cues. Generally, people of African descent are familiar with this but will rarely discuss it openly for fear of ridicule or being labeled crazy. In Western psychology, what do we know about intuition, telepathy, or the affective sensorium? The response may be "very little," yet these media of information and understanding may be paramount to the psychological experience of non-Western ethno-cultural groups.

Consider the following example. At a recent graduation ceremony, as I stood in the procession line with a Japanese American psychology faculty member grounded in her culture's *utamawazo* and epistemology, I stared off into the nearby collection of several thousand family and friends gathered for the ceremony. My eyes came on a student who had graduated several years previously and I was elated to see that he was alive and well, given his brush with a life-threatening incident several months before. My colleague had no outward sign of what I was looking at, what I was thinking, or what I was feeling. She suddenly asked me a question about the well being of this exact student, who was not in her line of vision and whom she and I had never before discussed. In the Western worldview, this would be characterized as serendipitous. In the African worldview, this would be indicative of the synchronicity possible in intuitive or emotional intelligence or preterrational consciousness informed, perhaps, by the affective sensorium. In other words, spirit conversed with spirit vis-à-vis the affective or intuitive sensorium. Words and nonverbal cues were not essential to the process of communication and shared experience in the moment.

These essential principles of the African worldview contribute to the ideological cornerstones of African psychology. They ground the person and community in an appreciation for and relationship to the mind-soul-spirit, life, death, universal order, behavior causation, and consciousness. Herein lies the grist for the contemporary rearticulation of an African psychology. How do we draw on these principles to articulate a contemporary psychology paradigm that resonates with the reality of African people throughout the diaspora? How do we draw on these concepts to design a model of human behavior and a praxis of intervention and prevention that promotes the well being and development of African people? How does the clinician provide an environment in treatment that validates the multiple ways of *being and knowing* experienced by African American clients? How can we as clinicians avoid engaging yet another version of colonialism under the guise of psychology? Consider the young client whose family seeks the professional assistance of a psychologist. The child presents as outwardly normal in behavior, affect, development, intellect, and social adjustment. The family is concerned, however, because the child presents a very active "fantasy" life rich with seemingly extraneous ideas and play friends and precognitions that are sometimes exceptionally accurate. The child's teachers are concerned about perceived levels of distractability that lead to musings of an attention deficit-hyperactivity disorder of some type, or worse, a psychotic disorder. The child further describes most things on a feeling level rather than relating to things in terms of concrete thoughts and actions. This child becomes a prime candidate for misdiagnosis, inappropriate administration of medication, and labeling. The real issue may not be any attention deficit disorder or a psychotic disorder, but a youngster who has not yet been socialized out of the use of her affective sensorium.

Summary

Western psychology orders its body of knowledge into discrete, yet overlapping, categories designed to explain human behavior, thought, and emotion, (e.g., physiology, psychology, cognitive psychology, motivation and emotion, learning, memory, psychopathology, social psychology, psychotherapy, community psychology, etc.). African psychology integrates itself into the broader human context of spirituality, divine order, social structure, philosophy, history, science and culture. As Kambon (1999) aptly notes,

> Many of the earliest known fundamental concepts of life, the universe, and human existence are conveyed in Kemetic cosmogony, such as concepts of natural order, infinity, procreation, dimensionalization, human-spiritual transformation, morality and justice, resurrection, reciprocity, complementarity, relationships and conflict-resolution, inter-generational obligation and responsibility, ancestral accountability, and numerous others. (p. 44)

African psychology contains many principles and concepts eschewed by Western psychology. In fact, these principles were consciously removed from the Western paradigm (Lindskoog, 1998). These include introspection and inclusion of constructs related to the soul and spirit and the centrality of such cultural constructs as interdependence, connection to nature, social collectivity in defining human functioning, and the consubstantial nature of things in the world—everything is related to everything. Regardless of Western psychology's decision to extract certain phenomena in its aim to define human psychological reality, these concepts continue to manifest themselves in the daily practice of diasporan African life and psychology (e.g., extended family; religious expression and practices; music, song, and dance; shared participation; social-affiliative emphasis; phenomenal time).[2]

What is the relevance of African psychology today? Among the many factors that make it a viable model from which African-centered psychology can draw are

1. The cultural retentions among Africans in the diaspora that warrant an African-based approach to mental wellness—such as the primacy of the communal self over the individual self, the centrality of spiritness and spirituality, the belief in the continued existence of departed family members and the maintenance of a relationship with them after their transition to the ancestral realm, the maintenance of African-based beliefs about illness and health, and the practice of an inclusive metaphysical epistemology.

2. Its capacity to assist in the process of maintaining alignment and authenticity with the essence of who we are as African people.

3. Its ability to reclaim that which is African in this emerging era of "alternative" medicine.

4. Its ability to aid in the liberation of the African psyche (soul-spirit) from the everlingering effects of hundreds of years of enslavement, oppression, and colonialism, empowering the African psyche with a conscious awareness of what was, what is, what can be, what can be seen, what cannot be seen, and what is beyond comprehension.

The objective of African psychology is the complete mental, spiritual, and social liberation of African people throughout the diaspora. African tools of knowing (epistemology) are not limited to the rules of Western empiricism that engage only tangible phenomena capable of being manipulated, rationally explained, and controlled. As illustrated in the Akan theory of reality and human beingness (Ajei & Grills, 2000), African psychology begins with the recognition that reality includes

- *nea wohu* (the observable or perceivable dependent on rational thought)
- *nea etra adwen* (that which transcends thought accessing knowledge beyond rational deliberation)
- *nea wonhu* (the imperceivable or unobservable, that which is incomprehensible)

These levels of reality have corresponding levels of human consciousness that can be accessed by the lay and the highly skilled or trained practitioner. These levels of reality and corresponding levels of consciousness compliment a comprehensive conceptualization of the self, of human beingness, and a more inclusive, dynamic model of the therapeutic process from prevention to diagnosis to tertiary intervention. In other words, African-centered psychology offers a holistic, life-affirming, efficacious model of healing capable of complementing the essence of Africans throughout the diaspora.

In the contemporary advancement of African-centered psychology, we must create a nosology and glossary of terms that synthesize and reflect African constructs, models, assumptions, and practices. As Ajamu (1997) aptly notes, "The most fundamental and deeply entrenched aspect of conceptual incarceration resides at the level of language." Such a nosology is emerging in the contemporary work of radical or constructionist Black psychologists. This nosology would move us closer to the practice of *sakhu sheti*, the deep, profound, and penetrating search, study, understanding, and mastery of the process of illuminating the human spirit. In the practice of sakhu sheti, we can penetrate and embrace more profoundly the multitude of concepts the ancestors have left us. In the practice of sakhu sheti we can penetrate the meaning and implications of the Laws of (Mis) knowing (Fuller, 1969) and (Non)being (Nobles, 1994).[3]

African-centered psychology, along with other African cultural constructs, should play a major role in the advancement of African psychology in the 21st century. African conceptualizations of the person and self hold promise for informing our understanding of adaptive, authentic human functioning and can contribute to the development of health promotion models and disease prevention among Africans throughout the diaspora. African conceptualizations have the capacity to:

- make significant contributions to the emerging paradigm of African-centered psychology
- redefine and expand the limited purview of human realities represented in Western psychology paradigms
- contribute to the application of African-centered psychology as a force for personal and social liberation (self-actualization)
- reveal that which is African psychology through the systematic investigation of traditional African cultural, spiritual, and medical beliefs and practices

But first we must understand its philosophical, theoretical, and epistemological foundations. Although this chapter presented a discussion of the African deep structure of African-centered psychology, the following chapter will delineate models that emerge from this African-centered perspective.

Notes

1. The term African is used to refer to Africans throughout the diaspora: continental Africans, African Americans, Caribbean Africans, Central and South American Africans, Africans in Europe, and so on.

2. See Barrett, 1974; Hilliard, 1997; Holloway, 1991; Kambon, 1999; Noll, 1992[91 in refs]; Pinckney, 1998; and Smith, 1994 for a more complete discussion of cultural retentions.

3. The Law of (Mis) knowing states that if you don't understand White supremacy, then everything else that you think you know will simply confuse you. The Law of (Non)being says if you don't exist according to your African essence, then everything you think you are will only be a diminishment.

3

Understanding African American Mental Health

The Necessity of New Conceptual Paradigms

Thomas A. Parham and William D. Parham

Our continued interest in providing psychotherapeutic services to African American populations has stimulated a dramatic increase in the number of presentations and publications that concern themselves with providing mental health services to people who are culturally different. Given the substantial increase in the amount of literature, presentations at professional meetings, and training seminars designed to help clinicians work more effectively with African American populations, it is surprising to note how many clinicians and academicians feel less than fully comfortable working psychotherapeutically with African American people (Allison, Crawford, Echemendia, Robinson, & Knepp, 1994).

A number of reasons could be cited for this apparent discomfort. The conceptual paradigms about the African American experience promoted heretofore have been faulty in their assumptions of what the experience entails and, therefore, have been limited in their ability to accurately depict the life spaces of African America. The theories and constructs on which traditional psychology has been built and advanced are inappropriate when used to understand and explain populations that are culturally different than those studied by the architects of many of psychology's theories. Certainly, several researchers (White, 1972; White & Parham, 1990; Parham, White, & Ajamu, 1999) have asserted that it is difficult, if not impossible, to understand the lifestyles of African people using the traditional psychological theories that were developed by psychologists of European American descent to explain the behaviors of European American people.

For example, early paradigmatic formulations of the counseling process suggested that African Americans, due to their deficient cognitive and higher-order reasoning abilities, could not engage meaningfully in the counseling experience and, therefore, could not reap the benefits promised by involvement in the process. Later assumptions suggested that counseling was sufficiently generic in that all people who participated in the counseling experience could potentially benefit. The belief in the generic applicability of the counseling process suggested, in essence, that a specific focus on African Americans and the counseling process was unnecessary.

And so, even as we sit here in the 21st century, it is hard to understand the psychology of a people who are culturally different when the professions of psychology and counseling remain handicapped or otherwise disadvantaged by their conceptual incarceration. Thus, in spite of the newfound sensitivity to treating culturally different people generally, and African Americans in particular, our disciplines continue to cling to conceptual paradigms they know to be faulty, inaccurate, or outdated. This should be clearer to you now, having read Chapter 2 and the introduction to a worldview of African descent people.

A second reason that might account for the apparent discomfort of many clinicians in working psychotherapeutically with African Americans is that there is not a clear understanding of who or what constitutes an African American. The journey from colored, to Negro, to Black, to Afro-American, to African American, to now persons of African descent represents an identity transformation of sorts and a change from accepting imposed definitions to asserting a posture of self-determination and self-definition. How an African American defines his or her identity intersects with the therapist's own race and identity to influence a client's behavior in the therapy session. Furthermore, the client's ethnic-racial identification is influenced by several factors, including the ethnic-racial philosophies fostered during their developmental years. European American therapists, as well as African American therapists and therapists of other racial-ethnic groups, also run into similar challenges in deciding how best to respond to the racial-ethnic identity feature of their African American clients.

An additional comment regarding African American identify seems warranted. Social science seems committed to depicting African Americans in the absence of understanding and appreciating environmental and other contexts within which African American communities grow and thrive. Viewing African American people as a homogeneous group versus seeing the richness of their heterogeneity renders most definitions of African American short sighted at best. Yet, within the framework of counseling, African American clients are accepted frequently under the premise that there are more similarities than differences. What perceptions might an

African American client hold of an African American therapist? That they are similar or do they differ significantly in the ethnic-racial identification? A more detailed presentation of these group identification premises will be forthcoming at a later point in this chapter when we discuss issues of therapist preference.

Related to the lack of a common definition or description of African Americans—and thereby, a lack of agreement about who or what is an African American—is a potentially compromised understanding of the relational dynamics between therapist and client. This potential for interpersonal dynamic confusion seems to be true across therapist-client pairings. Thus, if a qualitative appreciation of a group (e.g., African Americans) is absent, how, then, can their relationship (vis-à-vis therapy) to another group, namely Anglos, be fully understood? This potential for misunderstanding or feeling outright confused about relationship dynamics seems to hold true for therapists, irrespective of their racial-ethnic identification.

A closer examination of how race and ethnicity have been used in the therapy process will give us some additional insight into this dilemma.

The Ethnicity Factor in Psychotherapy

The ethnicity factor and its influence on the psychotherapy process has been studied for the past three decades and has received a noticeable increase in research attention during the past two. Studies to date have generally indicated that race and ethnicity influence a client's decision to seek therapy. These studies have also generally speculated that race and ethnicity affect virtually every aspect of the therapy relationship, including client-therapist interpersonal dynamics, assessment and diagnosis of the client, psychotherapy processing, therapy termination, and evaluation of therapy outcome.

Despite this attention, the degree to which race and ethnicity influence the many aspects of the therapy relationship remain unclear. Also, this lack of clarity perhaps was instigated because many believe that the most critical research question in this area is this: When, under what circumstances, with what therapist and client, and at what time, is the influence of ethnicity and race on the psychotherapy process most strongly felt? The answers that emerged were interesting, but were these the most important questions to be asked at the time?

Help-Seeking Behaviors

One of the initial ways race and ethnicity was thought to influence the therapy process was in the decision to seek help in times of psychological or personal distress. Help-seeking behavior refers to the verbal or nonverbal solicitation of assistance, guidance, or support to resolve an issue or problem a person may be facing. Considerable research suggests that African Americans will rely on more traditional support systems first (Block, 1980; Boyd-Franklin, 1989) in times of personal distress. Those traditional support systems might be defined as older relatives (i.e., grandparents, uncles and aunts, godparents, parents), community elders (former school teachers, ministers, church deacons, business people), or other individuals who are perceived as having gained wisdom about a specific problem through experience. In much the same way as therapy, these traditional support systems were thought to provide a listening ear, unconditional acceptance of a person's humanness, empathic consolation, occasional mild confrontation, confident reassurance, and, sometimes, practical advice.

The decision to access the traditional support system is bolstered by several critical elements. These elements include a personal relationship at its most fundamental component, in which the individual seeking help forms a close personal attachment to the potential help giver at some point in the past. Another critical factor thought to influence the process was the history of the help giver, recognizing that the potential help giver has a track record of being a viable resource, either to himself or herself or to others who may have been in need. A third variable in the decision to seek assistance from the traditional support system is the issue of trust. Trust, in this case, involved the development of a level of confidence and prediction in the person, without any fears or misgivings about the individual's ability to render assistance in the context of reasonable safety.

In some respects, it was thought by many people that potential African American help seekers make intuitive "leaps of faith" in believing that the likelihood of these variables being present in a potential help giver was increased when that help giver was of African descent. Consequently, race and ethnicity were thought to influence the decision to seek assistance, particularly if there was a match on ethnic or racial characteristics of the helper. Certainly, the literature seems to bear this out as White and Parham (1990), and Block (1980) before them, concluded that many Blacks failed to consider therapy as an option during times of stress because of the potential to being treated by non-Black therapists. In fact, as early as 1971, Vontress similarly argued that a counselor may be rejected by a Black client simply because he or she was White, thereby deciding not to seek the counseling and therapy needed. These reasons may account for the recent trends cited in the Surgeon General's report on mental health (U. S. Department of Health and Human Services, 2001), in which African Americans were more prone to use hospital emergency rooms in times of mental debilitation rather than more conventional outpatient services.

Therapist Preference

Another factor thought to be influenced by race and ethnicity was a client's preference for a particular therapist. Over the last three decades, this area of study received a significant amount of attention. In seeking to discover whether African American clients tend to prefer service providers who were African American or European American, much of the research was thought to focus on this issue. Several studies suggested that Black students preferred to be helped by a counselor of the same race rather than by a White counselor (Ponterotto, Anderson & Grieger, 1986), whereas other studies either contradicted these findings or suggested that, at best, race plays only a secondary role in the counseling relationship (Cimolic, Thompson, & Waid, 1981). Despite some inconsistencies, a majority of the research tended to indicate that Black clients showed a demonstrable preference for service providers of the same race.

Literature on therapist preference was further enhanced by studies that sought to explore less between-group comparisons (i.e., Whites vs. Blacks) and more within-group variability (i.e., Blacks versus other Blacks). Significant in this regard were the studies by Parham and Helms (1981, 1985) and Helms and Carter (1991). These studies sought to demonstrate that racial identity attitudes rather then racial self-designation were more important factors in predicting the preferences of clients for therapists. These studies helped to stimulate a host of research articles and manuscripts during the last 20 years that continue to demonstrate the salience of racial identity as an influencing factor in client preference. In fact, some of this research was thought to provide explanations for the rather consistent preferences by Black clients for counselors of the same racial and ethnic background. On a pragmatic level, the history of Black-White relationships in the United States was thought to predispose African American clients to be distrustful of White counselors (Atkinson, Furlong, & Poston, 1986). On a theoretical level, it was believed that communicator credibility, attractiveness, and influence all function similarly to affect the communication process between the client and the therapist.

Despite the fact that the disciplines of counseling and psychology have made significant advances in the understanding and treatment of the African American population, our work appears to be stalled in the ideas and paradigms of the 1980s and 1990s. This is particularly true as academicians continue the debate between the multicultural movement and the empirically supported treatment movement (Atkinson, Bui, & Mori, 2001). In order to move our work forward, particularly with African American populations, we argue that new conceptual models and paradigms need to be developed to help us to better understand the mental health of African American people. Clearly, as argued in Chapter 2, these new ideas must be anchored in a worldview that is essentially African centered.

New Conceptual Paradigms

A worldview is as much about a shared cultural experience as it is a set of ideas that give meaning to our experiences (Ani, 1980). In thinking about understanding the African-centered worldview, it is important to share three assumptions that guide our thinking for this text. The first of these suggest that the psychology of the people (i.e., the study of their souls or spirit, as opposed to the study of human behavior) can never be anchored in theories and constructs that do not support and affirm their humanity. Thus, an African-centered psychological perspective examines processes that allow for the illumination and the liberation of the spirit (Parham, White, & Ajamu, 1999).

The second of these assumptions suggests that because African-centered psychology is about the illumination and liberation of the spirit, the conceptual pillars on which the discipline is based must speak to the nature of one's humanity and also articulate how that humanity is expressed and revealed in the context of therapeutic interactions.

Third, we would argue that race and ethnicity might have outgrown their usefulness as meaningful constructs in the context of mental health. Rather, we would contend that we must begin to explore the variable of culture. In the United States, many see culture as symbolically represented by food, clothing, ethnic dress, dance, music, and holiday celebrations. However, if culture is to be a meaningful variable in our discussions, we cannot allow it to be reduced to such simplistic definitions. Culture is an organizing mechanism that forges a group of people into an ideological unit (Ani, 1994). Culture, in our opinion, is a complex constellation of mores, values, customs, and traditions that provide a general design for living and a pattern for interpreting reality (Nobles, 1986). Thus, in using an African-centered cultural perspective, one attempts to use African values, customs, traditions,and so forth as a lens through which our perceptions of reality are shaped and colored.

Accordingly, the African-centered worldview begins with the recognition that things within the universe are connected (the notion of consubstantiation). This sense of interrelationship between all things is essential for understanding the relationship between African American people and the environmental context around which their lives revolve. As such, any analysis of behavior must be understood in this context rather than solely on the focus of the individual. This notion of interrelatedness is also important for understanding the connection between the spiritual, cognitive, affective, and behavioral dimensions of the personality. Although some psychological perspectives seek only to focus on one isolated dimension of the personality, the African-centered worldview recognizes that a spiritual essence or life force permeates everything that is. Thus, the personality we develop is believed to be a manifestation of the spiritual, mental, emotional, behavioral, and biogenetic factors that interact with the environment in holistic ways (Kambon, 1992).

The African-centered worldview also focuses on the collective, rather than the individual, as the most salient element of existence. Thus, individual achievement and competition is valued less than efforts that contribute to the cooperation between people and effort that facilitates group survival (White, 1984). By using an African-centered worldview, we hold to the truth that all extensions can be made between the cultural worldview and understanding of a psychology that better explains the makeup and lifestyle of African descent people.

In thinking about any perspective centered in a cultural context, we are reminded of our days in graduate school, in our introduction to psychotherapy or personality courses. There, each of us was asked to think about and develop a personal theory that summarized our beliefs and guided our work with the clients we would soon be working with. Once we articulated our theory and delineated our beliefs, we could begin to see that all therapeutic work was guided by sets of philosophical assumptions. In a similar vein, it is important for mental health professionals and students alike to remember that they must begin to explore similar questions about the clients of African descent they see or will see in therapy. Consequently, using new conceptual paradigms to understand the mental health issues of African American people requires the exploration of several fundamental issues. These issues or assumptions include the nature of what it means to be human, the role of spirituality in the assessment of client functionality, the manifestation of identity in the context of historical and contemporary social realities, an analysis of what constitutes mental health for African people, and the role of the therapist-healer in the treatment intervention with African American populations. Let us briefly discuss each of these factors.

The Nature of Humanity

For African people, humanity can only be understood in the context of an inner relationship between each person and the divine force in the universe. Fundamentally, then, it was believed that man and woman possess a "spiritual anatomy" that sought out opportunities for growth and transformation from his or her physical presence (i.e., the body) and animating spirit through the development of moral and then, ultimately, the divine parts of the spirit. Thus, from an African-centered worldview, holding to the truth that "all beings are created in the image and likeness of the creator" helped African descent people to understand that the nature of all things in the universe was and is divine. This fundamental truth then becomes the core around which the psychology of the people must be developed. That is, we must recognize and embrace the divine nature of the self.

The Nature of Spirituality

Another modification that must be made is the understanding of the role of spirituality in the assessment of client functionality. Unfortunately, the discipline of psychology as it is practiced in the United States has adhered to a strange notion that there should be some separation between the sacred and the secular. In spite of the fact that psychology has inappropriately confused the principles of spirituality and religiosity, most clinicians are trained to believe that individuals possess a soul or spirit as part of their overall human makeup rather than understanding that an individual spiritness represents the core essence of their being. Spirituality, in this case, represents the energy or life force of each individual. Thus, in assessing the functionality of the clients we treat, our study cannot be relegated to manifestation of cognitive, affective, and behavioral phenomena. We cannot simply view people as objects with an emphasis on objective methods for studying and assessing them. The psychology of people of African descent really is about the soul or the spirit. As a consequence, most clinicians' efforts at treating African American people are contaminated by their desire to quantify or objectively measure every dimension of the personality, rather than seeking to understand and gain insight into the essence of the individual humanity and spirituality.

The life force or spirit, in our opinion, is best understood through an examination of individual and collective struggle by African descent people. Sometimes that struggle is with the self, sometimes that struggle is with another person, and occasionally that struggle is against a social force (e.g., oppression, racism, sexism, classism, etc.). Irrespective of the object, a person's spirit is characterized in the fundamental ways he or she engages life circumstances and synthesizes the life force in a way that allows for integration, transformation, and transcendence.

For African people, that struggle is frequently against forces of evil and oppression. In fact, West (1996) reminds us that spirituality is reflected in the ways African American people cope with unjustified suffering, unmerited pain, and undeserved harm. Once experienced, the question then becomes how a person achieves some critical distance, and then transcendence, from the pain and suffering in order to reengage the situation in an effort to overcome it and transform it. Clinicians then must understand that African spirituality is partially grounded in the transfiguring of personal and collective suffering and social misery. Understanding African American clients will require, then, some recognition of how a particular client has accomplished this transfiguration. The next step for the clinician, after understanding and empathizing, is to give voice to what West (1996) describes as the psychic scars, existential bruises, and ontological wounds reflected in the stories our clients disclose. In that way, we access their spirituality and help them to engage it on a more conscious level.

Identity

Another paradigm that must be reexamined involves how identity manifests in the context of the social realities of our time, including day-to-day existence. In previous writings, Parham (1993), among others, has argued that the central issue in the struggle for identity with African Americans continues to revolve around how one can maintain a sense of cultural integrity in a world that does not support and affirm our humanity as African people. Essentially, this assertion recognizes that the answer to the question "Who am I?" is always an admixture between individual evaluations from the person as well as influences from the social-cultural/environmental context in which the person's sense of self is nurtured and cultivated. To the degree that that nurturing is supportive, a likely outcome would be a positive self-identity. To the degree that that nurturing is contaminated with the dynamics of discrimination and racism (i.e., global White supremacy), then the development of that individual and collective identity must always be understood in the context of that social oppression.

In an attempt to explain identity development within this context, several models have emerged in the psychological literature as a means of explaining this phenomenon. Collectively, these models are identified as belonging to the school of "psychological nigrescence" (Cross, Parham, & Helms, 1998) or in some cases, as advancing the principles of African self-consciousness (Baldwin, 1990; Kambon, 1992). Individually and collectively, these models provide a very powerful interpretative lens through which to view the life experiences of African people (Cross, 2001).

However, in seeking to provide clarity on this phenomenon, two issues need to be revisited. First, we must understand that identity is more than a set of stages that characterize a person's racial attitudes. In Fanon's (1967) analysis, he asserts that there are three critical questions. These questions include: "Who am I?" "Am I who I say I am?" "Am I all I ought to be?" Fanon's analysis reminds us that our discussions of identity cannot be relegated to the identification and labeling of particular identity states. Rather, we must be concerned with how individuals achieve some measure of identity congruence from the context of their own life space.

A second issue that needs to be revisited is the question of how identity functions in the context of everyday life. In this regard, it is our belief that identity functions, among other ways, as a buffer against racism, oppression, White supremacy, and other social-cultural and environmentally oppressive phenomena. Identity functions as an experience of bonding that helps each individual to form attachments with others who share similar cultural practices. Identity also functions as a means of code switching, allowing each individual to adapt to a particular environmental circumstance that may be more or less supportive of their cultural identity. Identity functions as a bridge in helping individuals to transcend the limits of their identities in breaking down barriers that prevent genuine levels of intimacy and connection. Identity also provides a sense of individual pride and achievement in helping to create for each individual a picture of oneself. And last, identity functions in the context of an intergenerational continuity, in which individuals are allowed to relate to their past and present, and visualize the future.

Unfortunately, the identification with these models as "racial identity" constructs relegates our discussions to an assessment of how pigmentation and phenotypical features have become prominent aspects of our identity. If, however, we expect these models to have a larger social utility, then as we mentioned earlier, our focus must shift from racial identity to ethnic and cultural identity. These aspects of identity are those that grow out of shared struggles and collective heritages of people throughout the globe. In recognizing this distinction, one can readily see that a global view of African people shows that even as a few high profile members of African American communities advance to positions of high status, salience, wealth, and prominence, our collective status of political and economic conditions are substantially the same everywhere around the globe. The masses of Africans and African American people are at the bottom of the political economy. And so, if our models are to be accurate conceptions of our collective condition as African descent people, then we must begin to examine how the principles of culture and ethnicity are the core constructs of a collective identity that should compel and propel us nationally, socially, economically, and politically (Hilliard, 1997). As Dr. Hilliard says, "you cannot relate to a global geopolitical reality with a local identity."

Mental Health

Another conceptual paradigm that needs to be reexamined is analysis of what constitutes mental health for people of African descent. Essentially, it seems inconsistent to argue on one hand that the principles and practices of Eurocentric psychology fail to capture the essence of African American life while simultaneously using diagnostic manuals and personality instruments in assessing their mental health. In most cases, traditional psychological theories and constructs, as well as those instruments designed to measure various aspects of personality, have not been developed to explain the dynamics of mental health as they related to African American people. Consequently, if our therapists, counselors, and clinicians are seeking to assist clients in distress, help them to heal, and to otherwise return to a normal state of mental health, they are at a decided disadvantage. You cannot help an individual to be mentally healthy if you have no idea about what constitutes mental health for that person or his or her people.

In this regard, mental health can be defined as "a person functioning in accord with the nature, aim, and purpose of their creation" (Farrakhan, 1996).

Thus, assessing mental health requires that our clinicians and academicians understand the nature and essence of African people, particularly with regards to their spiritual core. Although these will be discussed more thoroughly in later chapters, one example of this is provided by Karenga (1990), among others, in his text titled *The Book of Coming Forth by Day* (1990). In his text, he recalls the five dimensions of African character as articulated by ancient Kemetic (Egyptian) society. These dimensions include divinity, teachability, perfectibility, capacity for free will, and the need to be morally and socially responsible. In using these constructs to define the character of African people, it is also necessary that we assess a degree of congruence between these dimensions and the ways in which these attributes are manifested within the life experience of African descent people. In essence, we are suggesting that clinicians must help clients to assess the degree to which they function in accord with their divine nature, their nature of teachability, the nature of perfectibility, the nature of free will, and the nature to be morally and socially responsible.

The Role of the Therapist-Healer

The fifth conceptual paradigm that needs to be rethought involves the role of the healer or therapist in treatment with African American populations. Before discussing this, however, mention should be made of how one's approach and role definition can be central in gaining the trust and cooperation of the client. Some clinicians approach counseling and therapy with an eye on being a "mental health" provider. Undoubtedly, this posture carries some baggage for some people (clients) seeking assistance who might be more comfortable with a service provider offering a more psychoeducational approach (i.e., teaching) as opposed to a provider whose approach is focused on "treating" an illness or some sort of pathology. That said, it is vitally important that we consider these "approaches" and what impact this focus might have on the process of counseling. In many counseling situations, the role of the clinician is guided by his or her theoretical orientation and assumptions about how and why clients will experience some relief and resolution from their particular predicament. For some, relief will occur through an exploration of residual baggage or unresolved developmental tasks from childhood. For others, relief is believed to come by fostering the therapeutic environment, which allows for the client to reexperience an atmosphere of empathy, genuineness, congruence, and unconditional positive regard. Still others will seek to challenge irrational beliefs that are believed to instigate excessive feelings of anger, anxiety, guilt, or depression, which in turn diminishes a client's capacity for effectively dealing with life situations. Irrespective of the theoretical orientation chosen, each has a specific set of culturally based assumptions around which the clinician organizes an intervention strategy. In a similar fashion, we again make the point that those who work with people of African descent need to anchor their intervention strategies in a set of culturally specific assumptions that inform both the direction of the therapy intervention and the role that the healer plays in facilitating that outcome.

Traditional definitions describe therapists as individuals who are trained to assist their clients in understanding and resolving life's circumstances that have led him or her to experience some measure of emotional distress (Ohlsen, 1983). The skills used in achieving these outcomes include listening, reflecting, interpreting, questioning, paraphrasing, summarizing, giving feedback, mild confrontation, goal setting, teaching, diagnosing, and conceptualizing.

Although it can be argued that these skills are essential to any mental health helping professional, it may be a stretch to assume that these are the only skills to facilitate a therapeutic process in which African Americans are concerned. In an African-centered reality, we wish to advance the notion that therapists are really healers. Healers are individuals who participate with clients, not simply direct and control them. Healers help clients confront their mental, physical, emotional, and spiritual debilitations. In rendering African traditions and constructs relevant to contemporary African American needs, healers, according to Hilliard (1997), must be involved in

- *Healing thyself*, by understanding how we as clinicians have ourselves been damaged by our confrontations with oppression or privilege. We cannot help clients confront their own pain until and unless we confront our own. Healers then, must consciously redevelop their minds, bodies, and spirits. Being a healing presence cannot be developed simply by the acquisition of degrees and certifications from state licensing boards.
- *Remembering the past*, by promoting congruence and harmony in a way that a client's consciousness, as well as that of the healer's, is properly aligned with his or her destiny. This is consistent with the African-centered principle of *ori-ire* or properly aligned consciousness.
- *Accessing the spirit*, by serving as a conduit for positive energy flow that is transferred and transformed into specific cognitive, affective, and behavioral strategies for helping.
- *Confronting the maafa*, by helping to restore health and wholeness to their lives by returning to the source of their energy. The *maafa*, in this case, is defined as a great disaster of death and destruction beyond human comprehension and convention (Ani, 1994). The chief feature of the maafa is the systematic denial of the humanity of African people. The healer in this case must examine the ways in which he or she has been affected by maafa experiences, and how those might affect him or her in rendering assistance in a counseling role.

It is also important to understand that the role and task of healers is not simply to access information, but to incorporate "wisdom" into the lives of their clients. The attribute of wisdom is particularly salient because traditionally Western training in psychology or counseling assumes that wisdom is synonymous with the obtaining of degrees or certifications from academic institutions and various licensing or credentialing boards. We would argue that wisdom must be sought and acquired through direct experience as well as consultation with traditional sources of knowledge and information in the communities of African descent people.

Hilliard (1997) provides one of the best examples in his text titled *SBA: The Reawakening of the African Mind*. In it, he reminds the reader that one of the oldest and most comprehensive texts in human history is the book of Ptah Hotep, the words of an ancient Kemetic scribe. Among the lessons that are most profound is the acknowledgement that none of us is born wise: We must seek wisdom and guidance by being open listeners (hearers of the word). Open listeners approach their task by acknowledging the importance of the message that people (i.e., clients) share. Thus, being a good listener and healer, according to the Ptah Hotep, requires one to *subdue arrogance* (by not deluding ourselves about an exaggerated sense of importance based on our education and training when compared to those who are less formally educated); *subdue pride* (such that we allow ourselves to become more vulnerable to new interpretations of reality); *aspire to perfection* (in seeking maximum congruence between what we teach and what we practice); and *being open to all* (such that we give real value and meaning to the lessons we learn from others' words and deeds).

Summary

The interest in providing more culturally sensitive treatment must be applauded. Clearly, the breadth and depth of information available that assists all of us to better understand African American populations has been a welcome addition. However, although we can now safely assume that heightened awareness and sensitivity levels of psychologists and counselors has increased, we are also aware that the knowledge required to make specific cultural interventions with African American people has not kept pace at the same rate. Consequently, we must do a better job of achieving a greater level of congruence between what we aspire to do as helpers and healers and how those aspirations are actualized in the context of our graduate and professional training and mental health treatment interventions. The need for new conceptual paradigms when working with African American populations is clear. The question is: Are we ready to start practicing what we preach? If so, then let's continue as we move to a deeper level of understanding about people of African descent and their personality dynamics.

4

Understanding Personality and How to Measure It

Thomas A. Parham

Any discussion of treatment issues with African Americans must first begin with an understanding of the personality dynamics of African people. At first thought, many clinicians would agree with such an assertion and then begin the process of analysis using a conceptual framework learned during years of graduate study or continued professional development. Perhaps a psychodynamic approach may be considered; maybe a more behavioral orientation might be used; or maybe a more humanistic approach with a client-centered therapy; or a rational emotive therapy slant might be employed. Regardless of which therapeutic approach is adopted and used, the clinician may be put at a disadvantage because each of those therapy approaches is rooted in a worldview that may be inappropriate for conceptualizing the personality dynamics of African descent people (Akbar, 1981; Azibo, 1989; Baldwin, 1990). White (1972) makes the clearest statement in this regard by asserting that, "It is difficult, if not impossible, to understand the behaviors and lifestyles of Blacks using traditional psychological theories developed by White psychologists to explain White behavior."

Rather than rely on traditional approaches, I maintain that attention should focus on conceptual frameworks that emerge from a more African-centered frame of reference. Essentially, it can be argued that regardless of which traditional approach to therapy a clinician adopts, he or she will have a difficult time promoting mental health because each of these traditional approaches are not normed on African descent people and each approach implicitly assumes a universality of the human condition without reference to a non-White culture. In light of this realization, it makes sense to build on the previous chapter by articulating my view of African-centered mental health. Accordingly, I will begin with a discussion of the concept of personality in an African-centered worldview, continue with issues in assessment, and conclude with a presentation of a conceptual scheme or frame of reference for counseling African American clients. That frame of reference begins with a definition of African American culture.

Culture

Culture has inspired many definitions over the past several years. For example, the dictionary defines it as "the integrated pattern of human knowledge, belief, and behavior that depends upon man's capacity for learning and transmitting knowledge to succeeding generations" (Webster, 1990). Fairchild (1970) defines it as behavior patterns socially acquired and socially transmitted by means of symbols, using customs, beliefs, techniques, and language. Nobles (1986) suggests that culture is a design for living and a pattern for interpreting reality. Using Nobles's definition as an anchor for our discussion, the relevant questions become (a) what are the rules for living that define and inform the African character and (b) what patterns do Black people use to interpret reality?

The African Personality

During the past four decades of study, the human personality is a variable that has also generated many definitions. In some respects, personality is used as a construct to describe someone's public image. In other respects, it is used in the context of social attractiveness, determining which people have good or bad personalities based on the way they respond to others as well as how others perceive them. In spite of the many descriptions given to the term *personality*, there should be a distinction made between what the personality is and how the personality is manifested in everyday life. Some traditional theorists would argue that personality is the scientific study of individual differences in thought and behavior as they occur in a given circumstance or situation (Ryckman, 1978). In fact, for Allport (1961), personality is the dynamic organization within the individual of those psychophysical systems that determine characteristic behavior and thought. Skinner (1974), on the other hand, suggests that one's personality is a complex organization of idiosyncratic learning history and unique genetic background. For Cattell (1965), personality is "that which tells what a man will do when placed in a given situation." In fact, Cattell developed a formula to illustrate his contentions that suggested that $R = F(S \times P)$. The formula contended that each person's response (R) is a function (F) of the situation (S) faced and the nature of one's personality (P).

Despite the difficulty in defining the construct, it appears that there is some convergence of opinion that suggests that personality is an abstract, hypothetical construct used to refer to an inner dimension of an individual that consolidates biological propensities with personal history in forming cognitive, affective, and behavioral responses to the environment. Although more traditional psychologists might adhere to such descriptions, I would contend that the African personality cannot be reduced to such scientific quantification and measurement, or defined so simplistically.

Fundamentally, remember that the ancients have taught us that there is a spiritual energy or essence that defines existence. For the Yoruba, this energy was defined as *ashe*, which was a spiritual command for the power to make things happen (Thompson, 1983). Borishade (2000) defines spirit as a universal life-giving, life-enhancing, nonsubstantial essence that is found in all living things. Spirit is understood as being a divine essence that is part of the Creator that permeates everything in existence, whether animate or inanimate. Spirit then becomes an individual's life force. If we further accept the notion that energy cannot be created or destroyed but only transformed from one form to another, then we invite ourselves to posit that the life force that permeates each physical body is not unique to that individual. Rather, it may be that what is really manifest in each person is a re-creation of an "old soul" whose spirit is destined to confront the challenges, pitfalls, and opportunities of this lifetime.

I also believe the African tradition further teaches that lying dormant in each person is an energy waiting to be cultivated into the full expression of each person's humanness in a given lifetime. As each person encounters his or her reality and is nurtured by it (parents, caregivers, situational phenomena), the manifestations of his or her humanness are reflected in the spiritual, cognitive, affective, and behavioral dimensions of the personality as they interact with others. What, then, constitutes the core elements of the African personality? Let's examine them along internal and external dimensions.

Internal Dimensions

The Essence Of *Maat*

In *Psychological Storms*, Parham (1993) argued that the core of the African personality is spiritness. The spirit spoken of here is not some religious vision or some mystical "hocus-pocus." It is, in fact, the life force or energy that is fundamental to every living thing that exists in the universe. Our spiritual essence reveals itself through our capacity to know and experience reality (what we refer to as consciousness). Our spiritual essence is surrounded by a veil of culture (another core element of personality), which, as Nobles (1994) explains,

> is a human invention or activity that is best understood as the process which represents the vast structure of behaviors, ideas, attitudes, values, habits, beliefs, customs, language, rituals, ceremonies and practices which, in turn, provide humans with a general design for living and a pattern for interpreting reality. (p. 2)

These cultural rules or principles, then, are intended to support and facilitate the full expressions of one's spiritual essence (sense of self).

These rules for living are reflected in various segments of ancient and historical African societies. The previous chapter discussed that in ancient Kemetic (Egyptian) society, for example, life-affirming principles were reflected in the spirit of *maat.* Maat represented the fundamental set of rules or principles that defined the natural order of social interaction. Maat not only laid down guidelines that determined the essential qualities for human conduct, but more important, it explained the parameters for the establishment of a oneness with the Creator. In one respect, maat was a yardstick or standard against which to measure one's adherence to divine law in all that one thought and felt, and how one behaved (i.e., mental health). These principles were intended to represent the power of the spoken word, but were also an aspiration of consequence between words and deeds. Maat represented all that was good and proper in life, and was expressed through the articulation of seven cardinal virtues. These included truth, justice, righteousness, harmony, order, balance, and propriety. In historical African societies, there are other principles that served as descriptions of the natural order of the universe. Among these were the notions of *consubstantiation* (elements of the universe are of the same substance), *community* (the group of the collective was the most salient element of existence), and *harmony* (that one should be in accord with the universe and the natural flow of things).

Another core element discussed in the previous chapter that must be included in any analysis or discussion of the African personality is an understanding of the nature of one's humanness. In his text titled *The Book of Coming Forth by Day*, Karenga (1990) informs us that the ancient Kemetic conception of the African (human) personality presumes that who we are is anchored in five fundamental propositions. At the core of these propositions is the *divine nature* of humankind. This principle of divinity was not an expression of man or woman as God, but rather a recognition that we are all made in the image and likeness of the Creator. Therefore, the nature of humans is assumed to be inherently good rather than evil.

A second proposition speaks to the human potential for *transformation to perfectibility*. This concept recognized our quest to strive toward a standard of personal excellence in all that we do. Also, whereas the manifestations of our spiritual, mental, verbal, and behavioral dimensions of our personality represent our beingness at a moment in time, recognition must also be given to the idea that one could aspire to be "more better" as well. A third proposition was the *capacity to be taught* and learn. This "teachability" of humans was reflected in the expectations that one would acquire wisdom by having been self-nurtured in the ways of moral and spiritual enlightenment.

A fourth proposition was the notion that each individual possessed the capacity to exercise *free will.* Essentially, this principle suggested that regardless of the social circumstances, every person made a conscious choice to respond to their reality in a particular way. As a consequence, each person would then become the beneficiary of that which he or she gave, highlighting the rule that "what goes around, comes around." The fifth proposition was the necessity to engage in *morally and socially responsible behavior*. This concept recognized the mandate to be correct in our conduct toward others and to strive to develop relationships that are based on truth and goodness, rather than deceit and evil.

Earlier, mention was made of an inner dimension of the personality that consolidates biological propensities with personal histories to help form one's response to environmental realities. As such, a core element in the discussion of personality is the biogenetic makeup of African American people. Kambon (aka Joseph Baldwin) (1992) provides one of the clearest articulations of this component by suggesting that the essential element of the biogenetic composition is the melanin molecule. This molecule, which is located throughout the different parts of the body in various concentrations, is not only responsible for the coloration of the skin but its primary influences on the body (especially the central nervous system) is believed to define much of the uniqueness of the African personality.

External Dimensions

Another core element of the personality is the *social-cultural context* (environment) in which the personality is nurtured and cultivated. The social-cultural context is composed of primary caregivers (parents), immediate family (siblings), extended family (aunts, uncles, cousins, grandparents), peers (friends), community (role models, business people), institutional agents (teachers, clergy, family physicians, police, etc.), society at large (other cultural groups), the media (television, newspapers, periodicals), and the zeitgeist (the social climate of the times). Each of these elements helps to construct a reality that is experienced by the individual as supportive and nurturing, unsupportive and stifling, or some combination of the two polarities. To the degree that one's environment is supportive and nurturing, there is congruence between and harmony with the spiritual and physical dimensions of life. Thus, African people are able to create for themselves cultural comfort zones that facilitate the affirmation of their humanness.

Crucial Energizing Forces Within the African Personality

In thinking about the energizing force(s) for the African personality, I would like to briefly discuss two. These include

1. The need to experience harmony and balance
2. Human capacity to grow, regenerate, and strive toward self-preservation

Harmony and Balance

In earlier writings, Parham (1993) has suggested that the biogenetic makeup of the African American personality helps to create for each individual the set of needs that require fulfillment and satisfaction. Furthermore, he suggests that the cultural distinctiveness of African people colors the very nature of what the need is, as well as what is necessary to satisfy the need at any given moment (p. 5). (In this instance, he uses the concept "need" to mean a psychological or physical requirement necessary for the sustenance and well being of the principal organism.) In this regard, the need for *harmony and balance* are two energizing forces that drive the personality. Harmony represents peace as well as the personality's need to be in accordance with the natural order. Harmony is both an outcome and a process in the sense that it represents both the essence of being and becoming. In her writings, Myers (1988) has suggested that reality is a union of the spiritual with the material. Similarly, harmony denotes a joining of parts of the personality such that arrangements are in accord with one another. The use of the term accord here is no accident, for it suggests that because accord implies conformity, harmony will require conforming to a set of principles (i.e., maat) in order to achieve peace.

Balance represents a synthesis of energy or forces that affect our lives. Those forces are both internal (forces we direct) and external (forces that seek to direct us). Balance also serves as an indication of stability that is produced by an even distribution of weight (force) across a specific plane. In essence, it describes the achievement of equilibrium when we successfully direct our energies to meet our needs and to align ourselves with the natural forces.

The need for balance is also reflected in the complementarity of differences. The wisdom of the ancestors teaches us, "life at its best is a creative synthesis of opposites in fruitful harmony" (Parham, 2000). Accordingly, a characteristic of the individual personality that might be effective in successfully responding to a given task or situation may be disastrous in another context. Thus, balancing the energy flow requires the use of a full range of spiritually based mental, emotional, verbal, and behavioral responses to a situation.

Growth, Self-Preservation, and Regeneration

Another set of energizing forces or drives that affect the personality are defined as *growth, self-preservation, and regeneration*. Adherence to the notion of consubstantiation (elements of the universe are of one substance) compels us to analyze specific characteristics that are common to every living thing on this planet. Whether our reference point is a plant or tree, an animal or human being, all living things appear to possess the capacity to achieve maturation over time (growth), the capacity to protect one's self from danger or harm (self-preservation), and the capacity to heal and reproduce the self (regeneration). As such, I would argue, as Nobles (1986) has before, that these attributes are central to the effective functioning of the African personality.

Assessing the African Personality

Having now discussed the makeup of various dimensions of the African personality, let us now turn our attention to issues of assessment. How do we measure this thing we call the African personality? We should acknowledge that there are few instruments available that adequately capture the dynamics of the personality of African descent people. What is available has tended to focus on the ethnic-racial identity dimension. Despite that limitation, however, some instruments do capture the essence of the personality within the context of an oppressive and racist society. Accordingly, we wish to highlight one of those measurement devices.

Racial Identity Attitude Scale (RIAS, Parham, and Helms, 1981)

Psychologically speaking, the social history of African Americans in the United States has been dominated by competing forces: The attempts of Whites to strip African folk of their Black consciousness on the one hand pitted against African American people's attempts to develop a Black consciousness on the other. Thus, given the ubiquity of the White emphasis on deracination, Cross, Parham, and Helms (1998) point out that, not surprisingly, African American history contains accounts of Black people who have tried to develop and maintain a sense of cultural congruence and personal identity. This process of trying to develop and maintain a Black identity in the context of social oppression has come to be known as the psychology of nigrescence. In his analysis of the nigrescence (racial identity) construct, Cross (1991) suggests that observers with a myopic historical perspective will trace nigrescence to the events of the late 1960s (Civil Rights) and the 1970s (the Black Power Movement). Cross (1991) further argues that a broader perspective allows one to recognize that the emergence of the nigrescence process dates back to the times of slavery and evolved step by step with efforts of White slave owners to deracinate their slaves.

> Given the ubiquity of the White emphasis on deracination, it comes as no surprise that within African American history are accounts of Blacks who, having first been deculturalized, experience revitalization through the process of nigrescence. (Cross, Parham, & Helms, 1998, p. 4)

Consequently, I agree with Cross's assertion that nigrescence is one of the most powerful interpretive lenses from which to view and comprehend the experience of African people in America. Thus, central to early concern raised in the literature has been the need to develop techniques and instruments for measuring the nigrescence construct.

The most widely referenced measure of the nigrescence construct was developed jointly by Parham and Helms (1981) and is called the Racial Identity Attitude Scale. This scale was originally designed by transforming the Hall, Cross, and Freedle (1972) Q-Sort into attitude items by requiring respondents to use a 5-point scale (ranging from 1 = strongly disagree to 5 = strongly agree) to indicate their amount of agreement with each of the 30 items. Subsequent revisions of the scale have continued the Likert format but have expanded the scale to include 50 items (Helms & Parham, 1990). Current versions of the scale consist of 30 items (RIAS-A) and 50 items (RIAS-B).

The development of the Racial Identity Attitude Scale was intended to be consistent with Cross's (1971, 1980) description of the "Negro-to-Black" conversion experience by suggesting that the development of a Black person's racial identity is often characterized by his or her movement through four distinct psychological stages, a transformation from pre-encounter to internalization attitudes. In the first stage (pre-encounter), an individual is prone to view the world from a White frame of reference as he or she thinks, acts, and behaves in ways that devalue or deny his or her Blackness. In the second stage (encounter), the individual experiences one of many significant personal or social events that challenge beliefs in the pre-encounter assumption. In the third stage (immersion-emersion), the individual begins to immerse himself or herself into total Blackness, clinging to various elements of Black culture and simultaneously withdrawing from interactions with other ethnic groups. At this stage, everything of value in life must be Black or relevant to Blackness. The fourth stage (internalization) is characterized by the individual's achieving a sense of inner security and self-confidence with his or her Blackness. The resolution of conflicts between the old and new worldviews become evident as tension, emotionality, and defensiveness are replaced by feelings of psychological pride, ideological flexibility, and a decline in strong anti-White feelings.

Although the Racial Identity Attitude Scale (and the newest revisions and editions [Cross & Vandiver, 2001]) has demonstrated significant import for measuring the nigrescence phenomenon, it is questionable whether the instrument accurately measures dimensions of the African personality. In fact, given the instrument's focus on attitudes that characterize Black people's adaptation to oppressive conditions in America, I would now hesitate to adopt such a conclusion. In order to accept such a premise, one would have to adhere to the fact that the stages of racial identity represent core elements of the African American personality. Given the previous discussion, in which core dimensions were described as spiritness, culture, maatian nature, biogenetic makeup, and the social-cultural context, such a conclusion would be inappropriate. Rather than viewed as a measurement of a core dimension, the Racial Identity Attitude Scale may instead be described as an instrument that allows us to assess how the social-cultural context of the personality influences the development of a particular set of attitudes and feelings in African descent people.

The African Self-Consciousness Scale (Baldwin & Bell, 1990)

In light of the need to develop specific instruments designed to measure the African personality, which is grounded in Afrocentric theory, Baldwin and Bell (1990) have developed an instrument designed to measure the African self-consciousness construct. As described in Kambon's (1992) text, the African Self-Consciousness Scale is a 42-item personality questionnaire conceptually organized around four competency dimensions of African self-consciousness and six manifest dimensions based on some major categories of African social experience. The competency dimension of the scale includes (a) awareness and recognition of one's collective African identity and heritage; (b) general ideological and activity priorities placed on African survival, liberation, and pro-active/affirmative development; (c) specific activity priorities placed on African self-knowledge, African-centered values, rituals, customs, and institutions; and (d) a posture of resolute resistance toward anti-African forces and threats to African survival in general. The six manifest dimensions cover the areas of education, family, religion, cultural activities, interpersonal relations, and political orientation (Kambon, 1992, p. 160).

Although the African Self-Consciousness Scale has demonstrated its importance in measuring components of the African self-consciousness construct, it, too, raises questions about its ability to accurately measure dimensions of the African personality. In my observation, the African Self-Consciousness Scale measures ideological and philosophical adherence to an

African-centered worldview. Consequently, it appears to measure *attitudinal* dimensions of the personality. On a more critical note, there are several components of the African personality described in Baldwin's (1990) model that are more difficult to find in the current versions of the African Self-Consciousness Scale. The instrument does not appear to assess the biogenetic makeup of the African personality, nor does it measure the spiritual dimensions of the personality, both of which would be assumed to encompass the basic "African nature" of the personality described in Kambon's (1992) writings. It is also interesting to note that the instrument does reflect an element of the struggle for liberation described in Kambon's writings. However, it should be noted that liberation is not a core dimension of personality, but an aspiration of an individual when his or her person(ality) is nurtured in an environment that is incongruent with an African-centered reality. Essentially, we continue to believe that it is important to distinguish between core elements of the personality and how that personality is manifest in the given social-cultural context.

In summary, I would argue that both the Racial Identity Attitude Scale and the African Self-Consciousness Scale fall somewhat short of measuring the core elements of the personality as described by Kambon (1992) and Parham (1993). However, both instruments do attempt to capture the degree to which people adhere to worldviews that are African centered versus European American centered. Despite the relatively few shortcomings, both instruments appear to have a considerable advantage over more traditional personality measures (e.g., MMPI, CPI) in several important ways. First, the Racial Identity Attitude Scale and the African Self-Consciousness Scale reflect concepts relevant to African American people. Second, both the scales attempt to define and measure a more comprehensive level of functioning representing both deviant and healthy attitudinal and behavioral adaptations. More traditional personality measures, such as the MMPI, are typically relegated to measuring pathology only, forcing the clinician to infer mental health from an absence of mental illness. Third, both instruments have been normed and standardized on African American populations, and report reliability and validity data that equals, if not exceeds, traditional personality measures.

Alternate Conceptual Frameworks

Earlier in the text, mention was made of how, with the increased interest in treating African American clients, efforts have been made to develop culturally specific paradigms to conceptualize their personality dynamics. These efforts have resulted in the introduction of classification systems that attempt to define constructs such as mental health and mental illness, ordered and disordered behavior, and the like. Examples of concepts generated by African American psychologists include *menticide*—the deliberate and systematic destruction of an individual's or group's mind with the ultimate aim the extirpation of an entire race (Wright, 1975) and *negromachy*—a confusion of self-worth in which one depends on White society for self-definition (Thomas, 1971). Among those who have been most articulate in a theory of personality dynamics is Akbar (1981), who developed a classification system for mental disorders. In his system, Akbar first defines ordered and disordered behaviors and then uses descriptions of attitudes and behaviors that correspond to an individual's maladjustment to socially oppressive phenomena.

Because space and chapter focus limit a more thorough discussion of existing conceptual systems that are culturally specific (Akbar, 1981; Wright, 1975), readers are referred to the original writings. However, mention should be made of a relatively recent advancement in the development of a classification system for diagnosing African American personality disorders. This contribution is reflected in the work of Azibo and his development of the Azibo Nosology (1989). Describing his nosology as a system for diagnosing disorders and pathology of the African personality, Azibo has accepted the challenge of consolidating various concepts and labels of personality disorders advanced by numerous Black psychologists over the past three decades. Although the system itself is less than complete (and will undoubtedly continue to undergo periodic refinements), the strength of the system is its alignment with an Africentric conception of the human personality. Furthermore, it provides at least a supplement to, and in some cases, an alternative to, classification systems like the DSM-IV that is currently used by clinicians to assess and diagnose mental disorders.

Conceptual Scheme for Counseling African Descent Clients

Given the previous discussion on the core dimensions of the personality, it seems logical to proceed with a summary of the key concepts including the essence of human nature, definitions of normal and abnormal behavior, therapeutic process goals, the relationship between the therapist and the client, the role of the therapist, and how and why people change. The following section corresponds to Figure 4.1 in which I highlight (with superscripted letters in text and in the figure) the scholars who have contributed to defining the terms used.

Key Concepts

Fundamentally, African American people experience *reality*[a] as a union of the spiritual with the material (Myers, 1988). Reality is experienced

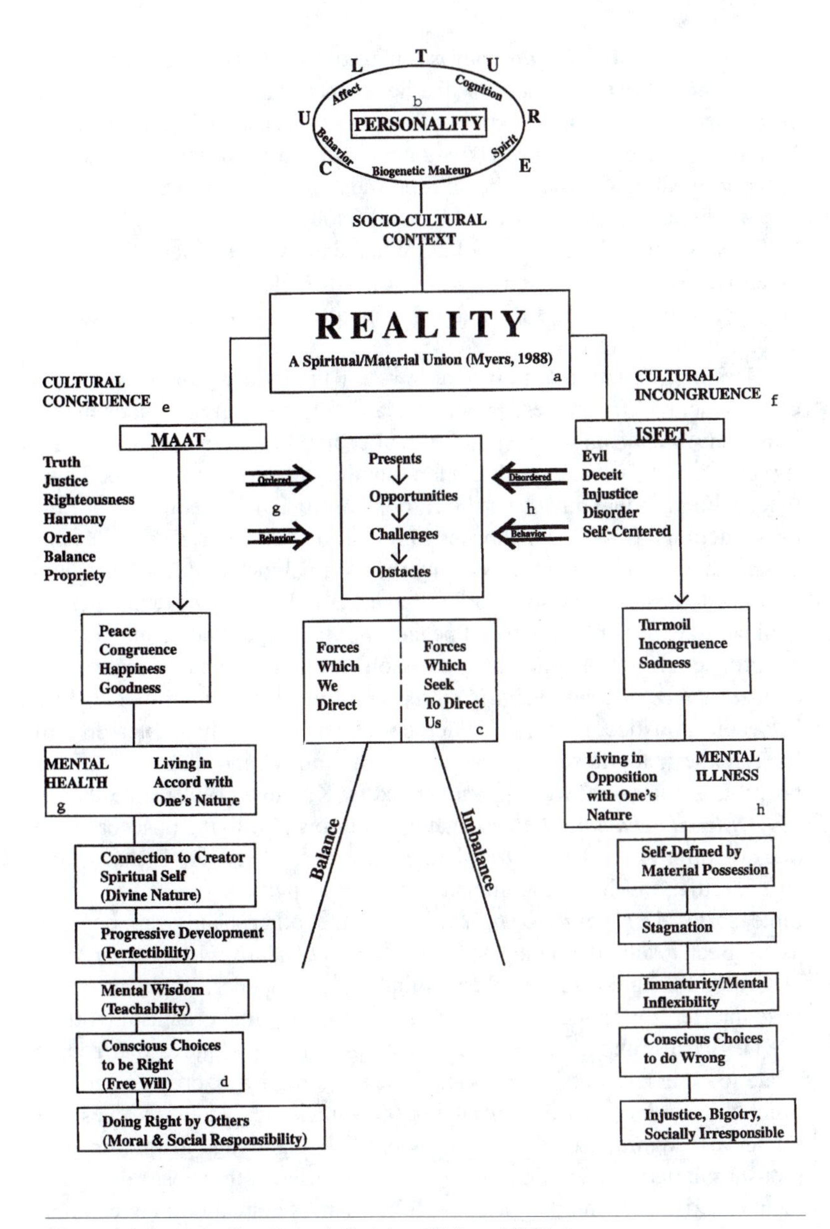

Figure 4.1 Reality: A Spiritual/Material Union

through the use of our five (maybe six intuitions) senses. The *personality*[b] we develop is a manifestation of the spiritual, cognitive, affective, behavioral, and biogenetic factors that interact with (join with) the environment (socio-cultural context). *Harmony* is achieved when the various components of the personality are in accord with one another; when the personality is in accord with the natural laws and order of the universe; and when the environment in which one interacts is supportive and nurturing. Because the basis of all things is *spirit,* recognition must be given to *forces*[c] (energy) that we direct (the ideas of will and intent) (Nobles, 1986), as well as forces that seek to influence and control us. When energy is summoned to meet a given need through interaction with the environment, forces from within and forces from outside are regulated in an attempt to achieve equilibrium and balance.

Despite the fact that universal laws for thought, word, and deed are ever present, African descent people are free to exercise independent judgment in choosing to respond to reality in a certain way. This capacity for *free will*[d] is basic to all human functioning. However, it is believed that each individual must bear the responsibility and consequences for his or her actions. If a person chooses to relate to reality in a *culturally congruent*[e] manner (i.e., maat), living by the cardinal virtues of the truth, justice, righteousness, harmony, order, balance, and propriety, then a person is likely to experience a sense of peace, happiness, goodness, and cultural congruence. If, on the one hand, a person chooses to relate to reality in a *culturally incongruent*[f] way, (*isfet,* representing evil) living by the values of deceit, injustice, evil, self-centeredness, and so on, then a person will likely experience falsehood, sadness, disharmony, and dishonesty. This position is consistent with that advanced by Karenga (1990) and others.

Ordered behavior,[g] then, is a natural outgrowth of living in accord with one's nature. As Akbar (1981) defines it, ordered behavior is that which sustains life, and helps the human organism to perpetuate itself and promote survival. *Disordered behavior,*[h] on the other hand, can be seen as a direct result of relating to reality in a *culturally incongruent* way. Disordered behavior is described as that which impedes, binds, or otherwise interferes with the maintenance and survival of the organism (Akbar, 1981). Because the nature of the African personality requires that people relate to others in morally and socially responsible ways, ordered and disordered behaviors may be reflected in the values each adopts. Values that reflect a recognition of the sameness in all living things in the universe (consubstantiation), a notion that the group or tribe is the most salient element of existence, and that personal fulfillment is gained through community service, are likely to reinforce ordered behavior. On the other hand, values that reflect an egocentric/self-centered approach, or ones that view personal worth in the context of material attainment, will likely reinforce disordered behaviors. The concepts of ordered and disordered behavior are important because they provide a gauge with which to measure each person's potential adjustments to life circumstances.

Existing in a particular space in time presents each person with various opportunities, challenges, and obstacles. If the personality is appropriately insulated in a culturally congruent space, yet is flexible enough to meet the changing demands of the moment, then harmonious adaptation to one's reality is an expected outcome. However, if the personality is reinforced by culturally incongruent values and principles, then the adjustments a person makes to the changing demands of a given moment may be inappropriate or otherwise lead to maladjustment.

Mental health, then, is analogous to living in accordance with one's nature or natural essence. One of the keys to mental health is the acquisition of self-knowledge. The awareness of who one is as a spiritual being is central to this notion. As such, a healthy personality requires the illumination of the spirit so that the energy or life force channeled through the cognitive, affective, and behavioral dimensions of the personality organizes to meet the needs of the organism as a whole. The manifestation of those dimensions is accompanied by a consciousness that recognizes the divine nature of the self, the ability to progressively grow, the ability to acquire wisdom, the ability to exercise free will, and the necessity to be morally and socially responsible.

In contrast to healthy adjustment, living in opposition to one's nature gives rise to psychological maladjustment and mental illness. The unhealthy personality lives in conflict with one's nature and is prone to spiritual darkness. Accordingly, the energy flow that is channeled through the various dimensions of the personality is misdirected toward environmental realities in ways that are improper. The manifestation of an unhealthy alignment of the personality is accompanied by a consciousness that defines the self as material, experiences stagnation, immaturity, is intellectually rigid, lacks awareness, and is socially irresponsible to others.

Chapter 5 takes a closer look at the African-centered worldview and human consciousness by exploring further the African personality from the African deep structure.

5

Reconceptualizing the Notion of Self From the African Deep Structure

Ezemenari M. Obasi

Introduction

The previous work of African American psychology played a revolutionary role in illustrating the shortcomings of Western psychology as a legitimate mechanism with the capacity to bring about optimal healing to the non-European American client. Previous chapters discussed the current state of affairs, mental health, and personality for counseling people of African descent. In the midst of a vast amount of citable literature that clearly illuminates traditional Western psychology's shortcomings when applied to the client of African descent, it is now time for African scholars to redirect their energy toward the African deep structure in which African philosophical assumptions, worldviews, ethos, and ideology serve as the foundation for the much-needed paradigm shift (Myers, 1987; Nobles, 1980). Although the previous work on Black psychology is important and necessary, one of the challenges of African psychology is to wield core African concepts that can be used to heal people of African descent today.

As African psychologists continue to grapple with an authentic paradigm for explaining the African experience, it is critical to ensure that its foundation is rooted in the deep structure of the African experience. African psychology cannot be viewed simply as a function of African authorship and African terminology. From inception, authentic African theories must be grounded in African deep thought and experience to truly be beneficial for people of African descent today. This point should be clear having now read the previous four chapters. Therefore, in exploring the

African deep thought, one can no longer avoid the necessity of addressing African philosophy, spirituality, and the study of nature (physics) in relation to new African paradigms that attempt to explain the nature of the African person.

In this regard, Nobles (1998) synthesizes the essence of our contention as he asserts that there are several assumptions that distinguish an African paradigm: (a) the universe is cosmos; (b) spirit is the ultimate nature of reality; (c) human beings are organically interconnected to the cosmos; (d) knowledge comes from participation and experience in the cosmic reality; (e) human relatedness is the praxis of our humanity; and (f) that the mode of our epistemological method is that of participation (equilibrium), relatedness (harmony) and unicity (balance between rationality and intuition, analysis and synthesis, known and unknown, and the visible and invisible). Although such theoretical parameters are clear and to the point, the real work is in the actual creation of the theories, for "where theory is founded on analogy between puzzling observations and familiar phenomena, it is generally only a limited aspect of such phenomena that is incorporated into the resulting model" (Horton, 1993, p. 198).

In searching for an African-centered psychological theory that can be used in the therapeutic healing process for people of African descent, it is clear that anything short of the illumination of one's divine soul, thus motivating one's life force to become more actualized, is unacceptable. With this in mind, it is my humble attempt to present wɔ ahoɔden (Twi for "to be healthy"), an African-centered theory that seeks to capture the dynamics of four important questions that have profound implications for African psychology:

1. How did Africans view the notion of *onipa* (Twi for "human being") before European contact?
2. In the context of precolonial Africa, what was considered normal behavior?
3. What effects did the *maafa—Kiswahili* for "disaster" (Ani, 1980)—process have on the African onipa?
4. What role can healers play in facilitating the realignment of the African onipa in an anti-African environment?

Before wɔ ahoɔden is presented, it is important to reintroduce some elements of African deep thought that are grounded in:

1. African philosophy
2. African concept of the person
   a. Akan
   b. Yorùbá
3. The study of nature: Physics' relation to African psychology

Once this foundation is established, the stage will be set to provide a framework that is practical for realigning one's *onipaness* to its divine possibility.

African Philosophy

Nobles (1972, 1980) suggests that an essential understanding of the nature of African ethos is to investigate and appreciate African philosophy. However, there is often a debate on whether or not African philosophy exists as a discipline (Gyekye, 1995; Hountondji, 1983; Wiredu, 1980) based on "Western standards." In spite of this, there is no question that African deep thought is prevalent throughout the African continent. Because Africans in America derive their most fundamental self-definition from several cultural and philosophical premises shared with several West African communities (Nobles, 1972), this section will draw primarily from the Akan people of Ghana and the Yorùbá people of Nigeria. In sharing these philosophical systems with you, I do not mean to suggest that their selection for discussion is indicative of their favored status among others that might have been chosen. However, they do represent cultural orientations that are both prominent on the continent of Africa and in communities across this country.

With that in mind, let us now focus on the question "What is African philosophy?" African philosophy is the study of a particular system of ethics, conduct, thought, nature of the universe, and so on, that has its basis in the culture and experience of African people. Nevertheless, as mentioned before, it is not merely philosophy produced by an author of African descent. It is the passionate discourse aimed at unlocking the wisdom encompassed in the African meaning of life and tradition that is of importance in this chapter. About this, Gyekye (1995) writes,

> A tradition requires that its elements (or most of them) be intimately related to the mentalities and cultural ethos of the people who possess the tradition; that these elements be related among themselves in a meaningful way; that they endure and be sustained; and that they be the subject of continuous pruning of refinement. (p. 37)

It is also important to state that African philosophy is not trapped in a capsule labeled "The Past." Because the African experience is fluid and not constrained to the linear concept of time, the contemporary African experience is just as important as the historical. In that spirit, let us now explore three specific dimensions of the Akan and Yorùbá traditions.

1. African views of the universe
2. The individual in relation to community
3. The notion of health and illness

One of the beauties of having the ability to think subjectively is illustrated in the onipa's capacity to formulate reflective views that bring meaning to one's life in this world and the cosmic universe. Since their existence, African people looked at the sky above and observed its stars, moons, sun, meteorites, clouds, rain, rainbows, and the movement of the winds (Mbiti, 1991). On Earth, these Africans were able to witness the cyclic progressions of life through the changes in the seasons and the transformations from seeds to beautiful trees. They began to experience the finite tenure of physical life (birth, maturity, procreation, death) and the infinite possibility of the spiritual life. They began to understand the meanings of love, hate, like, dislike, abundance, hunger, joy, sorrow, life, death, bravery, fear, community, isolation, pleasure, pain, and so on. These subjective Africans began to study the properties of the minerals and metals that saturated their surroundings. They brought about understandings in relation to the animal life forms that shared the Earth with them. "These experiences stimulated them to reflect upon their life and the universe in which they lived. The result was a gradual building up of African views or ideas about the world and the universe at large" (Mbiti, 1991, p. 34).

Although it may be deemed an impossible task to come up with an agreeable depiction of how the world was created, several similarities permeate African traditions throughout the continent. The universe is a created universe with the Supreme Being as the master architect. This created universe is both visible and invisible, yet the two are interconnected. It also is governed by order. As long as this order is not disturbed, the universe will continue to operate in a harmonious, rhythmic, and continuous fashion—with the seasons as evidence. Mbiti (1991) offers four dimensions of order: (a) Order in the laws of nature that allow events to be predictable—not random or chaotic; (b) moral order among people that produces value systems that support them to live in harmony among one another, with nature, with the universe, and with the Supreme Being; (c) religious order in the universe sanctioned by the Supreme Being in which the Supreme Being and other spiritual entities actively engage in the world's events; and finally there is (d) mystical order in the universe in which the practice of traditional medicine and healing tap into the power of the universe. Ultimately, the universe is viewed through the lens of human experience and it is the community's responsibility to live in harmony with it.

If we take a closer look at the community, it is obvious that a community is the summation of a group of individuals. However, survival of the fittest individual does not fit in the African paradigm of what it means to be a human in harmony with the universe. Communalism, according to Gyekye (1995), is an offshoot of the Akan concept of humanism wherein the welfare of the community and its member's interest are of utmost importance. Thus, to be human involves identifying with a group that will nurture a reciprocal relationship between the person and the community.

Understanding the responsibilities that one has to the other forms an integrated connectedness that through certain obligations in congruence with the survival of the group as a whole allows the person to obtain a sense of social significance that is crucial in maintaining good mental health. It is important to state that a person can simultaneously be unique and communalistic. However, "the conception and development of an individual's full personality and identity cannot be separated from her or his role in the group" (Gyekye, 1995, p. 161).

Finally, we come to the concept of health and illness. West Africans view the person's well being from a holistic perspective. If you take the Yorùbá word for health, *àlàáfíà*, it refers to more then just physical health. Àlàáfíà refers to a person's physical, spiritual, social, and psychological well being. If any of these aspects of a person's life is in a state of imbalance, then that person cannot claim to have àlàáfíà (Gbadegesin, 1991). Because the Yorùbá concept of the person, like the Akan, involves an interconnected-interdependent relationship between the body and soul, it is no wonder that they relate the capacity to be healthy with *ìlera* (strong body) and to be unhealthy with *àilera* (weak body) (Gbadegesin, 1991).

To be healthy is to have all aspects of human functioning in harmony with nature. This holistic approach is very important for identifying the therapeutic target of intervention. According to Gbadegesin,

> The task of the healer is to identify the cause of this imbalance and set it right. A healthy person, they say, is a wealthy person, and so the Yorùbá will do anything to avoid illness and if it occurs, to reinstate themselves to a healthy state because nothing compares to health [kíní tó àlàáfíà]. (1991, p. 127)

Failure to identify the true nature of distress will only have the potential to heal manifestations of the illness, as opposed to the illness itself, thus allowing it the capacity to rematerialize over time.

The ability to identify the cause of imbalance in a person's functioning can be a very difficult task. In many cases there are several causes and the answer usually depends on the healer's area of specialty. These causalities may include germs, psychological distress, forces in nature, one's ill actions, the spoken word, and so on. "The Yorùbá have a strong belief in the causal efficacy of a category of the spoken word: incantation … verbal utterances with particular tasks of changing the circumstances of life of a group or an individual for better or for worse" (Gbadegesin, 1991, p. 120). The Akan and Yorùbá concept of the person is both physical and spiritual in nature. At the same time, the universe is full of forces that permeate both the physical and spiritual plane. "Ability to make words perform such causal functions depends on how much of the essence of the forces of the universe is known" (Gbadegesin, 1991, p. 121). This reintroduces the profound implications speech can have on a person's health and the therapeutic process.

African Concept of the Person

The Akan conception of the person can be understood through the notions of *sunsum, ɔkra*, and *mogya*. Sunsum is the primary element of the person—spirit. Sunsum is the intangible element that accounts for the character (suban), disposition, and intelligence of a person (Appiah-Kubi, 1981; Ephirim-Donkor, 1997; Fisher, 1998; Gyekye, 1995; Opoku, 1978). It is also the "actor" or personae in a person's dream (Fisher, 1998; Gyekye, 1995; Opoku, 1978), thus having the capacity to leave the body and experience reality without the constraint of linear time. In this realm, the sunsum not only has the capacity to experience events in the past, present, and future, it can also relay important information or warnings to the person that may have profound implications in the world.

It is through *Onyankopon* (an Akan name for Supreme Being) that the sunsum reaches its subjective aim and is manifested into the ɔkra, or soul (Danquah, 1968). The ɔkra is the underlying part of the person that is a direct manifestation of the Creator (Appiah-Kubi, 1981; Ephirim-Donkor, 1997; Fisher, 1998; Gyekye, 1995; Opoku, 1978) that gives meaning to life. It is the living soul that constitutes the innermost self, the essence of the individual person (Gyekye, 1995). Ɔkra is often referred to as the guardian spirit that has the capacity to lend the person good or bad advice (Appiah-Kubi, 1981; Fisher, 1998; Opoku, 1978) and it is the embodiment and transmitter of the person's destiny (Appiah-Kubi, 1981; Ephirim-Donkor, 1997; Fisher, 1998; Gyekye, 1995; Opoku, 1978). Ɔkra cleansings are performed to wash away any filth that may have been accumulated through day-to-day life. With substantial significance placed on such rituals, the Akan elucidate the importance of maintaining both the physical and spiritual facets of the onipa in order to bring about a holistic notion of health. Unless the soul heals, the body will not respond to physical treatment (Gyekye, 1995). On physical death, the ɔkra will return to the Creator and the physical body will experience a cessation of breath—therefore, departure of the ɔkra from the body signifies death (Appiah-Kubi, 1981; Ephirim-Donkor, 1997; Fisher, 1998; Gyekye, 1995; Opoku, 1978).

Finally, there is mogya—or blood—that represents the most vital part of the physical body (*nipadua*). Appiah-Kubi (1981), Ephirim-Donkor (1997), Gyekye (1995), and Opoku (1978) all claim that mogya is passed down to the child through the mother, thus forming a physiological bond between them and the basis of the clan. It is also said that the *mogya* is responsible for the character that is transmitted from the parents to child.

However, after talking to several *okomfos* (Ghanaian traditional healers), it is my opinion that mogya is possibly passed down to the child by both the mother and the father. Intuitively, it is easier to picture the blood coming directly from the mother, because the development from an egg to a child all takes place within the mother's womb. However, the Akan have a saying: "When a man discharges sperm, it is equivalent to three bottles of blood." Because the sperm is the activating element that fertilized the egg, and is a potent source of blood (mogya), the child thus receives mogya from both parents, thereby explaining the apparent inherited characteristics from both parents.

The Yorùbá conception of the person is very similar to that of the Akan. Their concept of the person can be understood through the notion of *ara, èmí, okàn, orí, and ojiji*. Ara, the physical body, is formed by the divinity Orisha-nla. It is the medium—flesh and bone that we know through the senses—through which the person acts or reacts through the physical environment (Bascom, 1991; Gbadegesin, 1991; Idowu, 1995; Lucas, 1996; Opoku, 1978). At death, the ara will perish and return to the Earth whence it came (Gbadegesin, 1991; Lucas, 1996; Opoku, 1978).

Èmí is often referred to as spirit. The divinity Olorun breathes it into the ara—once Orisha-nla forms the ara—to make them living human beings (Bascom, 1991; Gbadegesin, 1991; Lucas, 1996; Opoku, 1978). Èmí is the divine active principle of life that links man to the Creator (Bascom, 1991; Gbadegesin, 1991; Idowu, 1995; Lucas, 1996; Opoku, 1978). Once èmí is activated throughout the ara, the body now has èmí (breath) and begins to *mí* (breathe) (Gbadegesin, 1991). Because èmí is imperishable and the activating force that animates the human body, it is often regarded as the uppermost part of the person. When the physical breath ceases to exist during physical death, this divine breath—èmí—will return to the Creator from which it came (Bascom, 1991; Gbadegesin, 1991; Idowu, 1995; Lucas, 1996; Opoku, 1978).

Okàn is directly translated as the heart, but is referred to as the heart-soul and recognized as the seat of intelligence, emotion, psychic energy, thought, and action (Bascom, 1991; Gbadegesin, 1991; Idowu, 1995; Lucas, 1996; Opoku, 1978). It is also thought to have the capacity to leave the body during sleep. Another important spiritual entity in the person is orí. Orí is translated as the physical-head and is the very essence of personality. Orí is the bearer of one's destiny and is the guardian protector of the person. It rules, controls, and guides the life and activity of the person (Bascom, 1991; Gbadegesin, 1991; Idowu, 1995; Opoku, 1978). The personality-soul in the person is a manifestation of the Supreme Being. The Yorùbá also recognize ojiji—shadow—as an essential part of the person. It is a constant companion of the person, a visible representation of the okàn that ceases to exist when the ara dies (Bascom, 1991; Idowu, 1995; Lucas, 1996; Opoku, 1978).

The Study of Nature
(Physics' Relation to African Psychology)

To appreciate the profound effects that good healing practices can have in the therapeutic process, it is important to examine the science of physics (from a holistic perspective) and the numerous implications it can have on African psychology. Physics, as it is formally understood, is the study of nature dealing with the properties, changes, and interactions of different forms of energy. Because all things in the universe are interconnected and predisposed to divine order, physics can be used as a technique, or tool, to bring about a deeper understanding of all aspects of reality. To view spiritual phenomena as merely supernatural events is erroneous if all things in nature follow the laws of divine order. Lack of knowledge is not a good enough reason to dismiss something as a possibility and label it as supernatural. Because physics is the study of nature, it can aid in bringing an abstract possibility into a concrete reality.

A good place to begin is with the notion of energy. Halliday, Resnick, and Walker (1997) define energy as a measure that is associated with a state (or condition) of one or more bodies. But, what is energy? In Western science, energy is described as being the capacity to do work. At its essence, it is all that was, is, and ever will be. It is the source that we draw from to perform our daily operations. As complex as it may seem, energy may not be visible, but its effects are certainly understood. We cannot go to a physics lab and make energy; we can only understand its properties to perform useful tasks. The law of conservation states that energy cannot be destroyed, but we constantly waste it. Because energy cannot be created, nor destroyed, it can only be manipulated from one form to another. Therefore, energy is the capacity of an object in a certain situation to perform useful tasks called work. The transferring of energy from one object to another is what is meant by work. Work ($W = F \times d$) is the product of a force (F) times a distance (d). In describing the transfer of energy from some distance (d), it is accepted that some force must cause this motion to take place. Newton's First Law states that if there is no net force on a body, the body must remain at rest if it is initially at rest. Fluctuation of work will create power. Power ($P = W/T$) is defined as the rate in which work is done, or the change of work per unit time. As a force acts on an energy source, energy is displaced some distance (d), thus creating work. As the change of work increases with time, so will the power that it has now created.

Imagine a match sitting in some gunpowder. In this situation, the gunpowder is a form of energy, but it is useless sitting in a pile unless some work is done on it. Lighting the match sitting on the gunpowder, representing a form of work, will cause an explosion, producing a large amount of power. The large amount of power is evident from the rapid change that the gunpowder undergoes when the fire (work) is added to it. Now imagine putting a turbine into a lake to generate power for lighting up your home. You would be unhappy when you realize that your lights do not turn on. A static source of water, or energy, cannot turn a turbine to deliver any power to turn on your house lights. Remove this turbine and place it into a river and now your lights turn on. This happens because your turbine now has an energy source (river) that is applying a force to it through work, thus producing power.

Given the above, where does spiritual phenomenon fit in and what is its relation to energy? Western science makes physical sense, but it also has its contradictions. How can one accept energy as being something that cannot be seen but experienced, yet no validity can be given to the notion of spirit? Spirit can also be described as something that cannot (always) be seen, but it is definitely experienced. Only one, who chooses not to experience spirit, can dismiss its existence as a true scientific phenomenon. Because what we perceive as massive objects is nothing but an illusion of bundles of invisible energy, why is it so difficult for people to deal with the possibility of spiritual phenomena as a concrete reality? I would argue that the main reason why Western science does not recognize the notion of spirit is not because it cannot see it—for it admits that energy cannot be seen (but mass can be seen!), yet energy is the foundation of all of its theories. The true issue is that Western science, and its practitioners, are in disharmony with spirit and therefore cannot experience it. As a result, these scientists have created religion to reconnect them to that which they once were.

Africans never acknowledged their people as being naturally born devoid of spirit. For the only parallel to such a being is one who is dead! Africans understand the notion of spirit to be an energy source that cannot be created or destroyed. This is apparent in their belief in reincarnation and spiritual immortality. This spiritual energy source is cosmically connected to all beings, and if understood, it can create a strong spiritual force—which leads to a strong spiritual power. By no means is this an attempt to illustrate that Western science is flawed. The only problem is that its holistic fruit became barren when planted into an anti-African soil.

Building on the notion that the nature of subatomic particles is essentially dynamic, is it important to ask the question whether everything in the universe is truly interconnected? The quest to define a mechanistic description of subatomic particles isolated from the influence of the world has been deemed an impossible task. As a result, physicists will be unable to precisely predict future events under definite circumstances. "Yes! Physics has given up. We do not know how to predict what will happen in a given circumstance, and we believe now that it is impossible—that the only thing that can be predicted is the probability of different events" (Feynman, Leighton, & Sands, 1965, p. 10). Quantum mechanics confirms the interconnectedness of a cosmic universe and makes it apparent in its recognition of all matter as a complex interaction between bundles of energy. Because energy permeates everything, it becomes senseless to think of the capacity to isolate that which is being studied in order to have an objective experiment. Bohr (1934)—who received a Nobel Prize in physics and created the Bohr model of the atom—stated, "Isolated material particles are abstractions, their properties being definable and observable only through their interactions with other systems" (p. 57), thus supporting the African notion of a cosmic universe where everything is interconnected. It is also imperative to appreciate that "true" objectivity—the capacity to analyze the world in self-governing parts that are autonomous from the observer—is impossible in a world in which everything is cosmically joined together through the forces of energy and, more specifically, spirit.

I would argue that spirit and energy is like elder and elderly. All spirits consist of electromagnetic energy, but all energy does not have the intellectual capacity of spirit. Electromagnetic energy flows in and out of our bodies all day long. There is no doubt that we, as African people, contain a personal spirit that is divine in nature, and that this spiritual essence is connected to all that exists throughout the cosmos. There is also no doubt that an unlimited amount of spiritual forces exist in our realm go unused and are wasted. Spiritual power is not going to jump in your lap and take you on a storytelling ride. The union of the spirit and person in sacred time and space occurs through the performance of rituals, through the living of a subjective reality that fuses one's brain, mind, feelings, and soul into the dynamic cosmic universe. When these rituals are performed, spiritual motion begins to take place, thus resulting in a force that is now doing work. Depending on the person's training and spiritual capacity, this work can be transformed into a strong spiritual power that can be used for positive or negative purposes. Spiritual energy is not to be played with, and cannot be summed up in some scholar's book. Life is experiential and until you begin to engage in spirit, nothing can be written in a book to give it its due. It is the challenge of the therapist to harness the necessary spiritual energy to heal the mind, body, and soul when counseling a client of African descent. This process may take a lot of work, but in the end, its results will exemplify an infinite, powerful change in the client that is priceless.

Four Questions

Given the above introduction into West African deep thought, it is now time to present and explore the concept of wɔ ahoɔden (Twi for "to be healthy"), an African-centered psychological theory that can be used in the therapeutic intervention of African people. Given the four essential questions that this theory addresses—(a) How did Africans view the notion of onipa before European contact? (b) In the context of precolonial Africa, what was considered normal behavior? (c) What effects did the maafa process have on the

African onipa? (d) What role can healers play in facilitating the realignment of the African onipa in an anti-African environment?—it is the purpose of wↄ ahoↄden to be used as a tool in the therapeutic process that seeks to realign one's onipaness to its divine possibility.

Wↄ Ahoↄden: To Be Healthy

Onipa (Human Being)

How did Africans view the notion of onipa before European contact? To date, psychologists have failed to clearly define and understand the nature of human beingness. Instead, significant amount of critical time is wasted on debates that ask "Does a Supreme Being actually exist" or "Is the Big Bang Theory truly responsible for the world as we know it?" "Is the person governed by nature or by nurture?" "Is everything predetermined or do we have free will?" In order to understand the onipa, one must first understand the African view of the universe stated above. With an understanding that a moral order exists among people that produces value systems that support them to live in harmony among one another, with nature, with the universe, and with the Supreme Being, there should be no surprise that the onipa is comprised of both a physical and spiritual component. It is the interconnected equilibrium between the body and soul that is responsible for true mental health. In an attempt to elucidate on the nature of the person in the African view of the universe, several African conceptions of personhood (e.g., Akan and Yorùbá) will be examined. By no means do I want to suggest that African societies were, or are today, monolithic. However, these groups of people have a remarkably close living tradition that dates back to ancient Kemet (Diop, 1974; Obenga, 1992) and are also comprised of a considerable amount of those Africans that were stolen to be bought and sold in the New World—our ancestors (Ben-Jochannan & Clarke, 1991; Mannix, 1962; Price, 1979). (Figure 5.1 provides an overview of the following elements to the onipa.)

The soul (Kemites = atum + akhu; Akan = ↄkra; Yorùbá = okàn/orí; Ewe = luvo; Ga = susuma) is a critical component in the therapeutic process as discussed earlier in the chapter. Given the body's interdependence on the soul, and characteristics of the body to respond to physical treatment, it will serve the healer considerably to conceptualize the dimensions of the soul that can be tapped into during the therapeutic process. The soul is the embodiment and transmitter of the individual's destiny (Akan = nkrabea; Yorùbá = kàdarà; Ga = shee mlí). One's destiny is the purpose, or message, that the Supreme Being sets for the soul. This purpose, or message, is to determine the manner in which the individual is to live in this world. A person's destiny cannot be avoided or altered without the Supreme Being's

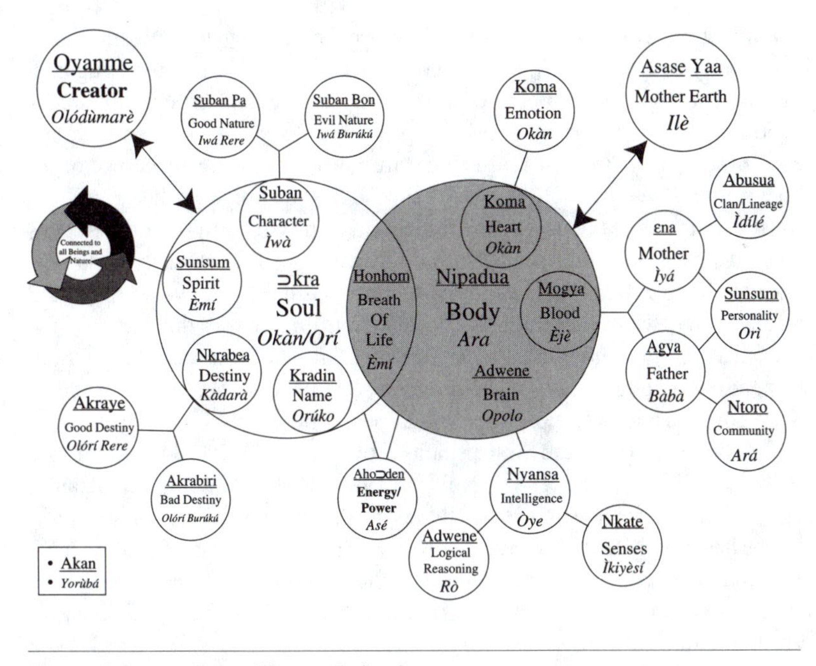

Figure 5.1 Onipa (Human Beings)

permission. The Supreme Being can alter one's destiny in a good way when one continuously exhibits good character. It can also be altered in a bad way if one continues to exhibit bad character. Therefore, it is through the notion of free will with good character that a good destiny is completed. Thus, bad character can lead to the undoing of a good destiny. The Yorùbá have a saying "that a good destiny is wasted by bad character." (Although the Akan and the Yorùbá tend to disagree on how one's destiny is obtained from the Supreme Being, they tend to agree that once the soul knows what destiny has been bestowed on it, a pact between the soul and the Supreme Being is reached.) Imagine if you knew that you selected when you wanted to come to Earth who your mother would be and what life circumstances and challenges you wanted to face. If this were the case, how would this affect our perceptions of our life circumstances and our capacity to enhance therapy? Would you continue to feel sorry for yourself when times got unbearably hard? Or would you recognize this as an opportunity to perfect a spiritual defect that has the capacity to be healed if the situation is approached correctly? If you knew that you had more than one chance to attain spiritual perfection, how might this affect your perception of stress and fear of the unknown in your everyday life?

Another important component of the soul is spirit (Kemites = khaba; Akan = sunsum; Yorùbá = èmí; Ewe = gb⊃gb⊃; Ga = mum⊃). The spirit is a nontangible entity that is responsible for the character, disposition, and personality of a person. A strong personality is said to be a remedy against illness. The quality of a person's spirit may be assessed through the observation of one's actions. A person's spirit may leave the body and experience other dimensions of reality that are not constrained to the notion of linear time. Dreams (night and day) are the best example of this. Here, the spirit may travel to the past or the future and bring back important messages that may have profound impacts on all aspects of life. For instance, a person may have a dream that a family member has died, only to wake up and discover that what was thought to only be a dream was the spirit of the departed family member letting that person know of the recent transition. Depending on one's view of the universe, this incident could be viewed as mere coincidence, intuition, or spiritual perception.

Because spirit is the first principle of life (Akbar, 1984; Ani, 1980; Hilliard, 1997; Myers, 1988; Nobles, 1986; Parham, White, & Ajamu, 1999), it is interconnected to all things in the universe. Trees have spirit. Water has spirit. Rocks have spirit. Animals have spirit. Some healers have the capacity to communicate to spirits in these different entities. That is why nature is so important when prescribing remedies for different sicknesses. For the nature of the sickness could have been a simple violation to some spirit's space, like cutting down a tree without asking its permission. To the extent that one's soul is in tune to different spiritual encounters, one's decision-making processes will be more efficient for producing results that bring one closer to completing critical tasks involved in one's destiny.

A person's character (Akan = suban; Yorùbá = ìwà; Ewe = n⊃n⊃me; Ga = jenba) and a person's name (Akan = kradin; Yorùbá = orúko; Ewe = nk⊃; Ga = gbei) also have important roles in relation to the soul. In this regard, a person's intrinsic character strengths and weaknesses are genetically transmitted to the child from the mother and father. As a child, the disposition of the parents dominates one's character. As one begins to mature through different developmental stages, personality and attitude will begin to have greater control over one's character. Spirit also has a strong influence on character.

A person's name is a symbolic representation of one's character and destiny (Fu-Kiau, 1991). Because a person's name is connected to the immortal soul, deliberate techniques, or rituals, are used in order to assure that one's soul is given its due through its name. It is believed that a correctly chosen name has the capacity to influence a child's purpose or character. Some Akan healers assert that a person's name can be used to revitalize or bring about harm to one's onipa. All this to say that a person's name can have insightful implications on life.

Scientists have had better providence in describing the physical aspects of the person. We are now in an era where parts of human functioning can be broken down into physiological chemical compositions that cause neurons to fire and excite specific regions of the body that cause a desired response to occur. Unfortunately, it still fails to illustrate the interconnectedness between the soul and the body. The body (Kemites = ka; Akan = nipadua; Yorùbá = ara; Ewe = nutilã; Ga = gbɔmɔtso) is created from the physical elements that exist on earth. The body is the vehicle that gives the spiritual entity experience and does not continue to live after death. However, through the customary funeral rites, the body is placed in the fetal position as a symbolic representation that the soul will now transcend into a different reality and that the body will now return to its original form as an accumulation of elements that make up the Earth.

One of the most powerful elements of the body is blood (Akan = mogya; Yorùbá = èjè; Ewe = vu; Ga = la). Biologically, blood is the extracellular fluid within the cardiovascular system. It consists of a yellowish fluid, plasma, whose weight is composed of 90% water, 8% plasma proteins (albumin, globulins, and fibrinogen), and 2% organic compounds and electrolytes. Blood consists mostly of red cells (erythrocytes), with a small composition of white cells (leukocytes) and platelets (thrombocytes). Blood circulates throughout the body carrying oxygen nutrients to the tissues while simultaneously removing carbon dioxide and other waste products. This same circulation is also responsible for dissipating heat that has been generated by oxidative reactions in cells. Another important function of blood involves the distribution of hormones. This process assists in maintaining homoeostasis and coordinating the activities of the organs of the body. It is through the transportation of white cells and antibodies (immunoglobulins) to the tissues that allows the blood to defend the body from pathogenic organisms and foreign substances (Bray, Cragg, Macknight, & Mills, 1999).

On the other hand, blood is the essence of human life that is inherited from the mother and father. The parents' spiritual, physical, and personality traits can be passed down to their children through their blood. It establishes a physiological bond between one's parents and ancestral lineage. Understanding the blood's role in spiritual and physical well being is paramount to the development of a healthy onipa. Realizing the important ancestral physiological connection that exists in blood and the African interconnected views of the cosmic universe, can people of African descent continue to experience Black-on-Black communal deaths through the lens of murder as opposed to suicide? In the Eurocentric worldview, the individual is seen as the center of the universe; thus to take a life is seen as murder. In the African tradition, a belief in the interconnectedness of people (even through blood) would render that act of homicide as suicide because to harm another is tantamount to harming oneself.

The body's strongest muscle, the heart (Akan = koma; Yorùbá = okàn; Ewe = dzi dzime; Ga = tsui), is responsible for the circulation of blood. Africans of ancient Kemet referred to the heart as the house of the soul

(Akbar, 1984; Nobles, 1986). It was also believed to be the central location of emotions and psychological reactions because its drumbeat was directly related to the current emotional state (beating fast when the person was excited and slow when the person was calm). As a result, the emotional state of the person can be taken as a function of the heart-soul. The Yorùbá view the okàn as the seat—or center—of intelligence (i.e., mind). Due to its dualistic properties—heart and house of the soul—the Yorùbá attribute similar properties to the heart, or okàn, as the Akan tribute to the soul, or ɔkra. In the end, the ancients made it clear in the scene of the "Psychostasia" from the Hu-Nefer Papyrus (Nobles, 1986) that one's fate would depend on the conduct and illumination of the soul.

Finally, we get to the brain (Kemites = akhu; Akan = adwene; Yorùbá = opolo; Ewe = susu; Ga = ansɔ), a high-powered neurological system that is responsible for putting the soul's will into action through the use of the body. It is responsible for the distribution and interpretation of information, and it also controls the body's sensory and motor operations. The brain grows and matures with time and is considered to be the house of intelligence.

In describing the dimensions of the body and soul, it is critical to make clear that the two are interconnected. When harm is brought on one system, the other system is affected. One cannot have good physical health and bad spiritual health and vice versa. The key to good health is to have these two systems operating amicably with one another. The ancestors of Kemet remind us that proof that these two entities are interconnected is the breath of life (Kemites = ba; Akan = honhom; Yorùbá = èmí; Ewe = gbɔgbɔ; Ga = mumɔ), which comes into existence during birth. When the connection between the body and soul ceases to exist, so will the breath of life—resulting in physical death. Breath is an invisible life force viewed as a spiritual activating principle in blood. That is why it is interesting to note that the Ewe and the Ga interchange the same word for the breath of life with spirit. To the extent that the body and soul are working in congruence with one another in a developed sense of harmonious precision, that person is said to be healthy, full of energy, and powerful (Akan = ahoɔden; Yorùbá = asé).

Healthy Ahoɔden (Energy)

In the context of precolonial Africa, what was considered normal behavior? An interesting phenomenon that continues to be prevalent in today's Western psychological circle is that although psychologists are very clear in identifying abnormal behavior, research leading to the definition of normal behavior is marginal at best. It is often puzzling to understand how one can rationalize a comprehensive scientific description of abnormal behavior and not engage in the process of describing normal behavior. If normal behavior is not clearly defined, what model—if any—are clients being

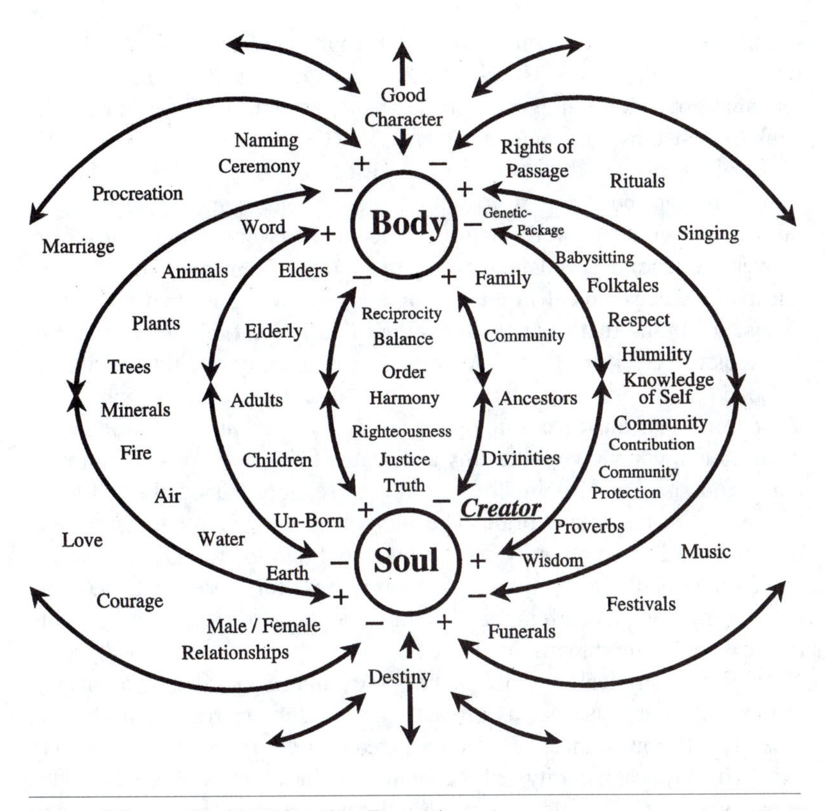

Figure 5.2 Healthy Ahoↄden (Energy)

aligned to? What is being used as an unbiased determinant that illustrates when the client is now psychologically, spiritually, and physically healthy? Being careful not to fall victim to "democratic sanity," scholars like Akbar (1994), Ani (1980), Hilliard (1997), Myers (1988), Nobles (1986), and Parham, White, and Ajamu (1999)—to name a few—have made it clear that the African way is to place such a responsibility in the hands of divine law. Healthy ahoↄden (energy), the capacity to nurture a healthy spiritual and physical base that is interdependent and manifested through one's actions, can be broken up into four major mutually supporting categories: maat, humanness, spiritual-physical maturity, and orí-ire. (Figure 5.2 provides an overview of healthy ahoↄden.)

The core of healthy ahoↄden is positioned on the cardinal virtues of maat as depicted by the Africans of ancient Kemet. Maat demands truth, justice, righteousness, harmony, order, balance, and reciprocity in the functioning of the sacred world, universe, governance, and human community. Maat is also manifest in the religious, cosmic, political, social, and anthropological domains (Hilliard, 1997; Obenga, 1996). With this vast insight of cosmic order, one can begin to understand and appreciate normal behavior on a cosmological level. The client can now be examined through the same lens that governs the universe (physics) as opposed to a linear measuring stick truncated by "democratic sanity."

To keep maat as a central theme for discussing healthy ahoↄden in relation to normal behavior, it is important to discuss what it means to be human. An Akan proverb states, "When man (woman) descends from heaven, he (she) descends into a human society." Humanness, then, is the harmonious engagement in one's community and culture that provides a design for living that ensures the welfare and interest of each member of the society (Gyekye, 1995). A person's community should provide an extended family unit that shares common cultural values, expressions, and aspirations that are in cosmological harmony with maat to produce an environment conducive to healthy ahoↄden. Humanness looks to communal events as a focal point for cultural expression and a vehicle for the acquisition of power and pride. The survival of the community is of great importance. The community should also continue to struggle to improve communal conditions that maximize humanness for those yet to be born, those comprising its current membership, and those who have passed on to the next revolving dimension of life.

Spiritual-physical maturity cannot be examined in a dichotomous perception of reality because, as previously stated, the spiritual and physical essence of the onipa must be interconnected in order for healthy ahoↄden to exist. The physical maturity that is conducive to healthy ahoↄden refers to the person's ability to progress from the unborn, to a child, to an adult, to an elderly, and to an elder. Physical maturity reaches perfection in the final stage that results in the nobility of being able to sit among the great ancestors, divinity, and ultimately, the Supreme Being. The cyclical progression through these stages is related to the dimension of perfectibility—the constant aspiration of becoming more self-actualized each day. This involves the transformation of being less physical and more spiritually oriented as symbolically illustrated by the Kemite's hor-em-aket (the so-called sphinx) or the Akan cosmological postulates: e-su, o-te, sunsum, ↄkra, honhom, onyame, onyankopon, and odomankoma discussed in detail by Danquah (1968).

Three cyclic stages of becoming serve as the foundation of spiritual-physical maturity: understanding, experience, and insight. The process of understanding speaks to the notion of having the capacity to recognize the constellation of an element's existence in space. It is through the process of understanding that a basic element comes into existence. This concept of understanding can be as concrete as realizing that one is an Akan, Yorùbá, Ibo, Mende, and so on, or as abstract as realizing that a person is a separate physical entity in a diverse constellation of spirit or energy.

Experience allows the element that was born into existence to evolve in space through the dimension of time. Experience brings a higher level of consciousness into existence. Free will is practiced through one's actions. Navigation through the universe begins to enhance the element's intuition, thus producing better decisions. Feelings begin to generate and reflect the element's observation of reality. Through the process of experience, memory is re-created. Experience allows an element to navigate through life to bring about a deeper understanding of its existence.

Finally, insight can occur when understanding and experience is mastered. Insight is the hallmark of becoming. Insight occurs through the recognition of reality, thus allowing the element to discern truth from falsehood. A sense of freedom is achieved at this stage. The element has now transcended the individual, linear, dichotomist logic that is prevalent in the process of understanding. Insight results in the view that the elements' true essence is just an extension of a greater source in which all is inclusive. The concept of insight results in the realization that one is a spiritual entity that is interconnected and interrelated to all that exists. Everything is now in the first place spirit but appears to be different because of the different complex combinational formation of the spiritual entity.

The previously described constituents (maat, humanness, and spiritual-physical maturity) are the nucleus of healthy ahoɔden. To the extent that the body and soul submits to them, the more wholesome and powerful the healthy ahoɔden will be. When looking at normal behavior, it is important to understand what guides a person's actions. Healthy ahoɔden is guided by the Yorùbá notion of orí-ire. Orí-ire is the quest of one's actions, thoughts, and feelings to operate in accord with one's destiny while being aligned in good character, humility, and respect for eldership. When orí-ire is directing one's actions, the body and soul is in harmony and spiritually connected to a higher consciousness. This is evident when a person's understanding of knowledge continuously transcends into wisdom. The greater the alignment that exists between one's onipa and orí-ire, the more efficiently the onipa will successfully navigate through the stages of spiritual-physical maturity.

If the whole world automatically submitted to these principles, we would be less dependent on psychologists. Because it is clear that mental, physical, and spiritual health is not always an automatic reality, it is the function of the healer to use these principles, and the client's capacity of free will, to prescribe a remedy to remove whatever disequilibria that are responsible for the client's distress.

Yare (To Be Sick)—Maafa Destructive Interference

What effects did the maafa process have on the African onipa? Part of what it means to be healthy is to have a clear understanding of what it means for sickness to become you—yare (Twi for "sick"). When one is able to identify a sickness, the next step is to identify its nature or origin. Fighting a

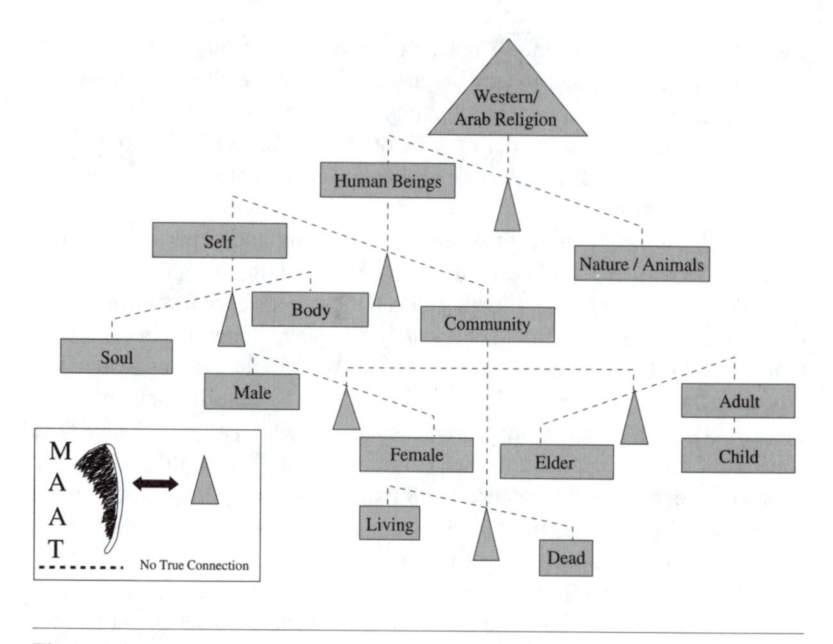

Figure 5.3 Yare (To Be Sick)

tle against a sickness full of unknowns leads to a speculating placebo remedy that may temporarily disguise itself as a cure, only to later expose its catalyst affect toward another unknown problem. When looking at the mental, physical, and spiritual health of people of African descent, one cannot ignore the affects of the maafa destructive interference to the healthy aho⊃den. Metaphorically, to do so will only lead to a healer's prescription to cure a branch, diseased of its ability to be radiant of its African onipaness, without understanding the true problem residing in the dirt that nurtures the roots of the onipa. (Figure 5.3 offers an overview of yare.)

Remember that the word maafa is Kiswahili for "disaster" and is the term often used to describe the multidimensional facets of the African holocaust (i.e., enslaved Africans, slave dungeons, middle passage, slave tamers, chattel slavery in the United States, and psychological slavery that continues to be pervasive today). The primary tool used to alienate Africans from their worldview was fear and a sense of helplessness. Physical death awaited many Africans who had the courage to resist, whereas spiritual incarceration was handed out to those who appeared to accept their situation. However, it is important to note that the African spirit often transcended these options through successful revolts (e.g., Maroon Societies), rituals, music, dance, symbolic speech, and so on, with the preservation of one's onipaness as a common premise. It is not the focus of this chapter to give a detailed depiction of the whole maafa process, but it is my belief that the institution of maafa is still in effect today. Traditional African spiritual systems are thought to be the practice of paganism, reducing African people into a subhuman class needing religion and such harsh treatment to save them. Through Western "objective" scientific practice, the human being is separated from nature to discover its vast mysteries, thus instilling a control-over-nature mentality that places the human being above nature. Within the human being, the individual self is disconnected and more important than the community as a whole, fostered by a survival-of-the-fittest mentality. In this new materialistic system, the body is more important than the soul, thus falling victim to the primitive pleasure principle. Men will also place their female counterpart in an inferior position. This can easily be exemplified in the wage difference between genders with the same job title. Adults are of most importance, whereas the elderly are thrown into nursing homes. Those living in the here and now are all that exist, thus little—if any—attention is given to the connection between those yet-to-be-born, those living, and those who have transcended.

Maafa destructive interference is simply a manifestation of people of African descent's willingness (through free will) to adopt a European worldview to interpret reality and govern their actions. In many cases, this is a yare mechanism, with attempts to be successful in a country that is run with a European ideology that has no intentions to affirm an African humanity and ways of being. If this statement is not true and cultural differences are truly embraced, why, then, is biculturalism truly necessary? An attempt to live a life that is not in alignment with one's cultural healthy ahoɔden can only result in yare behavior. Yare, the opposite of wɔ ahoɔden, can be organized into four major dimensions: *isfet*, zombieness, spiritual-physical immaturity, and *orí-ibe*.

When we look at the notion of *isfet*, we are taking a glimpse at potential causes of disordered behavior. Isfet is the opposite of maat. It represents a misalignment with the seven cardinal virtues (truth, justice, righteousness, harmony, order, balance, and reciprocity) and the five dimensions of character (divinity, teachability, perfectibility, free will, and moral and social responsibility), resulting in behavior that is in opposition to the 42 Declarations of Innocence. Isfet is characterized by a strong sense of falsehood and deception. A person aligned with isfet is surrounded by negative energy.

Zombieness is a term applied to a person who appears to be spiritually dead—a person who made the decision to accept spiritual incarceration with hopes of assuring a fruitful physical life. As a result, an alien design for living and interpreting reality has been adopted. The worldview has been assimilated to match that of the oppressor. A person in this state usually operates in isolation and is not connected to a greater African community. This person has no true connection to spirit or the universe. A fragmented understanding of self—and its relationship to the world—is developed. In the end, zombieness results in an internal sense of powerlessness and hopelessness.

Spiritual-physical immaturity speaks to the notion of operating from the lower self. In this case, the person is driven primarily by impulses that satisfy one's instinctual biological urges and result in physical satisfaction. Physical growth is so dominating—in comparison to spiritual growth—that there seems to be no true understanding of the spiritual-physical connection. This person has very few, if any, experiences with spirit, thus viewing spirit as an abstract possibility rather than a concrete reality. Because no true relationship is established with the spirit, the spirit becomes defenseless and is constantly in the mist of chaos. Intellectual growth eventually reaches a standstill and the person becomes quick to settle for less than what is possible.

Finally there is *orí-ibe*, the opposite of orí-ire. Orí-ibe occurs when one's actions, thoughts, and feelings are misaligned between one another and with one's destiny. In orí-ibe, the soul, body, and spirit are in constant conflict. Each entity wants to fulfill its needs with little or no regard for the others. Development of good character through discipline is neglected. This person is no longer operating under natural law. As a result, he or she is surrounded by misfortunes and accidents. This is that person who feels that the world is always picking on him or her, resulting in little or no direction with life's or personal goals.

Nya Ahoↄden (To Be Healed)— Reconstructive Interference

What role can healers play in facilitating the realignment of the African onipa in an anti-African environment? As we attempt to counteract the long-term effects that the maafa destructive interference has on the healthy ahoↄden, the most essential step is to identify the nature of distress. Once this is determined, the healer can begin to prepare a remedy to revitalize the power, or energy, in the person's onipa as a result of balance restoration.

When an onipa approaches a healer with an illness, that person may or may not know the true cause of the distress. Sometimes clients may know the true nature of their illness, yet it may be so devastating that they choose (consciously or unconsciously) to displace the nature of the illness on something more easily acceptable. As the healer begins to listen and participate in the therapeutic process, it is important to understand that the true nature of the distress can be both internal, external, or both. When we look internally into the onipa, the illness can have its roots in the onipa's soul, biochemical imbalance, cognition, emotions, beliefs, or character. Externally, the nature of distress can be derived from spirit, racism, environment versus onipa, maafa, behavior, or a sense of powerlessness.

Once the nature of distress is clearly identified, the healer must then be able to identify the most optimal target of therapeutic intervention that can restore the person's life force to its fullest capacity. Just like the nature of distress, the target of therapeutic intervention can also be internal, external, or both. Within the internal environment you have that which is tangible and nontangible. Science has overcome some significant milestones to explain the biochemical makeup of a person, although it is also clear that there is still a lot of room for discovery and improvement. It is through this technology that we are currently able to relate some mental health issues to specific physiological functions of the body. On the other hand, there is great work needed in the assessment of the nontangible internal aspects of the onipa. Spirit, dream, character, purpose, and identity analysis can and should be a fundamental part of the therapeutic process. Many of our healers become complacent with one therapeutic technique that may focus on only one target of therapeutic intervention (e.g., aspect of the personality) and miss out on critical information that could have been received from some of the other dimensions. It is such training that allows the healer, at the end of the therapeutic process, to diagnose an ill client as being perfectly healthy, particularly when that client is viewed through a different cultural worldview. The external environment, like one's family, friends, community, or culture, is also a critical target of therapeutic intervention, especially because they are often part of the nature of distress. The external environment can also offer alternative insights about the client that may have been unnoticed by the healer.

Once the nature of distress and the target of therapeutic intervention are identified, the healer can then begin to prescribe a remedy to the situation. A useful remedy can be deemed useless if it does not speak directly to the client. That is why it is important to understand how and why people change. The onipa, a synthesis of the soul and body, creates a combined consciousness that interprets reality for the client. It is through the notion of free will that the client then makes decisions that are either in accordance with maat, resulting in w⊃ aho⊃den, or in opposition with maat (in accord with isfet), resulting in yare. It is through actions that are in concurrence with isfet that cause the experience of the onipa, onipa's shadow, to become filled with unhealthy energy, thus making it become heavier (because mass is a form of energy as discussed earlier in the chapter). Physics states that energy is equal to mass times the speed of light squared. As the mass of the onipa's shadow becomes heavier and heavier, the client's internal energy level becomes filled with an unstable potential energy that can be directed into positive or negative actions. The challenge for the healer is to present a good remedy that will harness this energy and use it to aid in the therapeutic process. Health is then achieved when the onipa's shadow is in equilibrium with maat.

Finally we come to the question, What is the role of the healer? Although this issue is explored more fully in Chapter 7, it is important to mention here that the healer should provide an environment that is conducive to healing. A certain level of cultural and spiritual rapport should be established with the client to nurture a sense of education and empowerment. This speaks to the process of illuminating and liberating the client's spirit so that it has the capacity to assist in the healing process and achieving mastery over all aspects of human functioning. This results in a client that is more equipped to overcome personal and social tribulations. The healer should be able to help the client bring about congruence with the client's soul, body, and spirit by thoroughly analyzing the nontangible and tangible internal and external targets of intervention. Unstable internal energy that may lead to disordered behavior must be harnessed and redirected to aid in the healing process. Finally, the healer should appreciate one's cultural values and realign the client according to the divine principles of maat. The client should leave the therapeutic process with a validation of his or her personality, sense of power, and onipaness.

Having now presented and explored the sense of self from the African deep structure, Chapter 6 will continue this exploration by examining the self and consciousness using the Akan model as a point of reference.

6

African-Centered Conceptualizations of Self and Consciousness

The Akan Model

Cheryl Grills and Martin Ajei

The definitions and meanings ascribed to the self are the most basic, the deepest, and the furthest from awareness. "While assumptions about what a self is are furthest from our conscious awareness, they are also the most powerful and significant assumptions behind and beneath our behaviors" (Landrine, 1992). Western psychology operates from the model of a referential self (Gaines, 1982). This referential self is a separate, encapsulated self that is presumed to be the originator, creator, and controller of behavior. This referential self has unique abilities, preferences, needs, and desires that define and differentiate it from other selves. As such, the referential self can be described without reference to others or to context. From this independent self, Western concepts such as "self-awareness, self-criticism, self-consciousness, self-reflection, self-determination, self-actualization, self-fulfillment, and self-change are all possible, permissible, and indeed, expected in Western psychotherapy" (Landrine, 1992). In other words, in Western thought, this independent self is an autonomous, free agent.

Landrine (1992) argues that the alternative concept of the self, known to many sociocentric ethnocultural groups, is the indexical self. Here, the self "is perceived as constituted or 'indexed' by the contextual features of social interaction in diverse situations" (Gaines, 1982). This is true for Asian Americans (Marsella, 1985), Latinos (Marsella & White, 1982), Native Americans (Garrett & Garrett, 1998), and African Americans (Akbar, Saafir, & Granberry, 1996; Ani, 1994; Hilliard, 1997; Kambon,

1999; Nobles, 1998). The indexical self does not exist independent of its context and relationships. Further, the self is created and re-created within the context of relationships and situations or contexts within which it exists. This indexical self, then, is not a separate entity that can be referred to or reflected on in isolation, but rather is dependent on its connections for definition. It is also important to note that the indexical self is not limited to the physical world context and sets of relationships. It includes the "super" natural world of nature, the spirits, the ancestors, and God.

Akan Conceptualization of the Person and Consciousness

Culture provides an important lens through which an understanding of human psychological and social functioning can be attained. This understanding reflects a particular perspective derived from the experience of a group and will differ from culture to culture. An African epistemology emphasizes an affective-cognitive synthesis as a way of knowing reality. This reality does not limit itself to the five senses and rational logic as the only means for securing information and understanding. Knowing is not limited to linear reasoning. Knowing is not bound by space, time, the senses, cognition, and tangible verification or control of that which is known. Finally, the spiritual basis of all there is to know makes African epistemology distinct from that found in Western philosophy.

By way of example, let us consider the Akan cultural model. Akan conceptualizations of the person and consciousness are a direct extension of Akan metaphysics and epistemology. The fundamental structure of Akan cosmology is fairly well documented (e.g., Busia, 1954; Danquah, 1968; Grills, 1995; Gyekye, 1987; Rattray, 1923). The predominant interpretation of this view of the universe by traditional Akan sages, professional philosophers, and anthropologists alike reveal the following three essential features:

1. Existence is comprised of visible and invisible realms.
2. The universe contains a hierarchy of beings, all of which derive from *Onyame* (the Supreme Being). Next to Onyame, in order, come the *abosom* (deities), the *nsamanfo* (ancestral spirits), human beings, and physical objects.
3. The universe is endowed with varying degrees of force or power, all of which derive, ultimately, from Onyame.

Ontological and Epistemological Tenets

From the many cannons and postulates of the Akan doctrine of God, we will comment on a few that have immediate relevance for our understanding of the Akan theory of the person. Connected to the conception of God as the source of being is the reference to him as *Odomankoma*. Danquah defines Odomankoma as the infinitely manifold God, incessant, perpetual, interminable, the absolute container and content of reality (Danquah, 1944). God, in other words, is in all as all are in God. Second, although the Akan doctrine of God includes the conception of him as a transcendent being with no spatial or temporal limitations, he is believed to be immanent, manifested in objects and events that are susceptible to the limitations of the coordinates of space and time.

Although the Akan thinker contends that the universe is composed of visible and invisible beings, it is doubtful whether he implies that these aspects of existence are two distinctly separate categories, as the Western notion of dualism would suggest. Rather, the Akan thinker conceives of these two not as distinct realms but as two points on a continuum, constantly interacting with each other. This is because an *obosom*,[1] for example, which in a strictly dualistic interpretation of Akan cosmology will belong to the immaterial realm, is believed to be capable of physical manifestation and, as such, be susceptible to spatiotemporal coordinates. On the other hand, a tree, which in a strictly dualistic universe would be conceived as a physical entity, is believed constituted of a spirit by the Akan thinker. This makes a clear-cut dichotomy of the material-immaterial or spiritual-physical in Akan ontology implausible. And as will soon be seen, the idea of reality unfolding on a continuum has enormous relevance for the Akan theory of human nature, psychological functions, and the interpretation of thought, behavior, and emotion.

Commenting on the third postulate, that the universe is endowed with varying degrees of force or power, all of which derive, ultimately, from Onyame, Gyekye (1995) reports,

> This force or power is sunsum.... In this metaphysic, all created things, that is, natural objects, have or contain sunsum. Further every deity [obosom] is a sunsum, but not vice versa. Sunsum, then, appears to be a generic concept. It appears to be a universal spirit, manifesting itself differently in the various beings and objects in the natural world.

We will see that this sunsum is a central feature of African psychology.

Gyekye informs us of other senses in which sunsum is used:

> First, it is used to refer to any self-conscious subject whose activities are initiated self-consciously. In this sense, Onyame, the deities and the ancestors are said to be spirits [sunsum], that is spiritual beings with intelligence and will. Second, it is used to refer to the mystical powers believed to exist in the world. These powers are held to constitute the inner essences or intrinsic properties of natural objects, and are believed to be contained in those objects. (1987)

Thus, on Gyekye's interpretation, sunsum denotes either (a) a conscious being or (b) a power, derived from God, which constitutes the essence of all existents. Gyekye's analysis of sunsum has been upheld both by many of the traditional thinkers with whom we have discussed the subject and other scholars on Akan ontology.

To augment the perspectives of Gyekye (1995) and Minkus (1977) on sunsum, we would like to propose that the notions of a *conscious being and the activating essence of particular beings and things* are subsumable under *a power that constitutes the essence of all existents.* We are suggesting that we interpret Akan cosmology as asserting that sunsum, that internal element that empowers a human subject to initiate an act self-consciously, is a specie of a universal phenomenon. We can, thus, talk in terms of a "universal" and "particular" sunsum. On these terms, man is a being (at least part of) whose essence is a power (to act in the world) that is contingent on a universal natural power.

Universal sunsum, then, is a property intrinsic to all beings. What makes any existent what it is resides in its possession of this force: the attribute sunsum belongs to a human being by virtue of being human, and likewise to a tree by virtue of its being a tree. Therefore, on the principle of like attracting like, we can understand why that tree can be used to restore or to augment the energy in me or why it may be used as a tool to invoke the activity of an obosom. We may both contain the same sunsum essence and have a natural affinity to it.

Due to his or her belief in the existence of universal sunsum, and also that all sunsum derives from God, it is legitimate to argue that the Akan thinker conceives of being or nature as one. This divine energy (sunsum), made manifest in various beings in the perceptible and imperceptible world, constitutes the different modes in which God expresses Himself. Therefore, in this ontology, human beings, like all other categories of being, are just part of this being (God or nature). In consequence, we cannot plausibly separate being (as matter) from being (as spirit). God or nature-being is understood as reflecting a whole, or that which makes everything connected into a whole: I am composed of sunsum, and so is that tree, and both of our sunsum derive from one source: God or nature. What this notion of being as one simply means is that existence is composed merely of patterns of interactions within a whole, that each existing entity has the power to interact with every other entity and, as such, is a key to universal knowledge. We must note that this notion has serious implications for dualist theories of the person and also for the attribute of human consciousness. We have argued elsewhere (Ajei & Grills, 2000) that subscribing to this cosmology makes the events characterized as "paranormal" simply events not yet understood by our ordinary levels of consciousness. The significance of this discussion of sunsum and metaphysical consubstantiation will become more apparent after a discussion of African concepts of the elements of self. The Akan model is used to provide a concrete illustration.

Components of Self

Using Landrine's (1992) distinctions, African concepts of the self occupy both an indexical self as social role (the self and the social roles it occupies are synonymous) and an indexical self as receptacle (the self is a vessel through which immaterial forces and entities can operate and influence behaviors, thought, and emotion). In this indexical construction, "the self is not construed to be the center of cognition, affect, or action, and so is not the explanation for behavior" (Landrine, 1992). This is an important contrast with the Western referential self that shapes and defines Western psychology's theory and praxis.

From an African perspective, what, then, constitutes this sociospiritual indexical self and what distinctions can be made about *self as object* (the definition of self in terms of its incorporated elements and organization), *self as process* (influenced by a culture's epistemological system, a process by which we come to know ourselves and the world around us) and *self as essence* (self as an extension of ultimate reality)? How do these inform an understanding of human behavior and the functions, structure, and nature of the consciousness of those of African descent?

Self as Essence

Self as essence refers to the ontological belief among African people that the fundamental basis of human beingness is spirit. What makes one a human being is the presence of a spirit-based essence. One form of this spirit essence, referred to as the soul, is thought to be a spark of the divine, God. As such, each human being is connected to the source of all creation and to everything in creation. In a decisive manner, the concept of God, in every culture, indicates the values and ideals of human functioning upheld by that culture. For the African, the notion that the spirit-essence of man is a spark of God's divinity means that man partakes of the nature of God. The creative principle of the universe is one with man. This divine principle that is one with man reflects one's capacity to realize and seek to fulfill ideal conceptions of human behavior and functioning in community. Hence, the African Doctrine of God or, rather, the African theory of man's relationship with God, underlies these ideals.

Nobles' (1998) description of the characteristics of spiritness experienced as a human condition illustrates the African belief in the link between this quality and attributes of human behavior and functioning. Qualitatively, spiritness is experienced and manifested in a number of ways. According to Nobles (1998), it is

- experienced as an urge and desire for what is excellent, good, and right;
- eventuated in the ever-expanding love and feeling of "good will" for all life;
- that which makes for ethical character and conduct;
- the urge to kindness, goodwill, and fellowship;
- the "felt need" to love and be loved for no particular reason at all;
- the desire for order and the beautiful;
- the "impetus" for concern beyond self to other;
- the emotional "sense of the Divine agency" and relationship in human affairs;
- the compelling need to understand the nature of the Divine and thereby life itself and our meaning and purpose in life;
- the magnetic pull away from mere animal-physical existence toward that which is higher, nobler, better, and more excellent;
- the sense of inner "power" and dignity.

These qualities of spiritness constitute ideals and aspirations for which people ought to strive. Ultimately, these qualities will bring the self into complete harmony with the Divine Mind and, for the African, this is an important end that human life is intended to promote. In other words, the self as essence is a philosophical device fashioned by Africans to regulate human behavior so that well being remains the paramount aim of human functioning.

It is helpful to clarify the emergent African conceptualization of human beingness: the connate self (essence) and the embodied person (manifestation of self). The manifested self and corresponding processes and levels of consciousness can be viewed as derivatives of both essence and expression. Existence (in the form of essence) precedes expression (the state of being alive and psychologically conscious or cognizant). Essence reflects the essential nature, operating principles, and crux of human beings as persons; it is that which makes one human (Grills & Rowe, 1998). It is what the Akan call *ɔkra*, the Yoruba *emi*, the Igbo *chi*. Expression or manifestation in what Western psychology labels behavior, cognition, biological processes, and emotion composes the "outer envelope" (Nobles, King, & James, 1995). This outer envelope is the expression, the evidence, the indication, the tangible presentation or articulation of that essence. Western conceptualizations have restricted the purview of human behavior (particularly the reductionist view) to this outer envelope. The African conceptualization has concerned itself more with what is contained within the envelope and how it functions as an envelope in relation to its essence or inner context.

Self as Object

Self as object consists of the elements that constitute human psychological functioning organized into a dynamic system. It refers to the definition of self in terms of its incorporated elements and organization. The African concept of self, as summarized by Grills (1999) used the model of the atom to illustrate the core elements that constitute the person.

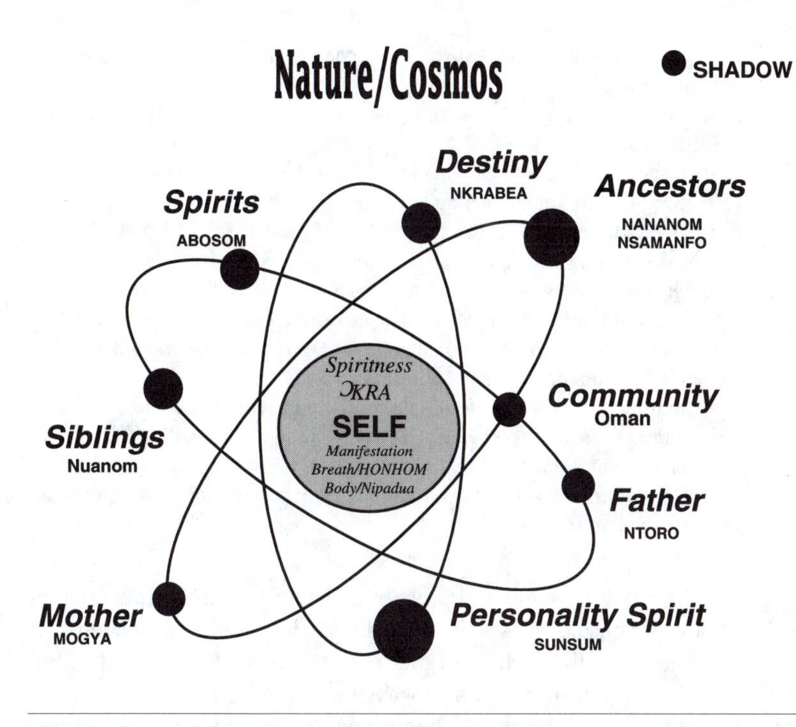

Figure 6.1 African Conceptions of Self

In the atom model, a "cloud" of electrons surrounds the nucleus. The farther these electrons are from the nucleus, the lower their density and the weaker the integrity and conscious capacity of the molecule (the self). Using Akan (along with Yoruba and Wolof) constructs, the nucleus is a compilation of elements that act in relation to each other and culminate in an existent: the living, manifest self. Orbiting around the nucleus of this model of an indexical self is

- Energy expressed as the soul providing a direct connection to the source of life and ultimate consciousness (e.g., the *Ɔkra*—the indexical self as a life force role).
- A destiny that can act as a "homing device," orienting the individual to his or her purpose in life and imbued with the capacity to influence consciousness (e.g., *nkrabea*—the indexical self in an existentially anchored role).
- A personality spirit (e.g., *sunsum*—the indexical self as spiritual role). Sunsum is in ontological unity with Ɔkra. It is also the governor of *tiboa* (the animal in your head), which may be translated as conscience.
- A shadow or personal double that remains in the spiritual realm while the self manifests in the physical world. This is consistent with the African concept of duality or twinness that recognizes that every thing has its corollary opposite such as male-female, dark-light, earth-sky, seen-unseen

(e.g., sunsuma—the indexical self referenced to its counterpart or double in the spiritual realm).

- Spirits or deities (e.g., *abosom* or *orisa*—the indexical self referenced to the spiritual realm).
- The person's ancestors (e.g., *nananom nsamanfo*; *egun*—the indexical self as referenced to a living and acting ancestral line).
- Formative, guiding, and protective energy of the father and his clan's spiritual guardians (e.g., *ntoro* and *egyabosom*—the indexical self as an extension of the paternal family and its spiritual resources).
- The ancestral blood line (*mogya*) that provides a container for the ɔkra and the spiritual connection to the maternal ancestors (e.g., *abusua*—the indexical self as multigenerational family role).[2]
- The environment in the form of a community providing a context of meaning, values, rules, and roles (e.g., *ëmanor*—the indexical self as social role).
- A broader cosmological net that includes nature providing the ultimate environment within which the person and his or her community are in constant dynamic interaction.

Together, the above form the basic core of human psychological functioning and the roots of consciousness with all of its potentialities and functions.[3]

When first developed, the old model of the atom was meant to illustrate how electrons orbit an atom. It was never an adequate explanation of this process and is no longer used, but it provides a useful heuristic for portraying energy fields and the relationship of different energy fields to the atom's nucleus, which in the African conceptualization is the core of the pseudo-individuated[4] self. In the model, a "cloud" of electrons surrounds the atom. The farther from the nucleus, the lower the density and the weaker the integrity and conscious capacity of the molecule (self). The nucleus consists of essence, which is soul and expression or manifestation, which is body and breath (*honhom*). Orbiting around this nucleus of the self are some of the elements noted earlier, especially nkrabea, abosom, nananom nsamanfo, and mogya.

The objective of this model is to illustrate the dynamic interactions of the components and mechanisms that constitute the person and his or her consciousness. The closer the energy components vibrate in relationship to the nucleus (a condition of coherence in the self and awareness by the self of its essence and expression), the greater the health and integrity of the nucleus self. Under conditions of congruence, the self can more readily access, engage, manipulate, and use the various realms of consciousness. For example, think of the last time you experienced an "intuition" inspiring you to do something, avoid something, be cautious about something, and you ignored it only to learn that this prescient idea was accurate. By ignoring it, unnecessary consequences followed.[5] The source of this "intuition" may have been your ancestors, your ntoro's divinities, the abosom, or your own personal spirit guardian. To continually ignore them is to cut yourself off from your own inherent mechanisms for understanding and navigating the world.

Consider another example that illustrates the importance of congruence between the elements of self. A client once struggled with a career-related decision. Intuitively, he knew that he enjoyed the labor and creativity associated with a particular profession but found himself moving toward a completely different line of work because it was more financially lucrative. His blessings flowed, things "came easily" whenever he pursued that which felt *right* and natural to him in the profession he liked. Obstacles, strain, and heartache followed him, however, as he pursued the more financially lucrative profession. In an African schema, questions about alignment of destiny and character might be raised to assist this young man in resolving the stress and depression that ultimately ensued. Was he in fact fighting against his own nkrabea in the service of the trappings of material gain that would come with the more financially lucrative job? What were the reasons for pursuing financial gain? Was it for the accumulation of material trinkets and toys? Who would benefit from this? What were the ethical issues attached to the profession he opted for that ultimately placed him at odds with his own career destiny? The more attuned one is to the multiple sources of insight, the multiple factors that contribute to an integrated self, the greater one's capacity to live an effective, healthy life.

The African view argues for the existence of multiple sources of insight and influence, contributing to an integrated self. The symbol of the atom is used to illustrate these multifarious components that constitute this core self. The strength or integrity of the core is dependent on the dynamic, vital, and harmonious interaction between the constituent elements that provide further definition and meaning to human beingness. In addition, these elements of the self are in a constant state of dynamic interaction with one another. When the components are aligned and the conscious self is attuned to these components, the person experiences alafia (the Yoruba concept of well being and good health).

As with the atom, electrons are necessary for coherence and viability. In other words, the elements that "orbit" the core conscious self are necessary to its balance and survival. Further, the atom is weakened—it is not as powerful—when it is not forming connections (bonds) with other atoms or molecules (other people and spiritual energy). The atom's electromagnetic field draws other atoms to it. Likewise, the healthy self has an affinity for connecting with others. To be healthy, a person must bond with and be connected to others, real and incorporeal. Considerably more work is needed to help us arrive at a deeper understanding of the meaning, function, and expression of the components, mechanisms of action, valence, energic aspects, chronology, and dynamic interrelationships between the discernable components of the person defined in traditional African psychology. Nonetheless, this conceptualization sheds new light on the cultural foundations, meaning, and importance of African American principles of connectedness, interdependence, and spirituality.

Self as Process

Self as process refers to the culturally informed mechanisms by which we come to know self, other, and context. This process leads to differential levels of consciousness. That we "know" via awareness, sentience, and rational process is a manifestation of the most basic level of consciousness. Through refinements in the relationships between the components of self, conscious manipulation and utilization of the elements of self, and intentional interaction with nonphysical reality, we come to "know" at more remote levels of consciousness.

African culture and psychology tells us that there are three levels of reality. And in consonance with this conception of reality, the Akan thinker offers a hierarchical order of the objects of knowledge and the pathways to it. The three levels of knowing in the Akan philosophy of knowledge are: *nea wohu, nea etra adwene*, and *nea wonhu*. We would like to expound on these categories of knowledge and suggest how they inform the self as process.

Nea Wohu

Nea wohu literally means the observable or perceivable. This category of knowledge represents knowledge derived from ordinary sense experience and rational thought. In other words, nea wohu is the Akan equivalent of both rational and empirical knowledge in Western epistemology. The sources of knowing at this level are *hu*, which translates into the English "see, observe," and *te* which translates to "hear." The verb *te* is also used to represent perception by other sense organs as well. Thus, *me te nka* (I feel) and *me te pampa* (I smell) denote sense experience other than by hearing. So far, *te* and *hu* have been shown to be the pathways to empirical knowledge. But these verbs are used also to represent knowledge procured through the pure activity of the mind. Thus, *mahu nea wokyere no* means "I understand what you mean" and *mate ase* means "I understand/comprehend the depths of it (of the subject matter)."

Nea Etra Adwene

The Akan word *adwene* has both a wide and a narrow meaning. Interpreted widely, it means "consciousness" whereas its narrow interpretation yields the English "thought." It is being used narrowly in the phrase *nea etra adwene* to mean "that which transcends thought." Thus, Akan psychology maintains that we can access knowledge at a level beyond rational deliberation. Two reasons, at least, make this position plausible. First, this is in consonance with their holistic metaphysics alluded to earlier. If reality comprises the visible and the invisible, and the visible is comprehensible through rational deliberation, then it is reasonable to suppose that there must be another way by which invisible reality could be comprehended. Second, experience is the basis of this strong belief in the human ability to know at a level beyond rational deliberation. In fact, most modern Akan philosophers, notably Gyekye (1987), Agyakwa (1974), and Oguah (1977) assert that, further to reason and sense experience, paranormal cognition is a third mode of knowing.

Several expressions in the Akan language illustrate the reality of this kind of knowing. If, for example, X is able to foretell the arrival of Y in a way that we will recognize as precognitive, and you ask X how he came to have this true belief of Y's impending arrival, he would say *na ne din da madwene mu*. In other words, "his name was in my mind." Another statement that could be made to answer the same question would be *onipa din ben ne ho*; in other words, "a person's name is attached to him." How do these statements reflect the assertion of the type of knowledge we refer to as *nea etra adwene*?

First, the notion of *din* (name) in both statements is instructive because, for the Akan and many African ethnocultural groups, naming has special spiritual significance. Among the Akan, a person's name has a direct bearing on the ɔkra (soul) through the medium of *kradin* (the name of the ɔkra). Every Akan has a kradin to signify the day his ɔkra entered the visible world in the form of a human being. Now, as said earlier, the ɔkra forms an ontological unity with sunsum. Therefore, *ne din da madwene mu* means that the person (the embodiment of ɔkra-sunsum) is in my mind. I was consciously aware of him. His persistent presence in my mind was indicative of his coming. The precognized event (his coming) was informed by the persistence of his being in my mind. Two things are implied here. First, the statements *onipa din ben ne ho* and *X din da madwene mu* could be considered to be inductive statements from observation: Each time X's person persistently occupies my mind, he turns up where I am. This means, second, that there is some sort of communication between the mind of X and my mind without my being cognitively aware of this. My awareness of the presence of X is my consciousness of this communication between our minds, but I am not cognitively-rationally aware of this communication. Although I am not rationally aware of this communication, experience tells me that it is reasonable to suppose that such communication takes place. Thus, there is awareness, but it is awareness at another level, an awareness which *tra adwene* (surpasses thought).

Similarly, an answer to how one came to have certain clairvoyant information would elicit the answer *esoo me mu* (it gripped me). It occurred to me suddenly and without any rational deliberation. In other words, it occurred to me intuitively. Such an occurrence demonstrates an important characteristic of awareness as *nea etra adwene*.

The term *oben* refers to someone who is extraordinary, possessing powers that an ordinary person does not have. It is the possessive state of the noun *aben* (well cooked). To be aben means one is very aware psychologically, is mindful of self and surroundings, and is intelligent with a well-developed mind. It denotes the possession of knowledge at the level of nea etra adwen. Oben implies an outstanding capacity or ability to know. A context in which this sense of oben would be employed is this: Suppose you go to an *okomfo* (Akan traditional healer) for consultation and, before you speak, he or she tells you of your mission to his or her shrine. Akan psychology will attribute the term oben to this okomfo because this okomfo has a profundity of perception that is beyond the ordinary. The profundity of perception attributed to the okomfo will reflect first, that he or she has reached the apex of knowledge in his or her field of activity and "the field" here is the field of reality, which comprises the visible and invisible realms. In the case of this okomfo, the oben clearly refers to his or her competence to know of events in the invisible realm. Hence, we refer to a version of knowledge of this type nea etra adwen. Clinically, this has appeared in the context of reflection or interpretation of client data, but in such a way that the shared material exceeds what the client has disclosed, hypothetically indicates things to come, and reaches into client past history information not yet disclosed or implied to the therapist. When this has occurred in the treatment setting, the clients have reported experiencing a deeper level of empathy.

Okomfo X aben ultimately means that X is well versed in the affairs of sunsum; that X can penetrate the realm of sunsum and manipulate it. What does this mean? It means that X's sunsum contains an abundance of tumi (power) and as a result of this, his or her perceptive faculties are heightened to a level from which the limitations of the visible world can be transcended and deeper insight gained into the fundamental principles that govern relationships between things and events in both realms of reality. This power under consideration here refers to psychic power. Here we maintain that the high psychic power of an obenfo (one who is well cooked), when activated, leads to a distinct perception of the fundamental relations in existence. Hence, this power is a gateway to knowledge of reality that cognition cannot reach.

The concept oben then suggests that a subject can possess capabilities for nonordinary knowing. We want to suggest, further, that this concept also is indicative of a holistic approach to knowledge. If to *ben*, by definition, is to be well versed in *any* type of knowledge, we can think of the subject of oben as being well versed in knowledge both at the level of nea wohu and nea etra adwen. The mind of such a person will be the juncture of a configuration of pathways leading to different forms of knowledge. Therefore, he or she would be the repository of holistic knowledge.

Nea Wonhu

Nea wonhu means the imperceptible or unobservable, but as we said earlier, the verb hu, in the Akan language, is also used to represent understanding and comprehension. Thus, nea wonhu may mean "the incomprehensible," and it is in this sense that we use it here. Strictly speaking, this is not a dimension of knowledge, but rather the suggestion of a level of reality—such as Onyankopon, the Supreme Being—the full knowledge of which is incomprehensible to the human mind.

These levels of knowing (nea wohu, nea etra adwen, and nea wonhu) have corresponding levels of human consciousness that can be accessed by both the layperson and the highly skilled or trained practitioner. In African metaphysics (Irogebu, 1995), these levels of consciousness extend from sentience (awareness through the physical senses) to what Grills and Rowe (1998) refer to as conscious preterrational consciousness (to engage transsentient reality with conscious awareness of self in an active relationship with that reality).[6] Typically, trance possession, as an altered state of preterrational consciousness, occurs as a nonconscious process in which the subject is not cognizant of the trance state activities. This was confirmed in our field study observations and interviews with highly skilled, practicing okomfos and their assistants.

Human Consciousness and the Significance of Sunsum

In the pursuit of knowledge, the African willingness to engage and include that which is empirically, tangibly verifiable *and* that which is not makes this an inclusive epistemology. The material world is not taken as the penultimate of reality. The Western mental fascination with the tangible object encumbers an identification that would bring us knowledge beyond the tangible. Schwaller de Lubicz (1998) notes that this inclusive epistemology is concerned with the esoteric (the inner meaning, the implied, but inexpressible in words) aspects of any given stimulus or phenomenon. A cerebral approach to knowledge leaves parts isolated from each other, whereas the esoteric approach aims for synthesis and an appreciation for the simultaneity of complements. Essentially, "when we look to the front, we feel that there is a behind. We cannot look in one direction without opposing to it a complementary pole, and although this pole is not sensorially observed, the awareness of it exists within us" (Schwaller de Lubicz, 1998). This is a fundamental principle of African psychology derived from the African philosophical principle of the complementarity of opposites, duality or unicity.

The question of culture and the contribution of culturally specific conceptualizations of consciousness have been increasingly examined with the hope of further illuminating the subject. Human mental activity occurs within a configuring framework of culture (Drummond, 1996) and we "experience our culture's collective understanding of what it is to be conscious" (Scott, 1995). Drummond (1996) suggests that our examination of consciousness should deal with the systems and phenomena that are located within the "labyrinthine folds of a brain-culture-physical reality manifold." This is consistent with an African cultural conceptualization, but we would extend the contextualization of consciousness to include the labyrinthine folds of a soul-spirit-physical-brain-culture reality manifold. Within this schema, consciousness at its most basic level functions as a process of perception and conception of the material-physical world. The *ultimate* essence and expression of consciousness, however, extends to the *nonmaterial* world.

In part, consciousness research in European American psychology has centered on physiologically based processes of human awareness contributing to a central debate in the field between proponents of the "hard" and "soft" approach to mental phenomena. The "hard problem" posits that human experiences are the result of neural activity. In this reductionist or materialist view (e.g., Crick & Koch, 1994; Dennett, 1996), human consciousness can be reproduced in computers (artificial intelligence) and all reality can be reduced to basic laws of physical science. Conversely, proponents of the "soft problem," often called dualists, believe that consciousness is beyond human understanding (McGinn, 1991). Consciousness is an "emergent phenomenon" (Scott, 1995) in which culture serves a central organizing function through which people experience consciousness. Chalmers (1996) elaborates by suggesting that a concept of consciousness should be a nonreductive, naturalistic, dualist theory that also involves an "extra ingredient." This extra ingredient has been variously described as chaos, nonlinear dynamics, quantum mechanics, and surprisingly enough, the soul.

An Akan, or a generally African worldview (Ani, 1980, 1994; Diop, 1989), would be more consistent with the argument that consciousness consists of something beyond simply the brain, its activities, and human sentience. It would be more akin to the emergent theory that rests on the assumption that materialism and dualism can coexist in a theory of consciousness with culture providing an understanding of what it is to be conscious. Such a view is consistent with the tenets of the model of the self presented earlier in this chapter. The African view would extend the bounds of the emergent theory, however, giving precedence to the role of the spiritual realm. As we have seen, spirit features prominently in African culture, psychology, and notions of consciousness. Consequently, Akan psychology conceives of material and immaterial not as distinct realms but as two points on a continuum, constantly interacting with each other. We have argued elsewhere (Ajei & Grills, 2000) that subscribing to this cosmology makes the events characterized as "paranormal" simply events not yet understood by our ordinary, sentient, rational levels of consciousness.

In the African view, consciousness is ultimately an attribute of spirit. One can know through proof (evidence), through reasoning (Descartes—good sense), or through African reasoning (plain, formal logic plus body sense—to be is to feel and think) (Obenga, 1997). This African reasoning is a synthesis of mind (spirit-soul essence), brain, body, society, and nature. It is not blind faith that maintains belief and respect for the traditional Akan and other African systems. The method of proof used in these systems derives from ritual or procedure. Priests and lay alike rely on what occurs after the intervention or procedure. *We know that they (deities or ancestors) have responded when the enterprise comes to bear fruit.* So it is not a system of blind faith but rather one that is verified by the presence or absence of its anticipated outcomes. The same logic applies to the belief in the esoteric elements of the human being. *We know of its existence (sunsum) by believing that certain consequences are produced by it.* Similar to Western science's belief that independent variable x causes the effect in dependent variable y with all other influences accounted for or held constant.

This conceptualization of consciousness, then, requires us to consider an analysis of the African concept of the person in terms other than the logic of Western science because this logic is based on a certain conception of the existence of space and time, and considers events as ultimately based on the activity of bodies in this understanding of space and time. The African thinker does not subscribe fully to these metaphysical canons. In this respect, the African conception of sunsum as an all-pervading force is relevant. This relevance is better captured by posing the question, "Are there not natural phenomena—forces in nature—that manifest themselves to one's sense experience only under certain conditions?"

The answer: There certainly are. Consider electromagnetic force. Electromagnetic theory was founded largely to explain "action at a distance." Elaborating on this theory, Einstein (1960) writes:

> As a result of the more careful study of electromagnetic phenomena, we have come to regard action at a distance as a process impossible without intervention of some intermediary medium. If, for instance, a magnet attracts a piece of iron, we cannot be content to regard this as meaning

that the magnet acts directly on the iron through the intermediate empty space, but we are constrained to imagine that the magnet always calls into being something physically real in the space around it, that something being what we call a "magnetic field."

According to Einstein, to explain some types of natural phenomena, physicists are constrained to imagine the intervention of some physical reality pervading all space. We can legitimately infer from this that, even in an uncompromising scientific framework as physics, the borderline between the physical and the nonphysical is not as clear-cut as mainstream logical analysis would like to affirm; an area between these two realms exists in which we cannot, with logical certainty, identify events as belonging here or there. All this is implied in Einstein's admission of imagining entities; for the activity of imagination, in traditional Western epistemology, is not a route to certainty. Electromagnetism (the imagined reality Einstein discusses) is not ordinarily perceptible to sense experience, but under certain conditions it emits photons and becomes a visible glow. Yet we neither conceive electromagnetism as an immaterial entity nor a physical substance with reduced physicality. It is a force of nature. Einstein calls it physical, and that is fine by us. However, we assert here that electromagnetism bears a striking resemblance to sunsum. Although electromagnetism has been largely understood by physics, there is no reason why sunsum cannot be accepted as a similar natural phenomenon as well.

Clinical Relevance

Entertaining these African psychology constructs—sunsum, ɔkra, nea atre adwen, and so on—forces us to reexamine the universality of many of the assumptions and models employed in Western psychology. For example, how universal and relevant are the following Western psychology practices to African descendants: criteria employed in assessment and diagnosis of mental disorders; strategies employed to help clients interact more effectively with their environment; approaches to death and grieving; indications of positive and negative treatment outcomes; emphasis placed on behavior, cognition, emotion, and biology in conceptualization, assessment, and treatment of the person; and target of interventions. What is the value added of African constructs and epistemology, particularly for those of African ancestry for whom cultural retentions keep these principles alive subconsciously and consciously?

Table 6.1 African-Centered Conceptualizations of the Self and Consciousness

Variable	*African-Centered Description*	*Clinical Relevance*
Sense of self	Derived from one's connection to others (physical and spiritual); it is not an individual dynamic	Examination of the legacy (biological, sociohistorical, and spiritual) left to the individual and family; this legacy can lead to opportunities as well as the need to address unfinished business to restore harmony and balance to self, family, and community.
Feelings (*Atenka*)	Are as important as cognitive process and provide critical feedback to enhance functioning and decision making	The affective sensorium becomes a conduit of information and illumination. What the client "feels" about something may be more than simple subjective emotional experience or projection. It may reflect knowledge derived beyond sentient process and is worth consideration in client discourse and decision making.
Survival	Connected to personal, familial, communal, and spiritual *tumi* (power)	Reconfirms important principle of interconnectedness; adds another dimension to concept of personal and community empowerment. Clinical interventions aimed at separation and individuation might do well to reflect on the implications of such a strategy for African Americans. Disconnection could be a direct threat to personal and family *tumi* and survival.

(Continued)

Table 6.1 *Continued*

Variable	*African-Centered Description*	*Clinical Relevance*
Language	The spoken word is power, is an art, is laden with levels of meaning.	Adds new dimension to the use of speech. What you say and how you say it matters. Further, in an African worldview, speech has physical power to cause and create. Examining the impact of others' speech on client well-being may be relevant. Who is saying what and what does this mean psychologically and spiritually to the recipient of bad speech.
Time	Fluidity of past, present, and future	The present is the past and the future. The future can be known in the present to inform or alter the future. Dreams, intuition (precognition), and *atenka* (vibratory feelings) are common pathways to future and past knowledge.
Universe	Interconnectedness and human beings are critical. The universe and human beings are mirror images of each other; to know the workings of the universe is to know the inner workings of the human being and vice versa.	Provides existential grounding to the individual; a tool of empowerment as the individual comes to recognize that the answers to all their questions and the power to resolve all their dilemmas are contained within them. Their ability to connect to the various aspects of the universe (cosmos, nature, living and nonliving matter) increase their capacity to tap into this knowledge and healing power.

(Continued)

Table 6.1 *Continued*

Variable	*African-Centered Description*	*Clinical Relevance*
Death	The beginning of another phase of existence; relationship between the departed and the physically living can be maintained; importance of remembering and being remembered	Can be useful in the grieving process as the client uses the knowledge that the departed have departed only from the physical realm, not the realm of existence. Knowing that they are able to maintain a relationship with those who have transitioned further affects resolution of the grieving process.
Worth (values and character)	Related to values; connection to and contribution to community; what one does with personal possessions, not the mere collection of personal possessions	Ethics and morals are paramount within the African American community (Gyekye, 1995). Values are patterns or forms of life, behavior, practice, or thought that are held and maintained by a people as most worthwhile and desirable. They guide people in their thoughts and actions. Social solidarity, harmony, and cooperation are values of great importance to African people. Proverbs are a useful tool to teach, examine, and reflect on various ethical standards.

How does the preceding discussion of ɔkra, sunsum, nkrabea, and others relate to the issue of praxis in the treatment of African American clients? We must begin at the level of conceptualization. The goodness of treatment and treatment fit relies heavily on the assessment and conceptualization in which it is grounded. The African-centered constructs provide the clinician with a broader lens from which to understand and assess client dynamics. As a first step bridge to praxis, we begin with the question posed by Parham, White, and Ajamu (1999): "How do African Americans construct their design for living and what patterns do they use to interpret reality?" They further suggest that the African American design for living can be seen in the adherence to particular value systems reflected in the following variables: sense of self, feelings, survival, language, time, universe, death, and worth. These eight variables provide a useful point of departure to examine the clinical relevance of an African-centered model of praxis. As illustrated in Table 6.1, using an African-centered frame for understanding the client provides the clinician with many more avenues for understanding, engaging, interpreting, and intervening with the African American client than is immediately accessible through the Western schema.

Conclusion

Turner and Kramer (1995) have shown us that racism and mental health connect with each other in at least seven major ways and these connections are themselves interrelated. Racism is exhibited in

- definitions of mental health and illness;
- theories of the etiology of mental illness;
- the evaluation process (assessment and diagnosis);
- the provision of direct services;
- the organizing and structuring of mental health institutions and programs;
- research carried out to understand the mental health problems of racial groups;
- the training of mental health professionals to provide direct service and organize intervention programs.

In addition, what diagnosticians regard as abnormal behavior cannot be separated entirely form their own cultural backgrounds—including their educational experiences and the professional orientations that provide frameworks for both definition and judgment of mental illness and health (Turner & Kramer, 1995). European American counseling and psychotherapy tend to assume universal (etic) applications of their psychology to the exclusion of culture-specific (emic) views (Trimble, 1990). What has been proposed here is further conceptual development of the emic view. In that regard, what this discussion has not done is provide the Western-trained practitioner with simple steps to follow that will permit intervention at the level of preterrational consciousness, develop the capacity of his or her sunsum, or interpret the contents of *dae* (dreams) from an African frame of reference. Rather, readers are invited to

- expand the range of their conceptualizations of the essence, elements, and functions of the self and consciousness;
- provide an atmosphere in treatment that is open to this level of reality and analysis;
- provide an atmosphere receptive to the client's preterrational experiences.

Inclusion of such data could contribute immensely to a client's resolution of presenting problems. This chapter is also an invitation to the discipline of psychology to expand its purview of human behavior to reflect the worldviews of a broader segment of the human race rather than the delimited view of Euorpean American concepts of reality and human psychological functioning. Sue and Sue (1999) advise that if counselors and therapists are to provide meaningful help to culturally diverse populations, they must reach out and acquire new understandings. An African-centered understanding of the self and consciousness is offered here. This culturally based understanding could lead to what Sue and Sue agree must happen next, the development of new culturally effective helping approaches.

The Akan illustration of an African-centered model of human psychological function and consciousness can take us one step closer to the development of a culturally effective helping approach with African Americans. What it offers are new tools for conceptualization from which praxis must stem. In the emerging African-centered paradigm, we see that to be maximally effective in the healing process with the African American client, the practitioner must connect at least five things:

1. Spiritual realities
2. Cultural realities
3. Historical realities
4. Sociocultural realities
5. Political and racial realities

Within an African conceptualization, consciousness reflects the combined influence of the soul, spirits, ancestral influences, and destiny as well as the factors typically ascribed to consciousness in Western schemas (biology, subneural biology and neuroscience, quantum physics, cognition, function, and cultural-environmental factors). Here, spiritness is as important as the physical manifestation of self. In the African-centered model, preterrational spiritual processes are a necessary building block in the construction of any model of consciousness. These spiritual aspects of self are central to the essence and expression of all forms and stages of consciousness and human psychological functioning. Within this context, reality is that which exists independent of the sentient observer and knowledge reflects a combination of perception and conception. Perception is the information garnered, in normal states of consciousness, through sentient means and the interpretation of sensed data. Conception is the manipulation of this data into meaningful abstractions that approximate what we believe to be "reality" (Grills, in press). Knowledge, and in part functional consciousness or awareness, is simply the collection of perceptions and conceptions. In this African cultural model, there are degrees of approximation to true "reality" that can be understood by an explanation of the essence, expression, and functions of consciousness operating at the rational and preterrational levels.

Theories of quantum consciousness most closely approximate our initial impression of what might be an Akan concept of the essence and expression of consciousness. In the double-aspect theory, a common substance or reality from which mind and matter or the mental and physical arise does exist. This substance-reality is "quantum reality." In the African sense, that quantum reality is spirit-energy, perhaps the sunsum referred to earlier. The source and origin of this energy is Onyakopon (God). God and the notion of cosmological consubstantiation (everything is made of the same spiritual interconnectedness) are the most basic components of African philosophy and psychology. As a result, for many African cultures, science and the spiritual are inextricably linked; spirituality is a reflection of science and science is a reflection of spirituality.

An understanding of the Akan and similar African schemas of the elements of human beingness should contribute significantly to African psychology's articulation of the core aspects of self and models of health promotion and intervention. It will also aid African people in the process of self-definition, mental and spiritual liberation, and empowerment. Using the Akan schema, the African American client can be engaged in the question, "Who am I in ways that differ from Western psychotherapy?" The trajectory of clinical questions to supply an answer consistent with an African conceptualization begins not with a consideration of genetics, environmental influence, personality, cognitive style, and learning. It begins with an identification of the divine source of one's being. It begins with a recognition of (a) the spiritual dimensions of the self, both personal and familial; (b) the connection to the community in the historical and contemporary sense; and (c) family origins (ancestral and contemporary). This is further supplemented by examination of genetics, environment, personality, cognitive predisposition, learning, and so forth. Further, it begs the question of character and moral fiber. Among the Akan and Africans in general, health and disease are inextricably connected with social behavior and moral conduct (Ackah, 1988; Twumasi, 1975).

What emerges from the Akan schema is the realization that within the African conceptualization of self there can be no "I" without a "we." The multidimensionality of self brings an appreciation for the layers of

Table 6.2 Self-Awareness

Who Am I?

Where in the World Am I?

How in the World Did I Get There?

Psychological Awareness of Self

1. *Who* are you?
2. How did you come to *know* that this is what you are?
3. Is this what you want to be?
4. Is this all that you will be?
5. What makes you you? What makes you a *human being*?
6. Are you just like everybody else or are you like no one else or are *you both*?
7. According to your African ancestors, before enslavement, what are some of the critical features of your *personality*?
8. Who would you most like *to be like* and why?
9. What are your *values*? What is important to you in life?
10. By what *principles* in life do you live?

Ancestral Awareness of Self

1. *Who* are your people?
2. Have you *studied* their lives and *learned* the lessons of their lifes' experiences?
3. Do you *venerate* their memory and respect their memory, sacrifice, and struggle?

Spiritual Awareness of Self

1. *Who* are you spiritually?
2. How do you *relate to the spirit* that is you, that is within you?
3. Do you *respect the spirit* that is you, which is an extension of the divine? How?

Destiny-Purpose Awareness of Self

1. *Why* are you here?
2. What did you come to *accomplish* in your *personal development*?
3. What *obstacles or challenges* must you overcome?

insight that must be brought to bear in any understanding of who a person is, what he or she does, and why.[7] This multidimensional self is sociohistorical, psychological, ancestral, spiritual, and existential (in the form of destiny-purpose). Table 6.2 presents some of the questions contained within dimensions that contribute to a full comprehension or awareness of the myriad factors that contribute to human psychology and agency. These dimensions of the self also point to sources of psychological distress and the potential foci of psychological intervention and healing.

Notes

1. An *obosom* (singular) is a spirit or deity. Abosom (plural) can intervene in the daily, life of individuals, families, and communities.

2. More must be said about the significant role played by mogya in maintaining the integrity of the self. The person you see is a physical manifestation of an essential spiritual trinity made up of okra, sunsum, and mogya, a homogeneous, spiritual whole in essence. This conforms to the Akan thinker's holistic conception of reality. The mogya or blood that courses through the veins of the living human being is vital to existence. The term mogya is composed of the two morphs *mo* and *gya*. "Mo" translates into English as the plural form of the second personal pronoun "you," whereas "gya" has two meanings. It can either mean fire, as in *dum gya no* (extinguish the fire) or it can mean "to accompany," as in *Mee ko gya no Nkran* (I am accompanying him to Accra). Interpreted thus, mogya can either mean (a) your fire—the fire that is in you and (b) that which accompanies you. From these, we would like to suggest a definition of mogya as "the energy (fire) of your life that accompanies you from the time of your birth." Defined thus, we can plausibly conceive of mogya as a spiritual element (a force) in people. The pronouncements of various Akan sages seem to support this view.

From notions such as "the food (e.g., the energy-giver) of the ɔkra," and the "dwelling-place of the ɔkra," we can ask how likely it is for the ɔkra to be "sustained" or "contained" by a vessel that is purely physical. But more important, what is implied in all this is a seemingly indissoluble bond between the ɔkra, sunsum, and mogya of a person. It appears to us, therefore, that for the Akan thinker, a person is essentially composed of a spiritual trinity. The blood you see is not just a compound of white and red cells. It is the physical manifestation of a soul that acts as the vital force of human existence.

3. Other concepts that can inform our understanding of the self are *dae* and *atenka*. Dae refer to dreams. Dreams, as an altered state of consciousness, are very important in the Akan schema. It is while in the dream state that communication will often occur with the spiritual realm via the sunsum and direct information from one's ɔkra. The majority of respondents in field interviews we conducted with Akan sages indicated that the ɔkra reveals information to the person in dreams. There was also considerable agreement that the sunsum is at work, literally, when one is asleep. Essentially, the mind is in contact with sunsum during sleep and one's own sunsum actively travels about in search of things, people, experiences that are revealed to you in sleep. It is believed that the mind in a wakeful state cannot reach into certain spheres of existence. It can't see beyond the physical. Yet knowledge of some realities in the nonphysical realm is essential for a person's effective functioning, hence the necessary dream state activity of sunsum. Dreams, beyond the mere cognitive and rest function noted in Western psychology, provide a type of revelation that can come from several sources (ɔkra, ancestors, abosom) and the recipient of the information from these sources is sunsum. These sources are also important in the illness and healing process, providing diagnostic and treatment information to patient and healer.

Atenka means to "feel" in a metaphysical sense, to have a premonition. If an event occurs and an Akan had thought of it or had a premonition, he or she uses this term to describe this foreknowledge. Atenka specifically means vibration. It relates to immediate awareness of something in an intuitive sense. Those who are spiritually initiated have more atenka than the ordinary person, but all people have the capacity to acquire knowledge through the mechanism of atenka.

4. This is referred to as a pseudo-individuated self because in African conceptualizations, one is never disconnected from the community of family, neighbors, ancestors, spirits, and the Divine source of existence.

5. My students shared the following examples: Y. took his mother shopping for a ceiling fan. He took the fan to his car and "something" told him to put the fan in the back seat of his car. He decided to ignore this thought and put the package in his front trunk where he always stores his things. As he drove his mother home, the hood flew open, shattering his windshield. V., a student, made plans to buy a new desk with some of her financial aid money. She budgeted exactly $150.00 for the purchase of a desk. When the check arrived, V. went straight away to the store to look for her desk despite a nagging voice inside suggesting that she not go out and buy a desk. She went anyway and ran into one obstacle after another, from one store to the next, which prevented her from buying a desk. She came home sulking and parked her car in a spot that she meant to be temporary. Her car was towed and the expense for its return was $150.00.

6. In the African deep structure of culture, there are many realms of existence that Ayoade (1979) refers to as the material-rational realm and the nonmaterial realm that can be accessed through preterrational consciousness. "Preter" is a prefix meaning "beyond" or "more than" or "past." Preterrational consciousness means consciousness beyond mere rational methods and is based on processes that are indicative of a higher mind. In this preterrational schema, the mind can look simultaneously at the future, present, and past, and possibly influence all. This quantum consciousness is an everyday, commonplace occurrence in Africa and is believed to be a cultural retention among many African Americans.

7. A similar conclusion would be drawn from other African schemas such as the Yoruba concept of the person (*enyian*) with its concepts of the divine breath (*emi*), soul (*emi* plus *ori*), shadow (*ojiji*), guardian spirit (*ori*), deities (*orisa*), personal destiny (*ayanmo ipin*); heart-spiritual source of emotion (*okan*), and ancestors (*egun*), or the Bantu's concepts of human kind (*mu-ntu*), or the Igbo with their concept of the soul (*chi*), ancestors (*eke*), shadow (*onyinyo*), or the Tonga in Zambia and their concept of *umuuya* (that which forces people to behave in special ways in keeping with the spirit), or the Dogon concept of the person (*dime*).

7

Counseling Models for African Americans

The What and How of Counseling

Thomas A. Parham

Given the substantial increase in the literature devoted to counseling culturally different people in general (Lee & Richardson, 1991; Locke, 1992; Paniagua, 1994; Ponterotto, Casas, Sazuki, & Alexander, 1995; Sue & Sue, 1999) and African Americans in particular, it is surprising to know how many clinicians and academicians feel stuck in articulating specific, and effective, strategies for interventions with this population. Although a number of reasons could be sited for this dilemma, I am prone to believe that the culprit lies in the focus.

When I refer to the "focus," I want to suggest that our training from traditional programs has led us to believe that the clinical and counseling skills learned can and should be applicable to all populations. Our newfound sensitivity to more culturally sensitive counseling methods, which ideally has been gained after reading the previous chapters, should remind us that this assumption can no longer be embraced. In fact, scholars representing other cultural groups have issued similar cautions. Yang (1997), for example, in delineating a series of "yes" and "no" assertions in support of an indigenous psychology, suggests that clinicians and researchers alike should not habitually and uncritically adapt Western psychological concepts, nor should they adopt any cross-cultural research strategy with a Western-dominant imposed etic or pseudo-etic approach. As such, I suspect that many clinicians are now, or maybe in the future will be, caught in a quandary about how to best serve their clients and how to employ the most effective intervention strategies.

Further complicating the question of how to serve African American clients is the realization that some clinicians may have participated in a course on multicultural counseling. There they might have been exposed to a didactically oriented "shotgun approach" to instruction in which the course was comprised of various theories and issues concerning multiple ethnic and cultural groups. Without even the slightest hint of culturally specific clinical training to supplement the course, most participants are still left wondering how to intervene therapeutically.

As a therapist and healer, my own experience suggests that two of the most important questions in counseling are "what" and "how." Consequently, strategies for intervention must include discussions of both what needs to happen and how it needs to happen in order to achieve desired therapeutic outcomes. Too often our focus is centered on what we need to do (i.e., be culturally sensitive) but stops short of describing "how" we need to do something. Having now been exposed to the wealth of information on African culture, personality, and consciousness in the previous chapters, it is now appropriate to turn our attention from theory to application. First, let's look at what needs to happen in counseling situations by examining the role and function of the therapist.

The Role and Task of Helpers and Healers

It is not unusual for young counseling students and even some professionals to approach the task of helping with great anticipation. After all, they are anxious to lend whatever expertise they have acquired to the resolution of the clients' presenting concerns. However, the desire to initiate a therapeutic relationship needs to be tempered until the clinician has taken the opportunity to examine more closely her or his role vis-à-vis the client. Earlier in the text, it was mentioned that in many counseling situations the role of the clinician is guided by theoretical orientation as well as the beliefs about how and why clients will experience some relief and resolution. Remember that for some, relief will occur through an exploration of residual baggage or an unresolved developmental task from childhood. For others, relief will come by fostering a supportive therapeutic environment that allows the client to reexperience an atmosphere of empathy, genuiness, and unconditional positive regard. Still others will seek to challenge irrational beliefs that are believed to instigate excessive feelings of anger, anxiety, guilt, or depression, which in turn diminish a client's capacity to effectively deal with life's situations. Irrespective of the theoretical orientation chosen, each has a specific set of culturally based assumptions around which the clinician organizes his or her intervention strategies.

In a similar fashion, you now ideally understand that those who work with clients of African descent need to anchor their intervention strategy in a set of culturally specific assumptions that inform both the direction of the therapeutic intervention and the role of the healer in facilitating that outcome. In fact, those assumptions articulated in earlier chapters of this book provide the lens through which we come to better understand our role as therapists.

Traditional definitions describe therapists as individuals who are trained to assist their clients with understanding and resolving life's circumstances that have led them to experience some measure of emotional distress (Ohlsen, 1983). Therapists, counselors, and psychologists—because they differ from lay people or friends—are expected to use an array of skills and techniques that are intended to facilitate some desired therapeutic outcome. Included among these skills and techniques are listening, attending, interpreting, questioning, paraphrasing, summarizing, giving feedback, mild confrontation, goal setting, teaching, diagnosing, and conceptualizing (Ohlsen, 1983).

Although it can be argued that these skills are essential to any mental health helping professional, it may be a stretch to assume that these are the only skills needed to facilitate the therapeutic process in which African American clients are seen. Recognition of this reality is provided by Atkinson and Wampold (1993), who suggest that White counselors and therapists working with culturally different (and by extension African American) clients need to bring a special sensitivity and competence to a therapeutic relationship. Although the issue of who certifies the standard of sensitivity and competence is a subject for further debate, there is little argument that these assets are a necessary part of the therapeutic interaction. Consequently, one of those competencies (assets) is the awareness of one's role as a healer.

Remember that healers are individuals who participate with the client in confronting the client's mental, physical, emotional, behavioral, and spiritual debilitation. In rendering African traditions and constructs relevant to contemporary African American needs, Hilliard (1997) reminds us that the task of the healer is to *heal thyself, remember the past, access the spirit, and confront the maafa.* In addition to these activities, remember that the role and task of a healer is to access and incorporate wisdom into their own lives. Fu-Kiau (1991) also helps us to understand the role and function of a therapist. In remembering that the essence of all things is spirit and that the spirit is energy and life force, that life force in each person constitutes a self-healing power. Thus, therapy becomes a process or vehicle in which individuals are helped to engage in a regeneration of their self-healing power. The transformative process of therapy, then, is an art of transforming a frown into a smile, a cry into laughter, self-doubt into self-confidence, personal isolation into social connectedness, mistrust into trust and responsible risk taking, and even silence and hesitation into articulate words.

Therapeutic Intervention

Thinking about intervening with a client in therapy, as a whole, can be a bit overwhelming for new, or even experienced, professionals. Therefore, it is sometimes helpful to collapse the exercise into more manageable, yet meaningful, parts. Allow me to illustrate with a case example.

Case Study

Melinda (a pseudonym) is a 15-year-old African American female high school student referred to therapy by her parents. They are concerned about what they describe as a depressed mood and the possibility of some suicidal ideation. Melinda shares with you that she is moody and temperamental and has some difficulty sustaining friendships. She also finds herself striking out at others for no apparent reason other than to hurt them. She has been in therapy twice before with Caucasian therapists, but each time her counseling was discontinued prematurely because of a failure to bond with the therapist. Despite that history, she wants to work on her emotional self so that her feelings stay more intact.

Assuming you have conducted a lethality rating with this client and it is low-negative, how might you proceed with Melinda to get her to really engage in the therapy process and develop a relationship with you? If we expect therapy to be a beneficial endeavor, how do we make the process more manageable?

In the initial stage of the treatment, a therapist usually tries to accomplish several things. What we want to do is (a) connect with our client; (b) facilitate his or her awareness; and (c) help the client in goal setting. In addition, we want to consider issues of assessment, helping clients instigate change, and allow some space for feedback and accountability. Given these priorities, we can now be clear about "what" we wish to accomplish in the therapeutic sessions. The next step then involves delineating exactly "how" we wish to accomplish these outcomes, using some specific strategies and techniques that are grounded in culturally based assumptions anchored in African-centered cultural norms and traditions.

It is important, at this point, that you have a thorough understanding of the African traditions and philosophical orientations that guide our work. You may recall from previous chapters that the ontological principle of consubstantiation has a central focus in African culture. The construct is meant to describe a belief that elements of the universe are of the same substance, that people and materials in the world are interrelated, and that all are governed by similar laws of nature and the universe. Whether your object of attention is a plant, insect, or, in this case, a human being, each is interrelated by three core conditions. All have the capacity to grow, all have the capacity to regenerate, and all have the capacity for self-preservation (Nobles, 1986).

Now, if we believe that these core conditions (capacities) have importance for the health and wellness of African descent clients, then our therapeutic work should be guided by recognizing that these conditions should be our compass for navigating our way through the therapeutic maze. First, let's explore "what" we desire to achieve in our work with clients.

Connecting with Clients

Among the myriad therapeutic tasks that confront the service provider, perhaps nothing is more important than establishing a relationship or connecting with our clients. Irrespective of one's clinical intuition or diagnostic conclusions, no effective work can occur without the development of a bond between the therapist and the client participants. In this context, service providers must recognize that the "bond" is a sacred thing, not to be taken lightly. It is at once the essence of trust, security, risk, vulnerability, sharing, commitment, and reciprocity. But how do we develop and nurture this bond? I believe that we must begin with an analysis of the cultural assumptions we make about relationships in general.

One of those assumptions is that relationships are fundamentally an interchange of spiritual energy and the clinician must tap into that energy and connect with it. Unfortunately, our material orientation to reality allows us to believe that relationships are formed with a mere handshake or by visiting one's office. This European-centered orientation to reality focuses on the physical-material realm rather than the spiritual. There is a tendency to maintain some objective distance between the provider and the client so that emotional and professional boundaries are enforced. As a consequence, relationships are often reduced to the initiation of physical contact rather than the joining of intellect, affect (emotion), and spirit in an atmosphere of harmony. Given that many of the African American clients we see are likely to appreciate more genuine connections, they may respond to a style that seeks to access their affective and spiritual core rather than simply the behavioral and physical dimensions of the personality.

Assessment

In the context of our traditional psychological and counseling training, we are taught that assessment is a systematic procedure used to ascertain qualitative and quantitative information on a specific person or attribute. It provides for both the measurement of a specific variable as well as an interpretation about what the data collected means. Assessment can involve the use of a specific screening tool, such as a test or measurement instrument, or something as simple as personal visual or auditory observations. In a culturally relevant sense, assessment allows the clinician to better understand both the diagnostic possibilities that surround a particular circumstance and the nature of the distress the client might be experiencing.

In assessing the psychological aspects of African descent people, care should be taken to avoid too much focus on identifying pathology and psychological debilitations rather than a more balanced approach that recognizes more positive aspects like strength, resilience, and resourcefulness. Consequently, beyond the traditional methods of assessment, it is important for us as clinicians to use our inherent sensitivities to better understand our clients (Paniagua, 2000). Also, we must both acknowledge and gauge the unspoken words, the unexpressed emotions in their body language, and the unconscious attitudes and beliefs expressed in their behaviors.

Facilitating Awareness

Awareness involves recognition of the forces that shape, color, or otherwise exert influence on the physical, psychological, and spiritual aspects of our being. Facilitating that recognition may involve helping our clients to be heard and understood. Often clients come to therapy not only frustrated by the situation they currently confront but also believing that they can't seem to find significant others in their lives who will listen to and understand that message.

Facilitating awareness also involves helping clients to understand their language. The messages clients share with us are often comprised of surface structure and deep structure meanings. Consequently, probing to the more deep structure meaning of the words they use and the tones they use to express them will undoubtedly create new and deeper understandings. Awareness is also heightened when clinicians can assist the client in exploring the dynamics of the past, current, and anticipated circumstances. Discovering how our experiences in life color and shape how we engage current situations and mentally plan for future ones is important as well.

Another element that helps to facilitate awareness is helping clients to access and manage their pain by acknowledging their fears. Fear, however natural to the human condition, alerts our beings to the potential for harm. Fear often incapacitates people from living life the way they would prefer. Clinicians must help their clients understand how that process occurs in their lives. In addition, facilitating awareness requires that we assist our clients to become more honest with their feelings. Often, people question their right to have emotional responses to life circumstances as well as the appropriateness of sharing those feelings with others, or even acknowledging them themselves. Awareness comes through verbalizing our thoughts and feelings in ways that are clear, truthful, and genuine.

Setting Goals

Goal setting within the context of therapy is extremely important. In fact, it is one of the most critical aspects of a therapist's work. Generally, goal setting focuses on defining a desired outcome and establishing some standard (i.e., time frame) that facilitates movement toward its realization. It can involve the outlining of general goals (e.g., feeling less depressed about life) or the articulation of very specific goals (e.g., exploring the racial-ethnic identity component of one's personality). Setting goals in a therapeutic sense is absolutely critical, but the process of crystallizing goals will require elements of realism, specificity (including cultural specificity), and perseverance. That said, it is also important to realize that goals, in some respects, can be statements of aspiration when couched in terms of personal attributes or behavioral objectives. In this regard, the goal(s) stated and the one(s) realized are likely the result of a blended perspective on what the client and therapist are each trying to achieve in relation to the other. Mention should also be made about the need to blend the focus of our goal setting between intrapsychic phenomena and sociocultural and environmental ones. This perspective acknowledges the fact that not all client distress is intrapsychic; some of it is caused by the oppressive, racist, discriminatory, and dehumanizing realities of the environment with which clients interact. Consequently, the target of our therapeutic intervention must likewise be sociocultural and environmental.

Taking Action and Instigating Change

If goal setting for the client and therapist involve defining a particular outcome, then taking action and instigating change are the procedural aspects for getting there. Taking action and instigating change involve both the commitment (conscious intent) to do something specific and the follow-through in that desired action or behavior. Because action and change involve psychological and behavioral dimensions, they require a personal sense of confidence and empowerment as well as a specific set of skills that the client is comfortable using. In a larger sense, however, a willingness to "do something differently" is related to both action and change. In fact, Nobles (1986) discusses three cultural dispositions that he believes are imperative for African descent people to master. These include

- *Improvisation*—the process of spontaneously creating a particular circumstance or event
- *Transcendence*—the ability to rise above or go beyond a particular circumstance
- *Transformation*—the ability to alter or modify the quality of an experience

These cultural dispositions are affected by a client's and therapist's belief in human possibility and potential, as well as a client's ability to maintain movement and momentum in the face of challenge and controversy.

Feedback and Accountability

Feedback is a process of providing information to clients about how well they are achieving their goals. It helps them to understand, in specific terms, the progress they are making on specific tasks, and particular places where they might be falling short. Feedback is an essential ingredient in therapeutic progress because the process itself provides the receiver of the information with opportunities to further engage the change process through periodic review and renewal of commitment.

Feedback must also be understood within the context of reciprocity. Such information is not only directed at the client through the therapist, but must also be given to the therapist by the client. In that way, clinicians know what a client is experiencing in the moment, but more important, what a client has found facilitative or not helpful about particular aspects of therapy. Feedback also helps to reinforce the notion of "aspiring to perfectability." Clients are reminded that successful interventions rarely occur as a single moment in time but rather in a series of successive steps, each of which brings a client closer to her or his goal.

Having now discussed *what* needs to happen in therapy, let us now turn our attention to the question of how we hope to achieve those outcomes. The task here is to provide you, the reader, with a set of skills and competencies that can be used to achieve some measure of success during the phases of the therapy process outlined above. Please refer to Table 7.1 for review during this section.

Connecting With Clients

Several techniques help to assist the therapist in joining with, or otherwise establishing a relationship with, the client. I would invite you to consider the following as examples.

Using Ritual

When used in the therapeutic context, ritual has potential to facilitate a process of joining or connecting for the therapist and client by helping each to develop a collective consciousness around the issue at hand. "Ritual" may be uncomfortable for some, and as such, it is important to recognize our own biases and assumptions about them and how such biases influence our willingness to employ this technique. They are not intended to evoke some sort of mystical hocus-pocus. Rather, rituals are used merely in an effort to assist the therapist in connecting with the client. Rituals can range from basic to elaborate. They can be as simple as a handshake or as elaborate as pouring libations (usually water) to

Table 7.1 Multicultural Counseling Skill Identification

Issue *Connecting With Clients Skills*	*Issue* *Assessment Skills*	*Issue* *Facilitating Awareness Skills*	*Issue* *Setting Goals Skills*	*Issue* *Taking Action/Instigating Change Skills*	*Issue* *Feedback/Accountability Skills*
Use of ritual (handshakes, libations, music, poetry, prayer, gift giving, story telling)	Understanding cultural strengths	Rephrasing (helping clients creatively synthesize opposites)	Examine culturally centered theoretical assumptions	Empowering the client (self-knowledge)	Examine congruence between goals and outcomes
Exhibit congruent realness (discuss a popular issue; self-disclosure)	Understand client distress from a culturally centered frame of reference	Understand functional behaviors	Become a subjective companion	Teaching clients to problem solve	Examine spiritual energy and sense of harmony/ balance
Be with a client (nonverbal affective responses)	Use of appropriate clinical instruments	Reflecting	Respect client's need for distance	Become a social advocate and engineer on behalf of the client	Remember the notion of "being and becoming" (perfectibility)
Create ambiance	Help client and therapist anticipate setbacks	Assess spiritual energy	Reframe (environment) (teaching improvisation, transcendence, transformation [Nobles, 1986])		
Shift context and setting (walks, be in the community)		Help clients understand their language and values	Help clients with culturally corrective experience (letting go)		
		Summarizing	Restoration of balance		
		Help clients understand their pain	Align consciousness with one's destiny (*ori-ire*)		
		Use of metaphor	Performing *sankofa*		
		Explore impact of social forces on client's life			
		Analyze defenses (obstacles to growth)			
		Assign readings			
		Help clients "know thyself"			

invite the spiritual presence of the creator and ancestors, or elders of the family, into therapeutic space.

In considering which ritual to use in a given situation, care should be taken to ensure that the technique is comfortable for both the client and the service provider. Once considered, clinicians may be guided by their own comfort zones.

Using Music

Maurice White (1998) of the musical R&B group "Earth, Wind and Fire" wrote that music has the language of the soul. It seeks to communicate its message to everyone who is open to receiving it. Music is comprised of vocal and instrumental sounds with rhythms, melody, and harmony. In the therapy session, music stimulates the senses so that the person's auditory organs process the music impulses. The sounds that result from the music stimulate feelings as each person seeks to align his or her awareness with the rhythm of the beat. Rhythms and beats, in turn, provoke a spiritual awakening that helps to establish the proper mood for the therapy session. Music also becomes central in the context of therapy because its rhythms help to illustrate the need for sustaining movement and momentum in the face of personal struggle. Much like there is a natural rhythm and order to life, music helps the listener stylize space and time in a rhythmic way; it helps a person to stay on the move spiritually, in the face of intellectual, emotional, behavioral, or spiritual pain. This is the essence of the installation of hope.

Poetry and Prose

Poetry is a language that stylizes words in a rhythmic pattern to reflect the emotional experiences of the writer and reader. Through the use of poetic verses and a sense of imagination, the writer and reader often engage the content of the message through symbolic representations of the subject. In a similar vein, poetry can serve as a stimulus to the client and therapist by providing each with a language to express their affective and intellectual sentiments, which relate to a particular issue.

Exhibiting Congruent Realness

The notion of "being real" seems almost common sense to most people, yet I suspect that the prospect is more difficult that one might imagine. Being real involves achieving a level of congruence between what we intend to do in a particular situation and how we actually respond or act in a particular moment. Being real invites the therapist to assume a posture of vulnerability, as the shelter of degrees, title, and experiences give way to his or her more human side. In this way, service providers are able to humbly engage clients on levels that are more genuine and egalitarian. Sometimes this is expressed through self-disclosure on the part of the therapist or something more basic like facilitating a conversation about other life events.

Being in the Present With a Client

The idea of being present-centered helps one to focus the shared energy between the client and healer in the present rather than the past or future. The immediacy of the moment provides the best gauge of how the client is experiencing the circumstance for which treatment was sought. Being present also provides the healer with valuable feedback to pass on to the client. However, rather than listen to and focus on the content of the message the client is giving, attention should be directed at detailing and analyzing the process dynamic, which is occurring in the therapy session itself.

Creating Ambiance

Ambiance is about creating a mood or atmosphere in the therapy session that assists the client in locating a personal comfort zone. Attention to this dimension of the process recognizes that individuals are, indeed, part of a larger social context from which they cannot be separated. Ambiance is created through cultural artifacts: music, artwork on the walls, smells, or anything that helps to engage the senses in that search for comfort. For example, a therapist might have a particular mask on display that might symbolize different emotions. Similarly, he or she may have a particular color scheme in the room or music playing that might invite the client to access a particular level of affect based on the color scheme or song represented.

Shifting Context and Setting

Traditional therapy in a Western-Eurocentric sense is usually conducted or located in a clinician's office or group room. Beyond the realm of personal comfort, this practice helps to ensure the privacy and confidentiality of the session, particularly when the "art of therapy" is restricted to individual conversation. In the African context, therapy can take the form of conversation but also might take the form of walking, drumming, laughing or crying, dancing, bathing, or even running. Therefore, because all of the activities that contribute to healing rest within a larger social context, therapists and healers might become comfortable with relocating therapy to other settings that allow the therapist to access those healing venues and activities.

Assessment

Several techniques contribute to a therapist's ability to accurately assess what is going on with a client in the moment. The following skills are offered as a way of assisting clinicians in making accurate and reliable assessments.

Understanding Cultural Strengths

Strengths are those skills or attributes that allow an individual or group to meet its needs. Strengths allow individuals to successfully confront and meet the challenges and demands placed on them by the larger social context. Assessing strengths is important for therapists because, too often, our theoretical orientations and our clinical intuitions are trained to only recognize, identify, and label pathology. However, being consistent with an African-centered reality requires that one look at those variables that allow a person to persevere through adversity as well as maintain some movement and momentum in the face of insurmountable obstacles.

Understanding Client Distress from a Culturally Centered Frame of Reference

In the African tradition, healers understand that there is a harmony, balance, and rhythm to life. Distress occurs when clients find that their energies related to the cognitive, affective, behavioral, or spiritual dimensions of their personality are out of alignment with each other. One must also remember that, unlike traditional therapeutic approaches that assume that the etiology of a client's distress to be an intrapsychic phenomenon, the African-centered tradition recognizes the social, cultural, and environmental factors that affect the psyche of African descent people. Consequently, a more holistic approach is required to truly understand client distress and psychological debilitations.

Using Appropriate Clinical Instruments

It is very difficult to accurately gauge or measure a particular construct if the instruments or devices a therapist is using are ones that are not normed and standardized on African descent people. Therefore, it is imperative for the therapist to use clinical instruments that, at the very least, have been modified by using more African-centered norms and standards, and, at best, have been developed with an African-centered framework in mind.

Helping Clients and Therapists Anticipate Setbacks

Setbacks in life occur when present circumstances run contrary to expectations. For African descent people who focus more on a present-centered frame of reference, care should be taken to help them project into the future in an attempt to explore both the possible negative and positive outcomes of a situation. In life, pain, struggle, and even tragedy are simply parts of "paying one's dues." Consequently, anticipating setbacks may help a client feel less frustrated when situations do not go as planned.

Facilitating Awareness

Specific techniques or skills that allow a therapist to increase a client's awareness of the issues going on are numerous. The following are offered as a way to assist therapists to achieve that goal.

Rephrasing (Helping Clients Creatively Synthesize Opposites)

In the African tradition, there is an expression that simply says "life at its best is a creative synthesis of opposites in fruitful harmony." In essence, this pearl of wisdom speaks to the necessity of helping clients balance their conversations about emotional distress with an awareness of the more positive aspects of that experience that is part and parcel of helping an individual arrive at the particular space he or she is currently at.

Understanding Functional Behaviors

In the African tradition, it is believed that all behavior is functional, that specific thoughts, feelings, and actions are intended to meet particular needs which emerge for the client at a particular moment in time. This skill requires a therapist to focus less on why a client might engage in a specific behavior and more on what a client might derive from behaving or responding in a particular way. Consequently, we as healers must concern ourselves less with why a person does something and more with what he or she gets out of certain behaviors.

Reflecting

Reflecting is related to the capacity for feedback, which allows the therapist or healer to give back to the client the essence of what he or she has shared in that moment. In addition, the feedback is characterized by a level of emotional or spiritual content that provides meaning and insight for the client of which he or she might have been previously unaware.

Assessing Spiritual Energy

Because African-centered therapists and healers understand that "whatever is, is in the first place spirit," they will know how important spiritual energy is in the life of a particular client. Facilitating awareness requires that a therapist be in touch with a client's spiritual energy and be able to assess that energy across domains (positive, negative) and intensity (high, medium, low). Because spirit is fundamentally energy and life force, therapists are required to understand where a client's energy level is and how he or she can access their self-healing power (Fu-Kiau, 1991). As Fu-Kiau reminds us, patients are like cars with batteries and are sometimes in varying needs of intervention in order to make them run properly. For some, the battery requires a simple jump start in order to reengage the vehicle. In other cases, the vehicle requires an extensive mechanical overhaul to put it back into running order. Similarly, human beings are known to have a reservoir of energy that requires tapping into and reviewing in order to ascertain where they are in their spiritual space.

Helping Clients Understand Their Language and Values

Helping clients understand their language and values is an important skill as well. Because African-centered therapists believe that ideas are the substance of behavior, helping clients to focus on the language they use in a particular circumstance provides important insight and cues into what a person is thinking and feeling.

Summarizing

Summarizing as a skill helps the therapist consolidate facts, observations, and intuitions discussed previously into a concise statement for the client. Beyond reflecting for the client the essence of their message they have shared, summarizing helps the therapist remind the client of the holistic nature of our reactions to life circumstances, and how interventions must be similarly structured.

Helping Clients Understand Their Pain

Clients oftentimes believe that emotional pain and distress are caused by the situational phenomena that they are confronted with. It is likely, however, that the particular situations have meaning and import for clients beyond the circumstances themselves and those dimensions of a problem must be thoroughly explored in order for clients to understand their pain. In essence, clients must be assisted with the process of not simply acknowledging their emotional feelings but rather digging deep into the cognitive processes that give meaning to life events.

Using Metaphor

Metaphors are merely figures of speech in which those phrases are used to suggest a similarity or likeness between the person or incident in question and the language being used. This figurative language is an important part of therapy because metaphor helps to identify deeper meanings in situations because the analogies used stimulate understanding at different levels.

Exploring the Impact of Social Forces on Clients' Lives

Because individuals do not exist in a vacuum, therapists must also take into account the sociocultural context in which clients are nurtured or developed. The social forces I speak of here are those societal energies that either perpetuate energy in a negative or positive way. For example, social forces of racism, sexism, oppression, and discrimination would clearly affect clients' lives in ways that would be meaningful for the therapeutic interaction. Conversely, those whose lives have been affected by social forces that engage struggle, instill hope, inspire optimism, and so on bring with them a new level of awareness that is important for clients as well.

Analyzing Defenses

Defenses are those qualities or attributes that help to protect the integrity of the individual psyche from harm or disorder. Because human beings have several needs (the need to grow, the need for self-preservation, the need for regeneration), anything that threatens the stability of that personality component will likely be defended by the individual. It is important for therapists and clinicians alike to examine ways in which individuals impede their growth possibilities by using specific defenses to ward off apparent threats to their psyche.

Assigning Readings

Reading is another technique the therapist can use to facilitate a client's awareness. The assignment of books and other periodicals allows clients to engage in the discourse on a particular topic in meaningful ways.

Helping Clients "Know Thyself"

One of the best things a therapist can do is help a client acquire more insight into self-knowledge. Too often, the sense of self is anchored in a distorted sense of reality that hinders and impedes the ability to become a fully actualized individual. Knowing oneself invites clients to discover aspects of themselves they may have been unaware of. These dimensions might include the personality (cognitive, affective, behavioral, spiritual, and biogenetic makeup), identity (answers to the questions "Who am I?" "Am I who I say I am?" "Am I all I ought to be?"), values (African-centered), or even the dimensions of their character and potential (maat).

Setting Goals

Goals chart the course for healing. They help the client review those strategies that help to bring some relief of distress. Specific skills and techniques that are associated with helping a client to set goals include the following.

Examining Culturally Centered Theoretical Assumptions

Theories are sets of abstract concepts that we use to make sense out of data that we see. In a culturally centered frame of reference, theoretical orientations serve as a road map that guide the clinician in setting specific goals for the client. It is important here that clinicians understand what specific cultural assumptions they are using to conceptualize client dynamics so that those assumptions can be used to assist the client in setting goals.

Becoming a Subjective Companion

Traditional therapy teaches that counselors and clinicians must learn to be objective outsiders. In an African-centered worldview, clinicians must become subjective companions who articulate very clear, understandable, and deliberate messages to their clients that reflect some level of adherence to culturally based assumptions. It is not uncommon for a therapist or healer to provide specific advice and counsel to the client rather than simply listening.

Respecting a Client's Need for Distance

On particular occasions, clients will come into the therapy process with a presentation of information that creates distance between themselves and the actual event. Rather than focus on confronting clients about their need for distance, African-centered therapists understand that healing can occur in the third person, much like it can in the first person.

Reframing

Another goal that is important for a therapist to use with clients is the technique of reframing (teaching the skills of improvisation, transcendence, and transformation). In this case, the therapist assists the client with changing the structure or quality of a known experience into something that is unknown and likely more beneficial for the client.

Helping a Client With a Culturally Corrective Experience

Therapists need to be culturally corrective, which requires the recognition of the interrelationship between the human organism and the law of digestion. Because digestion is an innate process of discrimination and analysis, the digestive system prefers to ingest food and then separates out that which is good and stores it from that which is bad and needs to be expelled. In a similar way, therapists must help clients understand those cognitive, affective, behavioral, and spiritual dimensions of their lives that they have absorbed or ingested into their minds, bodies, and spirits that are unhealthy and lead to disorder. The goal of therapy then becomes helping a client purge the thoughts, feelings, behaviors, and energies that do not support and affirm the humanity of that individual client.

Restoring Balance

Another important goal is to restore balance and harmony to an individual. Life circumstances, and an individual's adaptation to it, can cause an individual to become unbalanced in his or her energy flow. As such, the restoration of balance is an important technique in helping an individual to not simply synthesize opposites but to focus more creatively on balancing the energies within his or her life.

Aligning Consciousness With One's Destiny

Using the concept of ori-ire in goal setting is an important outcome because African-centered therapists understand that one's thought processes must be in tune and harmony with one's passions in life. This is an important goal in therapy as well. Thus, exploring one's passion, as well as those things that provoke a sense of urgency, are important.

Performing *Sankofa*

Sankofa is a ritual that involves periodic rebirth and renewal. In the context of a therapeutic setting, the goal of sankofa is to help an individual return intellectually, emotionally, behaviorally, and spiritually to the source of truth, harmony, and spiritual peace in their life.

Taking Action and Instigating Change

The following skills can assist clients in doing something to confront their circumstances.

Empowering the Client

The self-healing power in individuals is only partially realized if clients restrict their power to self-revelation. African-centered therapists provide encouragement and support for clients by helping them to believe and engage in some type of movement and momentum that can help them achieve some kind of change or mastery over a particular life circumstance.

Teaching Clients to Problem Solve

Problem solving is an absolute skill that can be taught to clients in need. Clients are taught to identify an issue and then to analyze those components of their problem situation they have control over and those they do not. Once identified, clients are encouraged to focus on those aspects of the situation that appear to be under their direct control or influence.

Becoming a Social Advocate and Engineer on Behalf of the Client

Often, the etiology of a client's distress is not intrapsychic but rather social, cultural, and environmental. If therapists are successful in helping clients to facilitate some healing, they want to be careful about sending them out into the environment still vulnerable to the same social pathology that instigated their desire to come to therapy in the first place. As such, becoming an advocate and social engineer on behalf of the client requires that a therapist makes deliberate attempts to access social services, institutions, and agencies on behalf of the client to help to transform those social entities into institutions that have a greater benefit and utility to the clients we serve.

Feedback and Accountability

These next skills are used to facilitate providing feedback and accountability for clients.

Examining Congruence Between Goals and Outcomes

Examining congruence allows a therapist to reflect on a time line for implementation that considers the level of progress made between stated goals and achieved outcomes. Once determined, they can then continue to encourage movement toward the desired outcome.

Examining Spiritual Energy and Sense of Harmony and Balance

Because there is a rhythm and an order to life, therapists will need to check back in with the client in order to examine how their spirit is doing and whether the individual has been able to achieve a sense of balance and harmony in his or her life.

Remembering the Notion of "Being and Becoming"

African-centered therapists understand that clients will sometimes get frustrated at the lack of progress, believing that whatever debilitation they came in to therapy with will be gone in an instant or after a short time. It is important to help clients understand that because each personality is endowed with the character of perfectibility, they must recognize the nature of being and becoming. Thus, clients need to be assisted in understanding that although they are in the moment, they are always in a state of becoming more self-actualized.

Summary

In this chapter, I have sought to analyze a therapeutic process from its most common denominators. Clearly, practitioners and students alike struggle with how to be more culturally competent when working with diverse populations. Competence is not simply an activity that you either do or don't have but rather is a series of microskills that, when strung together, allow a therapist or healer to be effective in the moment with clients who are culturally different. I argue that the role and task of healers is fundamentally different in an African-centered reality. In addition, I have raised the notion that the two most important questions in therapy are "what" and "how." Consequently, those questions are used to create a model of skill development that are functional strategies and skills that both clinicians and students can use to be more effective with African American populations. Last, in order to assist you, the reader, with this skill development process, an African-Centered Assessment Form has been provided in Appendix A. You are invited to use the scales to gauge your current and continued level of skill development.

8

Counseling African American Fathers

A Program for Active Involvement

Michael Connor

Having now focused on using specific skills and techniques for intervening with African American clients, let us now turn our attention to the application of this knowledge with a specific subgroup of the population. My focus here is on some promising work with African American fathers who, as a group, represent a critical element in the mental health and viability of African American families.

Donte (a pseudonym), a 23-year-old high school dropout with no relevant work experience, impregnated his girlfriend of three years. He was taking courses at the local community college, with no focus at matriculating toward a degree. Donte enrolled in courses that he thought might be interesting but tended to drop them after a few weeks when the class requirements became more demanding. He took no exams, wrote no papers, and only attended classes when convenient. He stayed at home with his parents when he was not spending time at a girlfriend's home. He had several girlfriends and throughout the relationship had been "cheating" on the woman he had impregnated. He indicated she was unaware of the other girlfriends and that she thought he was at his parents' home when not with her. Donte's parents, although in a long-term relationship, have never married. There are three children from this union. Both of his parents have a college education and his father has maintained "outside relationships" over the years. Apparently, his father came and went as he pleased, frequently not coming home for several days at a time. Donte indicates he has a good relationship with his father and sees him as a "good man and role model." He refuses to discuss how he feels about his parents' living arrangement, their having never been married, or how his mother might feel about the situation.

Although Donte has never worked, he states he is pursuing his dream of becoming "an entertainer." Specifically, he says he wants to be a rap star or a deejay. He did enroll in a course for radio engineering and volunteered some time working at a local public service radio station; however, there have been no offers of employment in this chosen field. Donte has no medical insurance for himself or for his child. He has no car and either catches rides with friends, uses public transportation, or drives his mother's car. He occasionally gets money from his parents to give toward his child's care. He did not attend any prenatal care visits, has never taken his child to the doctor, has not prepared any meals for her, gone grocery shopping, or purchased any clothing for her. He says he is able to care for her needs but tends to have his mother feed, bathe, and change her when the baby is with him.

The child delivered seven weeks early by cesarean section. She was maintained in an incubator for the first six weeks of her life. Although Donte was present at the hospital the night his daughter was born, he left shortly after the birth to spend the night with another girlfriend "to celebrate his accomplishment." He did not visit his child during the six-week stay in the hospital, saying that seeing her in an incubator made him "sad." The child's mother was at the hospital daily for several hours interacting with her child. Within eight weeks of the birth of his child, the child's mother returned to work full time stating she did not want to accept welfare benefits.

Jamal (a pseudonym), a 22-year-old high school dropout, impregnated his girlfriend while in high school. Neither of them completed school and he has been struggling since the birth of their daughter. Jamal attempted to maintain a relationship with his child, seeing her several times each week as his schedule allowed, providing some child care, nurturance, food, and clothing as he could afford. He had endeavored to develop and maintain a relationship with the maternal grandparents as well. Jamal was working part time washing cars. He grew up in a single parent household and had little contact with his father; however, an uncle and his maternal grandfather were active with him throughout his youth. These men, although initially disappointed on hearing that Jamal was about to become a father, took time to discuss his responsibilities to this child and to the mother of his child. They impressed on him the seriousness of his situation and suggested he "step up to the plate and act like a strong African man." Although Jamal's mother never married, she openly discussed her belief in the institution of marriage and of maintaining responsibility to those who are dependent on him. She has been active in her church, works full time, and began attending vocational school (she wants to be a practical nurse) when Jamal was in high school. She has never spoken negatively about Jamal's father and she is in a long-term relationship with a man whom she plans to marry after she completes her vocational training. Jamal has maintained a good relationship with his mother, his uncle, and with his grandfather.

Before reviewing the use of specific skill sets as intervention strategies, this chapter presents an overview of some of the social science literature pertaining to young African American fathers. Much of this research focused on perceived deficits, especially the impact of absentee fathers. This deficit-oriented review is followed by a brief review of research that focuses on Black fathers who are involved with their children. Information gained from involved fathers is incorporated in the development of an African-centered counseling-education intervention model (the Program) designed to enhance fathers' involvement in the lives of their children and the mothers of those children. The intervention model is presented and discussed, along with the experiences of Jamal and Donte, two composites representing issues and situations shared by young fathers who participate in the Program. The sharing of this model also represents how the notion of shifting "context and setting" can be applied in a specific program with this population.

Social Science and Black Men

As noted, much of the social science research on African American families accepts the deficit perspective, focusing on perceived deficiencies (while at the same time ignoring such realities as the impact of White privilege, White supremacy, and White racism). In fact, over the past decade, the major trends on which researchers have focused when looking at families of color are "overall declines in the rates of marriage . . . higher proportions of unwed mothers, higher percentages of single-headed households, and higher numbers of poor families" (Taylor, Tucker, Chatters, & Jayakody, quoted in McLoyd, Cauce, Takeuchi, & Wilson, 2000). In their scholarship of fatherhood review, Marsiglio, Amato, Day, and Lamb (2000) note "materials are typically drawn from White middle-class sources and are seldom representative of contemporaries from different ethnic, racial, cultural, and economic backgrounds." When studying African American fathers, these researchers suggest using "special sampling strategies that include fathers in jail, prisons, and the military." Interestingly, no suggestions or directives are offered to study married African American fathers who reside with their children!

For African American males, the deficit approach has fostered research focusing on father absenteeism and the resultant problems for children and women. For example, Parker and Kleiner (1966) suggested that many issues such as delinquency, homosexuality, and mental disorders can be attributed to a father-absent family environment. Lynn (1974) suggested that children reared in father-absent homes are more likely to exhibit delinquency, experience poor masculine development, and demonstrate compensatory masculine development in their teens. He also said that father absenteeism is associated with drug addiction, alcoholism, suicide attempts, and lower scholastic performance. Biller (1971) notes that boys reared in father-absent homes gravitate to gangs and gang activities. In a later article, Biller (1981) writes that lower-class Blacks in father-absent homes suffer in terms of sex role orientation. These males, and Black males in general, are denigrated by Black females (mothers, sisters, aunts, grandmothers, etc.), thus contributing to potential problems in future male-female relationships. Apparently, neither Black males nor females feel good about Black males. In these homes, there is much family instability and there are many financial problems. Lamb (1986), in summarizing the research on males in father-absent homes, concludes that they have problems with sex role and gender identification, problems in their school performance, and problems learning to control aggression.

Schulz (1969), in writing about Black men growing up in a Midwestern inner-city community, suggested that African American fathers have problems providing effective role models for their sons due to their marginal participation in the society at large. He writes that Black teenage males seek out peers "on the street" with whom to identify. Status on the street is important if there is no status at home. Liebow (1967), observing the plight of unemployed inner-city Black men (many of whom had fathered children), addressed the issue of lack of employment opportunities for African American men. He noted they experience problems getting work; the work is too hard; without cars, getting to job sites is impossible; and the jobs that are available are "dead end." Scanzoni (1971) acknowledged that two thirds of Black families were headed by men in 1968; he says that many stereotypes exist regarding the Black family because of the social scientists' focus on the one third that are headed by females and then their generalized findings to the population as a whole. Scanzoni attempts to shed light on the remaining two thirds (the "intact" male-female headed families). However, his book tends to focus on perceived deficiencies. For example, he noted that the literature "is replete with the alleged 'inability' of the (Black) father to move his sons toward goals" (p. 96). He notes that African American men came to believe they were inferior after being told they were for so many years and after being systematically excluded from opportunity.

Each of these works contains some accuracy regarding the specific African American population that was studied. However, Liebow and Schulz focused on the problems of low-income Black males, generalized their findings to African American males across socioeconomic status, tended not to study mother-father pairs present in Black families, tended to look at those males in which pathology was present, tended to ignore inherent strengths in Black families and in Black men, and tended not to deal with the issues of White supremacy, White privilege, or White racism (which African American men confront on a daily basis). This failure to deal with White supremacy, racism, privilege, and the resultant discrimination is most apparent in Scanzoni's work; he acknowledges the problems and then ignores any meaningful attempt to study, comprehend, or deal with the magnitude White racism has on African American families. Had the African American males in these studies sought, or been referred to, typical Eurocentric counseling or therapy, they likely would have received psychotropic medications (to control their perceived anger, hostility, suspicions, depression, or anxieties) or one of several "talking" therapies (to explore intrapsychic confusion, unresolved childhood conflicts, problems with authority, or self-hatred, for example). If the men rejected these mental health approaches, they likely would have been considered to be avoiding their problems and blamed for not being willing to participate in their own change programs.

Adolescent Fathers

Regarding adolescent African American fathers, research is somewhat limited in scope. Seemingly little is known about those who experience successes, and this population, in general, is provided few services compared to those available for adolescent females.

Barret and Robinson (1982) suggest there are several myths regarding adolescents who father children. These myths include that they are worldly wise and know more about sex and sexuality than most teenage boys; they usually have fleeting, casual relationships with the young mother and experience little emotional reaction to the pregnancy; they are rarely involved in the support and rearing of their children; they complete school and enter high-paying jobs, leaving their partners to fend for themselves; they are psychologically different from teenage boys who do not become fathers during adolescence.

Hendricks (1981), when studying adolescent dads, found that they came from large families; often their fathers were present; they became dads at 17.8 years of age; about half had unwed sisters with children; about a third had brothers who were unwed dads; a fourth of them were born into single-parent homes. He also found they were not involved with church; they were working; they had completed high school; they saw nothing wrong with what they had done; and they were concerned about their children's and the mother's future. These teens were also found to be "unrealistic" about parenthood. In another paper, Hendricks and Montgomery (1983) found teenage fathers to be accepting of fatherhood; they expressed love for the mother and their child; they were concerned about the child's future; and they were not concerned about having had a child "out of wedlock." Robinson, Barret, and Skeem (1983) found no difference in locus of control between unwed adolescent fathers and nonfathers. Redmond (1985) found that teenage fathers and fathers-to-be want to know and understand what's going on in their girlfriend's lives. These teens indicated a willingness to help with physical care, financial care, and they showed affection for their children. Furstenberg (1976) found that teen males expressed an interest and desire to help with their children. Barret and Robinson (1985) found teenage dads maintained a positive relationship with their girlfriends and their families and they planned to meet certain social, educational, and financial expectations for the mothers and children. Brown (1983) found African American adolescent fathers to be concerned about financial support for their children, to have problems continuing their own schooling, to have problems with their girlfriend's parents, and to be experiencing anxiety about their own futures. These males were not perceived as being exploitative of their girlfriends. Although the above studies may be indicative of a specific subsection of adolescent fathers—which contradicts stereotypes of the population—it is a population that would likely benefit from proactive services designed to aid them in handling their responsibilities.

In attempting to predict at-risk teens, Robbins, Kaplan, and Martin (1985) found low-income males experiencing school problems and that those who were popular were vulnerable. Their sample of minority youth was not low on powerlessness or self-esteem as Lewis (1968) formulates in his "culture of poverty" conception. Other researchers are finding relationships between teenage pregnancy, school drop out, vocational unemployment, crime, and delinquency. Gibbs (1984) writes that unemployment among African American youth was 48.3% in 1983; the rate of delinquency was 21.4% in 1979; drinking and substance abuse were increasing; 44% of Black children under the age of 18 were living in female-headed homes in 1980; and 15.4% of Black youth in the 16 to 24 age group were high school dropouts. Sklar (1986) says that unemployment is a major contribution to teen pregnancy, especially for low-income and minority males. Sullivan (1986) writes that the lack of employment is related to teenage childbirth, leaving school, criminal activity, drug and substance abuse, suicide, and poor mental health. He also says that for inner-city youth, the lack of work is a fact of life. Bumpass, Rindfuss, and Janosik (1984) note that early parenthood and "illegitimacy" is associated with lower educational and vocational attainment, marital instability, larger families, and poor mental and physical health. Malson (1984) states that the situation is so bleak that many African American males have given up looking for work and thus will never be able to financially care for their children.

Gordon (1986) notes that teens receive negative sexual material from television that tends to project sexual information that is sexually irresponsible (rape, violence, and infidelity). Churches have not been at the forefront in educating teens about their sexuality and it is unlikely that teens are reading material that adequately informs them in this area. Thus, the primary purveyors of information (home, school, church, the media) are not accurately or adequately offering information that might help to resolve the problem. Inadequate education and information is likely to be related to our high teenage abortion and pregnancy rates (Connor, 1987b, 1988). Few teens use any form of contraception when they first become sexually active (less than one in seven, according to Gordon) and many report they are embarrassed to get information about contraception (Stark, 1986). Others report they did not think they could get pregnant (Chilman, 1983).

Involved African American Fathers

In reviewing existing research that considers fathers who are involved with their children, Cazenave (1981) indicates that African American men believe responsibility is the key to manhood. His sample (54 Black fathers employed as letter carriers) also indicated that ambition, firm guiding principles, and being an economic provider are important. Glick (1981) writes, "As the income level of men increases, the proportion of men with intact first marriages tends to increase" (p. 117). He notes that stability seems not to depend on being well to do but rather on not being poor. Hunter and Davis' sample of African American men, in responding to what they thought manhood was about, listed humanism, self-determination and accountability, pride and spirituality, and family relations (from McLoyd et al., 2000).

Connor (1986) surveyed the attitudes toward children and mates of 136 working class African American men in an urban Southern California area. The sample ranged in age from 20 to 45 years old. He was interested in determining Black males' perception of their roles as fathers; Black males' perception of their roles as mates; Black males' perception of other Black men's roles as fathers; and Black males' perception of gender-related child-rearing differences. In Connor's sample, they tended to perceive themselves as being actively and positively involved in both the lives of their children and the mothers of those children, and they did not espouse child-rearing differences related to gender. However, these African American men tended to see other Black men lacking regarding both children and mates. They perceived other men as having problems getting along and being meaningfully involved with both children and relationship partners. Among other explanations, this finding might suggest the population was not involved themselves and were projecting this lack of involvement onto others—a defensive posture. However, an equally plausible explanation is that these men (perhaps the African American community in general?) have accepted the popular and widespread notion that Black males are not involved with their families and, therefore, do not perceive any meaningful interaction when viewing other Black fathers. Psychologically, this implicit acceptance has dire consequences for the community at large in terms of acceptance of the negative stereotype and behaviors that might follow. The impact of this acceptance on young African American males in search of and in need of positive role models is immense.

A primary weakness of the above study (other than general problems using self-report inventories) was that only males were sampled. In a follow-up study (Connor, 1987b), African-American male (N = 277) and female (N = 138) respondents were asked to complete an expanded questionnaire regarding Black male attitudes toward children and mates. Interestingly, the results were much the same as the previous study—African American men see themselves meaningfully involved with their children and mates, but see other Black men as lacking this meaningful involvement. Black women perceive Black men to be meaningfully involved with children and mates. The support from females seemingly casts doubt on the notion of pathological projection as a defense for African American men.

Lessons learned from involved (adult) dads suggest they are willing and able to communicate with their children and with the mothers of their children; they share household and child rearing responsibilities; they are committed to an ongoing relationship with their child(ren); they put time and energy into their responsibilities; and they attempt to obtain and maintain gainful employment. Many of these fathers want to learn about parenting and they make taking time for their children a high priority. They seem to be in a "partnership" with their children's mothers, doing things together. Spiritual development tends to occupy an important aspect of these men's lives and they practice their faith on a regular basis. These men also tend to be active in sports and recreation, often with family or friends. They play an active part in family decision making and those who are most successful in their family relationships tend to understand, accept, and encourage active decision making with their spouses. These fathers allow themselves to be tender—although primarily with their daughters (hugging, kissing, holding them). Interestingly, Sullivan (1986) found that the African American community expected teenage fathers to participate in caring for their children. In fact, he found that local standards exist for judging young fathers who do and those who do not attempt to provide care for their children. Those who do not provide for their children incur disrespect in their neighborhoods. As Kunjufu (1986) writes,

> Our boys do not know when they are men, and it is the responsibility of men to teach them. If men do not fulfill this responsibility, boys will continue to define it from a physical perspective, i.e., making a baby, getting

into fights, and the consuming of drugs and alcohol, desiring fancy clothes, and cars. (p. 37)

The Program

The following male involvement in an African-centered counseling-education program attempts to combine information learned from involved fathers with historic African values and teachings. The Program attempts to instill cultural significance offered by our ancestors as a means of focusing and motivating youth to understand who they are and what they can become. As discussed by Jeff (1994), "Afrocentrism is based on African institutions, the most important of which is family" (p. 103). He suggests seven ethical principles that affect the family, including respect, responsibility, restraint, reciprocity, religion, rhythm, and redemption. Parham, White, and Ajamu (1999) discuss the character-building tenets of maat, "a standard for collective subscription toward living and being together as a people" (p. xv) and they note "the African worldview promotes … collective orientation to people, family, and social interactions" (p. 15).

The Program embraces these African-centered principles and includes both a "Rites of Passage" and a "Male Mentoring" approach to provide service to young Black fathers. Rights of Passage involves completing a set of tasks by different age groups of young men, which culminates in special, culturally relevant recognition programs, ceremonies, and events (rituals). Male Mentoring is based on development of one-on-one relationships between successful male role models and young adults. This education-counseling intervention program involves recruitment and outreach, four skills training components, follow-up, and referral. Successful participants enter follow-up at the conclusion of the skills training. The education and training is offered in a group context, with 12 to 15 participants in each training session. It is important to maximize group processes to foster the Afrocentric principles of caring and sharing, interdependence, support within the community, respect, and an orientation toward living and being together. The program also adheres to the African-centered notion that manhood is not defined by chronological age alone but by mastery (Parham, 1999). Therefore, participants are expected to achieve genuine progress when mastering specific functional areas of the curriculum modules. The suggested format is first to formally present the information to be shared. Facilitators are strongly encouraged to consider the use of visual aids and appropriate language. After the formal presentation, discuss the presented material and encourage everyone to share their perceptions and reactions. Be willing to stay as long as possible to cover all questions that might arise, but keep the participants focused on the material at hand.

At each step of the Program, success is acknowledged and celebrated, as are specific "milestones" in the participants' lives. That is, a child's birth, a birthday, a first step, a first word, a marriage, a completion of an educational or training program, are all honored and celebrated in the African tradition.

Participants can be recruited from a variety of sources, including but not limited to schools, barbershops, social service organizations, word-of-mouth, churches, job sites, the mothers of the fathers' children (a major way of getting the information to the males), and so on. They will likely come from populations that Axelson (1993) refers to as "poor Blacks" and the "Black underclass." Contemporary social programs refer to these men as "at risk"; however, in this intervention program, they are perceived to be "at promise." Participants are encouraged to enroll immediately on receiving information pertaining to the program. Getting men to participate can be the most difficult aspect of the program. Many are unaware that they have problems or that something can be done to aid them. Some have had no appropriate male role model to show them how fathers act and what they do. Many have not learned how to ask for or accept help even as they recognize it is needed. Too many have seemingly accepted Eurocentric norms that have resulted "in the dehumanization of African people" (Parham, White, & Ajamu, 1999, p. 23). They may have accepted their plight as being natural and reasonable. Thus, the outreach workers must be particularly sensitive and knowledgeable about the problematic histories of African American males in an oppressive environment. Outreach workers are the first line of attack for the program and must represent, demonstrate, embody, and live the very principles the Program attempts to convey. Therefore, young Black men who may be fathers and who are putting forth energy and effort to positively affect their babies are needed for this front line work.

During enrollment, it is important to be sensitive to the reading and writing levels of each potential attendee. Complete any enrollment forms for the men, as necessary, in an unobtrusive manner. Initially, the fathers are screened for suitability for training and those not accepted should be referred to other community programs. For example, men abusing substances are not appropriate for the education-counseling intervention and should be referred to relevant treatment programs. The Program should maintain a record for these men and invite and encourage their participation on completion of their treatment program (this is also true for those men who are facing incarceration). Maintain contact to reinforce potential training involvement on completion of other obligations.

Skill components include parent training, personal-legal issues, educational issues, and jobs-vocational training. The training takes place over four weeks with one topic being presented each week. A group format (the village) is used so that the fathers share and learn from one another. When special circumstances arise that cannot be resolved within the group, referrals are made to the counseling component of the Program.

Parent training represents the basis and the most critical component of the intervention model. The theory is that if a Black man has a child, he is a father and must participate with and in his child's life, irrespective of his legal situation, his level of education, or his vocational status. To do otherwise reinforces the Eurocentric perception of Black male pathology (absentee Black father) and continues to diminish the vitality of the African American community. Because many African American males consider themselves to be community minded, this is essential. However, they are encouraged to remember, as Haki Madhibuti reminds us, that you cannot pretend to believe in supporting the Black community and not believe and engage in supporting strong Black families because the family is the smallest and most salient element of community. In this manner, the Program will help empower Black fathers to establish and maintain significant attachments with their children, in part through a redefinition of what constitutes appropriate and successful African American fathers. Ideally, an African American male, trained in child development and who is also an involved father, should conduct this training. He will need to model the behavior he will be teaching.

During this training, first determine at which "stage" of parenting the men are in vis-à-vis their children. Then, offer parent-child interaction issues pertinent to that stage of development. For example, if participants are at a "pregnant" stage (that is, their wives or girlfriends are currently pregnant), focus on topics such as personal feelings of fear and anxiety, or joy and excitement that surround the pregnancy itself, prenatal development, prenatal medical visits, prepared child birthing, preparation for delivery, the value and need of male participation and involvement with babies, neonate and infant needs (sleeping, changing, feeding, holding, appropriate stimulation, bonding), and so forth. Additionally, the fathers should learn certain developmental landmarks of infancy (e.g., feeding, rolling over, crawling, standing, babbling, walking, etc.). The importance of health care, the role of stress, and how fathers affect the health and development of mothers and children should be emphasized. Men who have older children and therefore have previously gone through the "pregnant stage" will tend to share their experiences as they remember and reminisce about their own children.

Should several of the participating fathers have children who are at the toddler stage, the training focuses on toddler activities, including self-feeding activities, walking, controlling eliminations, learning to dress oneself, developing communication skills, child-proofing the home, positive approaches to discipline, and so on. If the fathers have children who are at the early childhood years, the focus would be on helping children develop personal capabilities—helping them to learn their social roles and responsibilities, learn self-discipline through the establishment of daily routines, and the like. Routinely, the discussions regarding discipline raise numerous issues for which time should be taken to thoroughly cover this very important child (and parent) developmental topic.

Generally, the participating fathers will likely have children representing several developmental stages. Should this be the situation, commence training at the children's earliest developmental level and work through the early childhood years. I find that those men with older children tend to readily share their experiences with the fathers who have younger kids, but those with younger children tend to have difficulty relating to older children's issues. Thus, a community of interactive and sharing fathers can emerge. The primary goal of this component is to help and encourage each man to become a more involved and competent father. Finally, regardless of the level at which this training originates, the fathers are encouraged to read to their children on a daily basis for a minimum of 10 minutes. This activity is demonstrated and modeled for the participants.

It is important to provide tangible incentives for each male who attends. These items can be exchanged for a small item for his child (diapers, formula, milk, etc.). The goal is to provide concrete evidence that his involvement and motivation is valued and rewarded.

Should any of the men raise issues beyond the scope of the training pertaining to parenting situations, they should be referred to counseling. This counseling component is essential as it may be the first time a participant has recognized and requested help. Obviously, a trained African American counselor is needed to deal with the issues. This African-centered therapy can be modeled along the guidelines presented in Chapter 7. Specifically, it is essential that the therapist *connect with the client.* This skill is particularly important here in order to help the client engage in the therapy process and avoid replicating the problems of early termination. Depending on the specific age of the client, care should be taken to use appropriate and relevant rituals, music, proper ambiance, and congruent realness. Use of appropriate *assessment techniques* and being sensitive to the client in order to *facilitate awareness* are two techniques that can lead to the *setting of reasonable goals*. The goal setting, in turn, allows the client to take action and to *instigate change strategies*. Care should be taken here to balance the need to address the client's external environmental realities with those that promote the client's acknowledgement and acceptance of personal responsibility (consistent with the notion of free will in the context of maat). Thus, providing *feedback* that *encourages accountability* is critical in any growth situation. It is also important to acknowledge that counseling at this stage of the process may help to buffer some of the information the men will receive at later stages of the training process.

The primary goal of the second week of training is to share with the fathers information about their *legal rights and responsibilities* to their children. A second goal is to help them with problem-solving/coping strategies.

Ideally, an African American attorney who specializes in family law and an expert in domestic violence (preferably an adult African American woman) should participate.

The attorney should encourage the men to establish paternity by explaining why it is important, valued, and imperative for both them and their children. Establishment of paternity affords fathers certain rights for custody, visitation, child-rearing participation, and decisions about the child's future. It also provides children with potential knowledge regarding their past and future.

Therefore, the attorney will provide education about legal rights, with focus on access to children, joint custody (primary custody in some instances), how to affect the legal system in positive ways, and so forth. This facilitator will also discuss and advocate commitment to financial support. Pecuniary support of children is mandated by the courts and one cannot avoid this fiscal responsibility. The attorney will explain to the men that it is better that they develop their own system of payment rather than relying on the legal system. African American men should try and avoid the criminal "justice" system throughout their lives. It should also be impressed on the men that fathers who financially support their children are more likely to maintain contact with them than fathers who do not provide support. In addition, it obviously takes financial involvement to rear children.

During this week, problems pertaining to domestic violence and the impact it has on our communities are discussed. We find that a mature African American woman is most credible and compelling in presenting this information. Perhaps she reminds the men of their own mothers or grandmothers whom they do not want to see "beaten down." Techniques of conflict resolution, stress reduction, and compromise-negotiation strategies are shared, discussed, and demonstrated. The fathers are encouraged to discuss and practice listening and hearing skills with one another to help them develop positive interactive approaches with their children and with the mothers of their children. The topic of controlling children's behaviors is revisited with discussion and demonstration of the difference between discipline and punishment. It is important that the men come to understand the impact that domestic violence has on their children, their mates, and themselves.

As during the first week, reinforce the men for completing this segment of training. Again, the reinforcers should be tangible items or services that they can give to their child(ren).

The focus of week three recognizes that the level of education of African American men is directly correlated with their ability to work and to support their children. Therefore, assess each father's educational background and present (encourage) each participant with the opportunity to improve and enhance his educational training. For example, those fathers with minimal reading skills, as noted during enrollment, can be referred to adult education programs. One approach is to have a teacher from adult education visit the intervention program and share his or her available services. Men who do not have their high school diplomas can be offered GED information and training (and adult continuation education). It is important to help the participants locate student resources from local community colleges or universities to serve as tutors (perhaps members from African American fraternities or other service organizations), thereby providing assistance for the men in the Program.

Apropos, those fathers who have graduated from high school might be offered information regarding vocational training, community college, and university opportunities. In addition, providing the participants with a field trip to a local educational institution so they might "experience" a campus (be it adult school, junior college, vocational school, or university) is another worthwhile endeavor. They should walk the campus, visit admissions offices, student unions, libraries, classrooms, and so on. During this phase of the program, it is also important to help the men focus on the difference between education and training (the latter occurs is most educational institutions) and the degree to which exposure to certain types of information has contaminated their consciousness in ways that are not personally affirming. Remember that Carter G. Woodson was clear that yielding control of your mind to alien sources would have you seeking an inferior status even before one can be provided for you.

Finally, educate the fathers about their own personal health issues and offer opportunities for physical examinations as needed. This should include reproductive and contraceptive information; information about safer sexual practices and sexually transmitted diseases; data concerning essential hypertension, diabetes, and prostate cancer; the impact of tobacco (including second-hand smoke), alcohol, and other drugs; and healthy lifestyles and nutrition. Perhaps, as the men understand their own health, they will develop an appreciation for the health and well-being of their children and the children's mother.

As before, reinforce the fathers for participation; however, use "activity" reinforcers this week. These reinforcers provide the participants with the means to engage in an activity with their children (e.g., *going* to the movies, *visiting* the African American theater or museum, *taking* their children to a local theme park, *making* a picnic, etc.). This reinforcement stresses the importance of doing things with one's child, depending on and appropriate to the age of the child.

Most of the programs servicing men as fathers tend to focus on *jobs and vocational training*. Although this might be a reasonable approach, it can be argued that it is shortsighted and limiting because this approach reinforces males as primary (exclusive) breadwinners at the expense of emphasizing parenting skills. Given the historical problems pertaining to African American males' marginal participation in the country's workforce (due to racism and oppression), equating male value and participation in family life from a financial vantage point may put African American men at an obvious disadvantage. It can be used to control, manipulate, and disparage them. When the job situation looks bleak, so does the parenting involvement. Tucker, Chatters, and Jayakody (from McLoyd, Cauce, Takeuchi, & Wilson, 2000) write, "Employment factors are critical to African American family formation, but they represent only one set of factors."

Broadening the role of dads by placing primary emphasis on consistent, competent, and focused paternal involvement, while dealing with vocational-job training secondarily, might enhance father-child bonding and foster ongoing consistent male involvement. It might also serve to empower Black men by taking personal-individual control of the definition of "manhood." That is, the ability to provide consistent financial support is an important aspect of the definition of fatherhood, but it is secondary to consistent child involvement.

The goal of the fourth skills component—vocational training—is to help the fathers learn how to prepare and present themselves for the job marketplace to further enhance paternal involvement with children. This component is designed to offer men requisite tools for securing employment and includes training for the following: searching for jobs, making career decisions, finding the right job, assessing personal skills and attributes, writing resumes, completing applications, and interviewing for jobs. A distinction should be made between a job and a career. Too many fathers are encouraged to be content with a "good" job rather than develop their career aspirations. This point is key as men should be encouraged to explore their passions and dreams as consistent with the principle of ori-ire, seeking to align their consciousnesses with that passion (destiny).

In addition, attempts must be made to place the fathers in existing viable programs to enhance their earning capabilities. Obviously, the goal is to place the dads in employment positions that are career oriented to ensure longevity in the workplace. Long-term employment is needed to assure that Black fathers are able to continue financial support of their children and themselves. Although the primary focus of the Program is parental enhancement, the importance, impact, and relevance of employment skills training is both recognized and appreciated. However, as noted above, emphasis is on presenting this component in the context of caring for and providing for one's offspring. That is, one of the major goals of gainful employment is to support one's children. During this fourth week, attempt to link appropriate fathers with African American men who are working at a job to which the participant aspires. Thus, the men can receive firsthand information and encouragement from those who have benefited from training and education, and who are making use of their skills. This format provides for a mentoring system that is important to the development of the participants, attempting to pair participants with individuals who are actually working in a field of interest. Effective mentoring can offer a model for generative relationships, allowing those who have achieved some relative success to "give back" by modeling appropriate behaviors to and for those who are attempting to survive and thrive in an often hostile environment. Ideally, these mentors may take on an elder role and develop some of the healer's capacities.

On completion of the skills training, the men will enter *follow-up*, whereby activities with their children and with the mothers of their children are monitored. It is important that they implement the information shared during the training *after training is completed*. The goal is to continue to enhance their level of child interaction; to offer ongoing aid and support so they might continue their educational pursuits; to reinforce them for using problem-solving, conflict-resolution, and negotiation skills; and to support and encourage their attempts at providing for the financial well-being of their children. In addition, the graduated fathers are invited back to the Program to share their successes and their challenges with new Program participants and with the Program staff. As funds become available, some can be hired to work in the Program. All are encouraged to refer their friends and acquaintances to the Program. All become a viable part of the village.

With the successful completion of the skills training, the participants and their families are invited to an annual "graduation" celebrating their combined and accumulated successes. This culturally imbued Rites of Passage program honors the men and their attainment and can take place between Fathers' Day and Juneteenth. The day will celebrate men in the lives of their children and their mates. All participants are supported in the wearing of traditional African garments. Each will be acknowledged at the ceremony; each receives a certificate of completion and a Kente Cloth. In the African tradition, music is available and food is served at this function. Because it is important that fatherhood be valued and celebrated throughout the year, additional social activities that strengthen continued positive interactions with family and one another are also encouraged. Any guest speakers should acknowledge and reinforce the positive behaviors that the men display.

As noted above, incentives are used during each step of the training to reinforce the fathers' participation. The incentives are items or activities the fathers can use for or with their children, including (but not limited to) diapers, formula and baby food, infant-toddler clothes, shoes, books, and educational toys, strollers, car seats, plus educational recreational activities. The value of any "in-kind" contribution the fathers make toward child care should be discussed, acknowledged, and appreciated. If space is available, a "baby-toddler store" can be maintained on the training site. This is a space where the reinforcers can be stored so that the incentives are immediately available when earned. Relationships can be formed with community businesses that might be willing to donate items to the program. Donations should be acknowledged formally to the sharing merchant(s) in local newsletters and other publications.

Finally, *counseling services* are a vital aspect of the Program. These services must be culturally appropriate and sensitive to the needs of the fathers. The types of situations that may arise can include concerns and fears about one's ability to parent; relationships with women other than the mother of one's child; relationships the child's mother is having with other males; credit issues; learning issues; issues pertaining to the ability to love and be loved; issues relating to one's own father or mother; and so forth. Although one of the Program goals is for the fathers to develop a willingness and capacity to trust one another enough to share these very personal issues, as Boyd-Franklin (1989) notes, some of the men may not be able to do so (for others, it may not be appropriate to do so). It is recommended that first preference for the counselor be a mature, intact, trained African American man who is a father. His hours will need to be flexible, as the men should be seen as soon as they become cognizant of their issues. It is critical that this counselor is knowledgeable of and sensitive to the African-centered concepts discussed in this book. We are aware that it is likely that many of the men will have to first complete a series of counseling sessions prior to their enrollment in the Program. Thus, the counselor plays a pivotal role in the Program's and the participants' success. He is in a position to introduce and educate the men about their issues and offer some solutions at the same time. The counselor must work directly with the Program and share the Program's goals and objectives.

Case Study

Jamal and Donte began the intervention program together, along with 10 other men. The participants ranged in age from 18 to 38; each had at least one child and two were married to the mothers of their children. None of the men had continued their education beyond high school, six were working full time in minimum wage paying jobs, and five had "contact" with the criminal "justice" system. Each of the working men made some contribution toward financial support of their child. All acknowledged paternity and seven had some consistent contact with their children, seeing them at least weekly.

Donte and Jamal did not know one another until they met the first night. Each of the men was confronted the first night about their perceptions of what it takes to be a man. Donte had problems integrating himself into the program and sharing his story with the other men. He tended to be either defensive or withdrawn, denied responsibility for his actions, and had difficulty hearing what the others were saying. Because the mother of his child had experienced difficulty balancing the demands of work and single parenting, she had returned to her parents' home (some 300 hundred miles away) where help was available. Donte expressed anger toward her and her parents for "making it difficult" for him to have a relationship with his child. Currently, although Donte continues to make demands of the mother about what she does with the baby, he does not provide child support, has visited her once in ten months, and is openly hostile toward her family who does provide support for his child. During an interaction some three weeks into the program, Donte was confronted by several participants who attempted to help him see some problems in his position. Namely, because he was not providing for his child, perhaps he should be thankful his child's mother and her parents were taking care of his "responsibilities." After sharing the perception that he believed he was acting as a "strong African man" to his child and that he did not "accept the White man's notion of manhood," he was told by one of the other participants that he, in fact, was living a "hip-hop cliché" and was "the very stereotype of what White men perceive Black men to be." Donte did not accept this feedback and withdrew from the program, maintaining his notion that "men are supposed to make babies and women are supposed to raise them." After some protracted discussions with staff, Donte was persuaded to return to the program (with a different group of men) and to attend some individual counseling sessions. Although progress is slow, he now occasionally sends some money to aid in the support of his daughter. Unfortunately, because of his lack of responsible behavior, the child's mother filed a complaint with the local district attorney and Donte is now in "the system." He has been ordered to pay more in child support than the mother had originally requested, he is in arrears in that child support (for which there is no statute of limitation), and he has been granted limited visitation. His child seems to be thriving in his absence.

Jamal, also, was initially quiet, but seemed quite interested in some of the experiences two of the older participants shared. Soon he was asking questions and seeking direction. He availed himself of the materials and was particularly interested in child development information that he attempted to use with his daughter. Jamal owns an older car, rents a two-bedroom house close to his mother's home, and has recently discussed the possibility of renting the house with an option to buy. He would like to spend more time with his male friends, hanging out, talking, and playing some basketball, but time demands and family commitments take precedence. He now reads to his child daily, takes her to school before heading to work, helps with her homework, and puts her to bed nightly. Jamal also helps with meal preparation, has cut down on television viewing, and has enrolled in two classes at the local community college. His wife also works full time and wants to return to school to improve her chances of providing for their child and the family unit. Jamal and his wife acknowledge myriad problems in their relationship, but verbalize a desire "to work on things."

Jamal reported conversations with his wife are "easier and less stressful" and they seemed to be "making plans to provide for an easier future." Jamal reported his mother, uncle, and grandfather are pleased with his growth, and he thought he could see a way out of a life of poverty. His mood and activities tend to be upbeat, which attracted the attention of a local businessman who indicates a willingness to discuss employment when Jamal completes his education.

Discussion

According to Jeff (1994), "Afrocentricism serves to bind people together and reduces competitive conflict and tensions while building strong character and self-esteem." It can offer "youths positive values . . . [and it] fosters knowledge and human development." This "worldview is holistic, vital, interdependent, and oriented to collective survival" (White & Parham, 1990, as quoted in Ivey, Ivey, & Simek-Morgan, 1993). Sue and Sue (1999) write that African heritage "stresses groupness, community, cooperation and interdependence."

Service programs geared to foster positive change in the African American community, including the development of responsible behavior toward one's children, would do well to incorporate African-centered values as discussed by the cited authors.

Apropos to African American fathers, community service programs must be focused and clear about the objectives, methods, and goals. Although there is the need to be "comprehensive" in scope, it is important to be realistic because resources and abilities are limited. Use referral agencies and programs as necessary and available. Develop a willingness to work together to resolve the issues affecting the community. Do not fall into the trap of attempting to be all things to the population you are trying to service. Rather, know what you can do and do it well.

In closing, I offer four points for consideration when working with African American fathers. First, although the study of and the service delivery to young Black males who are experiencing severe difficulties is important and might offer useful information for remedial activities for them, it is argued that this approach does not suggest meaningful ways to eliminate or improve the overall situation of the African American community. The resources required are simply too great and the energy expended is very taxing on the community. Jamal was likely to become another statistic in the community. He had not demonstrated himself to be an outstanding student or athlete at his high school; he had impregnated his girlfriend; he resided in a single-parent, female-headed household without his father being present; and he had no marketable skills. However, Jamal had the maturity and motivation that allowed him to avail himself of the rewards of the Program. Although suffering numerous problems, his background included a developmental history that involved two strong Black men and a focused single mother. He was able to hear the information made available and accepted responsibility for his youthful behavior. Somehow he understood the commitment he owed his child, her mother, his family, the community, and ultimately himself. He seems to be attempting to make the best of his situation and is trying to turn his life around. Jamal was able to confront the maafa.

Donte, on the other hand, seems lost. Although his mother and father were in his life and they were "educated," there seems to have been little appropriate adult role modeling available to him. Certainly, his father does not represent the best that African American men have to offer. Donte seems confused about what represents adult male behavior. He is immature, self-centered, and self-indulgent. It is unlikely the Program can provide the direction and support he requires until he recognizes there is a problem—and it is he. Although it is important not to give up hope on Donte, it is also important to recognize that appropriate change is unlikely for some time. Unfortunately, usually the "Dontes" receive services at the expense of the "Jamals," and over time, the "Jamals" become the "Dontes." Thus, greater time, energy, resources, and effort are required to effect change in their lives and, in all likelihood, we lose them, too. On the other hand, should Donte desire to make changes in his life, the African-centered model is appropriate. We can view him as "at promise." In therapy, Donte could be seen with his family, on an individual basis, or in a group. The first task is to connect with him, regardless of the counseling setting. Although perhaps misguided and confused, he possesses the potential to more fully and directly participate in his life and in his decisions. He has demonstrated himself to be bright (he has enrolled in some college courses, albeit he fails to complete them). Thus, the therapist could meet with him on campus or at a community event.

In assessing him, it is important to keep in mind that he may be experiencing difficulty with his parents' relationship—in particular, his father's lack of formal commitment to his mother. He may be disappointed, angry, embarrassed, frustrated, or confused. It is unlikely that he has had appropriate positive male role models to demonstrate how adult men and women interact with one another. Donte could be led to explore his feelings and perceptions without "putting down" his father. Or he may desire some satisfaction with some reasonable confrontation with his parents. At any rate, because he has mentioned "strong African men," he should be afforded the opportunity to meet and interact with some.

As Donte's awareness is raised, the African-centered therapist can begin to help him understand his functional behaviors, his defenses, his pain, and his spiritual energy. As he becomes more aware of himself, Donte can be aided in the setting of goals, including the letting go of his misguided perceptions of what Black men are. As balance is restored in his life, he will be able to take action to instigate meaningful change. The therapeutic task is to help Donte to problem solve. There is no need to seek and use a "therapeutic" label, no need to diagnose. In the current context, we simply want Donte to come to grips with his responsibilities to his child, to the mother of his child, to himself, and thus to his community.

Finally, the therapist (and others in the community) will provide ongoing feedback to the congruence between his goals and the outcomes. Assuming Donte is able to successfully resolve his issues, he could be a valuable asset in reaching other young males who are similarly confused.

Second, one can wonder just what can be gleaned from studying negatives in order to develop positives. For the high rate of African American adolescent pregnancy and out-of-marriage births, perhaps we might gather information regarding adolescents and young adults who do not impregnate (or get pregnant) to suggest a direction that improves the overall situation for our community. Perhaps they possess a clear understanding of their African heritage and are simply exhibiting the responsible behavior expected and anticipated of them. Studying young people who are having difficulties can offer direction for developing programs to aid them in the situations they confront, but that may not help much in the eradication of the root problem. What might be done to help them avoid getting into difficulty in the first place? What are young African Americans who are not evidencing these problems doing? Certainly, those experiencing problems cannot and should not be ignored, but perhaps there may be a need to become more socially proactive in problem-solving issues affecting our community.

Third, attempts to understand African American fathers who are involved with their children can suggest directions for programs to aid those men who are not involved. Although it is important and valuable to understand how families mired in deficits might respond to their environments (and to provide services), many African American fathers have been consistently and directly involved with their families over the years. These African American fathers tend to be routinely ignored and treated as though they do not exist. Thus, their stories are neither told nor heard. It is important to consider "involved" fathers' experiences to get a more complete picture regarding circumstances to understand families who reside in a set of different realities. These men seem to understand that an important aspect of being a man is demonstrating consistent love and support of one's children. For them, it is "masculine" to feel comfortable expressing love for their offspring.

Finally, it seems appropriate to end with a word about the importance of counseling for individuals like Donte and Jamal, who represent a population of potential clients typically underserved by the mental health system. First, the Donte's and Jamal's of the world are not likely to seek therapy voluntarily. In fact, many African descent people obtain counseling via direct referral from the courts or the schools. Given this reality, agency heads will need to consider the most appropriate means available for outreach to the Black men in their community and invite them to avail themselves of these services. Second, the implementation of the model described in this chapter requires a degree of collaboration across professional disciplines. Thus, mental health service providers will need to work with colleagues from the fields of health, law, education, criminal justice, and the clergy in order to set up a comprehensive intervention model. Last, the delivery of counseling services in particular will require the presence of clinicians who are both knowledgeable about and skilled in the use of African-centered counseling and therapy interventions. With better outreach, interdisciplinary teams, and culturally competent service providers, the men in communities across this country have a much better opportunity to take full advantage of these valuable services.

9

Raising the Bar for What Passes as Competence

Thomas A. Parham

Undoubtedly, the ability to work effectively with African American populations will require a level of skill and competence that is unusual in our profession. Unusual not simply because there are so few mental health professionals of African descent but also because professional clinicians and counselors, irrespective of ethnicity, are not trained in culturally specific models and techniques. Nobles (personal communication) is indeed correct when he asserts that putting "shoe polish" on Freud will not make the theory any more African centered. Likewise, because clinicians of African descent employ traditional forms of therapy, such does not necessarily constitute Africentric psychology.

Throughout this text, the contributors and I have argued that there exists an African-centered philosophical framework that has import for the treatment of people of African descent. We have also argued that this framework must be built around a core set of assumptions and beliefs about the nature of reality, the makeup of one's personality, the nature of distress, how and why people change, and what role healers and therapists should play in treating African American people. Kambon (1992) reinforces this point by suggesting that African-centered psychological theories must meet certain critical requirements and expectations that are relevant to both historical and contemporary conditions of African people. In laying out these requirements, Kambon suggests that an African-centered approach or model (a) must be Africentric ideologically and philosophically, and must include a biogenetic influence or determinant in the African personality formula; (b) must explain the basic African nature; (c) must explain how European cultural oppression and White supremacy and domination have affected personality functioning; (d) must explain, or at least suggest, how to maintain order or normal functioning in the African personality; and finally, (e) that the model should have explicit liberation implications and consequences for the African mind. Given Kambon's admonition about the development of a truly African-centered model of personality in mental health, this text has sought to remain true to the spirit of those core assumptions. Having now reviewed the text, readers may be asking, "What is it that has kept clinicians and counselors from developing the type of knowledge base represented by the material in this book?" Indeed, it now seems appropriate to explore the notion of how we raise the bar for what passes as competence.

Raising the Bar for What Passes as Competence

Agency heads and psychological practitioners interested in more cultural relevancy have used some very basic standards to confront the need to diversify the profession. When African Americans have been the clients in question, the strategy selected for promoting progress has tended to mirror those of decades past.

Over the years, the cultural sterility in society's institutions was so pronounced that "full integration" became the order of the day. Whether buses, schools, restaurants, or public accommodations, pressure was brought to bear on making these institutions more culturally diverse. Unfortunately, what was proposed as integration was really desegregation, and that became the strategy to achieve equal opportunity, and more recently, diversity progress. The problem here is not simply one of definition but one of belief in possibility. The progress we have sought and have made in the mental health field has been seen as a plateau rather than a process in need of constant innovation. Thus, once we achieve some measure of progress (e.g., desegregate a staff), that act, in and of itself, is oftentimes assumed to be the ultimate goal. Therefore, too many in our profession become satisfied in their efforts and content in their initial outcomes. Unfortunately, many of these strategies represent what we are now calling a "low-bar" approach. A few examples might help to magnify this point.

The Circumference of Our Experience

Some years ago, during the National Convention of the Association of Black Psychologists, we were blessed to hear an invited keynote address by the Honorable Minister Louis Farrakhan, the then and current leader of the Nation of Islam. Among the many profound pieces of wisdom he shared

that day was a statement that said, "He who prescribes the dian
knowledge, (also) prescribes the circumference of your experienc
Essentially, this statement argues for a personal analysis to asce
what ways have our thoughts, beliefs, behaviors, and spirits been harn
or restricted by our adherence to simplistic definitions of progress.
example, the faculty and staff compositions of our academic institution
and mental health centers have historically lacked the diversity necessary to represent a truly integrated workforce. Therefore, efforts were employed to hire staff that reflected the composition of diversity needed. In some cases, institutions and agencies were successful in these efforts and now considered themselves "diversity conscious" and truly integrated. Although these achievements do represent some measure of progress, they nonetheless are indicative of a low-bar approach. We must understand that desegregating a staff is a far cry from true integration. Raising the bar asks how have the policies and practices of academic departments or mental health institutions and agencies changed as a function of the changes in the demographics of the personnel?

Another dimension of our desegregation practices is the degree to which people believe that skin color and competence are synonymous. Many agencies assume that hiring African American clinicians or faculty members necessarily yields an individual who can, in fact, be effective in working with African American clients. Without screening for such things as knowledge and skills, how can agency heads be confident in a clinician's ability to meet a client's needs or, for that matter, a faculty member meeting the true diversity needs of a program? Clearly, more African American clinicians must be hired, but they, like their White counterparts, must meet standards of cultural competence. The circumference of our experience must be expanded to consider these questions.

Another dimension of the "low-bar" approach is the issue of curriculum and training. In recent years, academic programs have become more sensitive to the needs of diversifying the course offerings for graduate and undergraduate students. In response to this need, programs have come to offer a course in "multiculturalism" to students in general. Unfortunately, too many instances of curriculum diversity (desegregation) are limited to a single course over one semester. This is regrettable, indeed, because most of the courses allocate a week or two of a semester for each dimension of diversity represented. Consequently, if one were striving to be competent in understanding the psychological dynamics of African descent people, there would be great difficulty fulfilling that expectation with so little preparation. After all, how can one engage in a minimum of five years of graduate study to become a reasonably competent psychologist, counselor, or other helping professional, and yet learn everything about people of African descent in one or two weeks? The bar of competence is too low, and we must find a way to increase the scope of our experience.

If clinicians embrace the notion of moving beyond desegregation, it begs the question of what a competent clinician should look like, whether or not they are of African descent. How do we raise the bar for what passes as competence? Parham (1999) articulated a set of core competencies for those working with African American clients. His work was able to embrace the framework provided by Sue, Arredondo, and McDavis (1992) as they laid the foundation for multicultural competencies. Competencies are thought of as a set of skills or attributes that allow a counselor or therapist to respond effectively to the demands of a particular situation or circumstance. Developing levels of competency for working with African descent people requires an ability to increase one's awareness about personal biases, assumptions, attitudes, and worldviews; specific knowledge of African people's culture, history, worldview, language, and experiences; and a repertoire of skills that allow one to effectively intervene in personal and social circumstances. This is the essence of the Sue, Arredondo, and McDavis (1992) work. However, Parham extended the utility of that model by providing a level of cultural specificity that was particular to an African-centered ideological framework.

Given the information that has been presented in this text in the previous chapters, these proposed competencies are a way of consolidating that information into manageable categories that professionals and students alike can use as a gauge to assess the degree to which they are in compliance with these standards of practice. In suggesting that these competency guidelines should be "standards of practice" for African descent people, it is important for you, the reader, to remember that unlike the competencies proposed by Sue, Arredondo, and McDavis, these competencies have not undergone review by any professional associations or been embraced by professional organizations. Despite that lack of consensus validation, these competencies do represent a consolidation of the information provided by a host of scholars and practitioners (Akbar, 1984; Franklin, 1975; Kambon, 1992; Myers, 1988; Nobles, 1986; Parham, 1993; Welsing, 1991; White, 1984; White & Parham, 1990) who believe in the correctness and appropriateness in applying standards built on an African-centered philosophical framework.

As you can see from Table 9.1, the competencies are divided into three domains: Awareness, Knowledge, and Skills. In addition, each domain is represented by a set of core competencies that are absolutely essential for any clinician working with African American people. We invite you to examine these characteristics and actively work toward incorporating these into your existing repertoire of skills. Although the process of increasing your competence is certainly an individual responsibility, it does not have to be an endeavor you pursue individually. In fact, it is recommended that professionals and students alike consider taking coursework and receiving supervised clinical and counseling experience within the context of a group setting. In that way, participants learn from the knowledge base and experiences of those who are also involved in that course of study.

Table 9.1 *African American Psychology Proposed Practice Competencies*

Awareness	*Knowledge*	*Skills*
• Therapist must be cognizant of his or her own personal biases and assumptions about African descent people.	• Knowledge of African psychology and history in ancient Kemetic, historical African, and contemporary African American societies.	• The ability to maximize congruence between healing messages and proper conduct.
• Therapist must be aware of how they have been affected by the maafa, (a great disaster of death and destruction beyond human comprehension and convention).	• Knowledge of the central components of an African-centered worldview.	• The ability to connect with, bond with, or otherwise establish rapport with African American clients.
• Therapist must be aware of his or her own role as a healer.	• Knowledge of the principal of *maat.*	• The ability to conduct and participate in rituals.
• Therapist must have access to his or her own cultural memories about the majesty of African life and culture as well as the pain and tragedy of historical and contemporary Black suffering.	• Knowledge of the limitations of traditional European American psychological perspective when applied to African descent people.	• The ability to hear both the surface structure and deep structure messages that clients communicate.
• Therapist must be aware of how people and elements in the universe are interconnected.	• Knowledge of how science has been used as a tool of oppression.	• The ability to administer and interpret culturally appropriate assessment instruments.
• Therapist must have a sense of his or her own essence as spirit and be in touch with his or her own spirituality.	• Knowledge of the limitations of traditional approaches to therapy.	• The ability to advocate on behalf of clients to social service agencies and institutions.
• Therapist must have a relationship with the divine force in the universe.	• Knowledge of the characteristics and dynamics of personality development.	• The ability to use theories and constructs in forming diagnostic impressions.

(Continued)

Table 9.1 *Continued*

Awareness	*Knowledge*	*Skills*
• Therapist must have strong knowledge of himself or herself and provide answers to three critical questions: Who am I? Am I who I say I am? Am I all I ought to be? (Fanon, 1967).	• Dimensions of the soul.	• Ability to help a client set therapeutic goals in the context of an African-centered cultural reality.
• Therapist must have a sense of his or her own ethnic consciousness that is not simply anchored in race (biology), but in the shared struggle and collective heritage of African people.	• Dimensions of African character.	
• Therapist must have a vision for African descent people that embraces the transformative possibilities of the human spirit.	• Models of nigrescense.	
• Therapist must be aware of how to move from possessing intellect to dispensing wisdom.	• Models of African self-consciousness. • Knowledge of assessment instruments that are appropriate for use with African descent adults, youth, and children. • Knowledge of limitations of traditional assessment instruments when used with African Americans. • Knowledge of therapeutic rituals.	

(Continued)

Table 9.1 *Continued*

Awareness	*Knowledge*	*Skills*
	• Knowledge of diagnostic nosologies used to clarify disordered behaviors in African Americans. • Knowledge of ethical principles influencing African descent people. • Knowledge of how traditional ethical standards of some psychological and counseling associations may be culturally inappropriate for African descent people. • Knowledge and geopolitical view of African people and their condition in America and throughout the diaspora. • Knowledge of what racism and White supremacy are and how individual, institutional, and cultural racism impacts the lives of African descent people. • Knowledge of traditional help-seeking behaviors in African Americans. • Knowledge of communities, institutions, and resources that provide both tangible and intangible support to the African American people. • Knowledge of the dynamics of family in the African American community.	

SOURCE: From Parham, T. A. (1999). African centered cultural competencies. In T. A. Parham, J. L. White, & A. Ajamu (Eds.), *The psychology of Blacks: An African centered perspective*. Upper Saddle River, NJ: Prentice Hall. Reprinted with permission.

In developing a larger repertoire of skills, it is important to remember that those skills cannot be limited to the individual domain. Competencies must be applied to the organizational, institutional, and societal levels as well. Healers cannot merely address psychological debilitations in an individual context; they must understand that interplay between people and institutions.

This book began with an assertion that the field of African psychology had taken center stage for cultural diversity initiatives. As contributors to this book, we acknowledged that the level of scholarship and the amount of information now available to assist clinicians in understanding the mental health needs and issues of people of African descent was very extensive. We also cautioned that the road to becoming a more culturally competent therapist and healer was not an easy one and that the task of increasing one's skills could not be completed without extensive study, training, and supervision. By inviting you, the reader, to begin or continue down that road to greater levels of cultural competence for African descent people, it is our hope that the information contained in this text will help to make that journey more rewarding and beneficial.

Appendix

AFRICAN-CENTERED SKILLS ASSESSMENTS

Connecting With Clients

1. Use of Ritual __________________________________
(Identify)

Ritual initiated by client	Ritual mutually discussed	Ritual initiated by therapist

Nonculturally based ritual		Culturally based ritual

2. Creating Ambiance

Few, if any, artifacts, music, artwork		Environment rich with cultural trappings

3. Shifting context and setting

Remain in office/rigidity of function		Interaction and consultation with community/diversity of role

4. Exhibiting Congruent Realness

No personal sharing	Appropriate self-disclosure

Assessment

1.

Focus on pathology	Understanding strengths
Extreme difficulties adjusting to change or misfortune	Capacity for resilience, resourcefulness
Imbalance and disharmony	Balance and harmony
Internal distress causing debilitations	External stress causing debilitations
Use of instruments that are not normed on African American people	Use of instruments normed and standardized on African descent people

Facilitating Awareness
Client

1. Rephrasing Client Communications

Parroted client statements	Restated implied message

2. Focus on Client Strengths

Identified client problems	Identified and mentioned client strengths

3. Creatively Synthesizing Opposites

Maintain imbalance in statements	Restore balance to statements

Therapist

1. Understanding Functional Behaviors (Needs)

2. Understanding Client Value System

Imposing one's values on client	Accepting client values and communicating your understanding of them

3. Respecting Client Need for Distance

Confronted client about distance	Allow distance to remain

Setting Goals

1. Being a Subjective Companion

Remaining an objective outsider	Deliberately influencing client

2. Reframing (Improvise, Transform, Transcend)
   Social Change Within Environment

Encouraged intrapsychic adjustment	Encouraged social change; empowerment
Focus on client only	Engage family and community

3. Respecting a Client's Need for Distance

Confronting language expressed in the third person	Allowing appropriate distance

4. Facilitating a Culturally Corrective Experience

Allowing socialization to remain intact	Help client to purge

5. Restoration of Balance

Energy remains anchored in only one domain of the personality	Helping a client to achieve balance and harmony

Taking Action and Instigating Change

1. Empowering the client through self-knowledge

Little or no self-exploration	Teaching a client about their cultural essence

2. Teaching clients to problem solve

Exploring limited choices; providing client with direction	Exploring full range of choices and options. Inviting client to decide on course of action.

3. Becoming a social advocate and social engineer

Little or no contact with social systems	Contacting specific agencies or departments about policies and practices which negatively impact the client

Feedback and Accountability

1. Examine congruence between goals and outcomes

2. Examine spiritual energy and sense of harmony

3. Remember the notion of being and becoming

References

Ackah, C. A. (1988). *Akan ethics*. Accra: Ghana Universities Press.

Acosta, F. X. (1980). Self-described reasons for premature termination of psychotherapy by Mexican-American, Black-American, and Anglo-American patients. *Psychological Reports, 47,* 435–443.

Adebimpe, V. (1981). Overview: White norms in psychiatric diagnosis of Black parents. *American Journal of Psychiatry, 138*(3), 275–285.

Agyakwa, K. O. (1974). *Akan epistemology and Western thought*. Unpublished doctoral dissertation, Teachers College, Columbia University, New York.

Ajamu, A. (1997). From tef tef to medew nefer: The importance of utilizing African languages, terminologies, and concepts in the rescue, restoration, reconstruction, and reconnection of African ancestral memory. In J. H. Curruthers & L. C. Harris (Eds.), *African world history project.* Los Angeles: Association for the Study of Classical African Civilizations.

Ajei, M., & Grills, C. (2000). Sunsum as conscious energy: A viable scientific postulate. *Psych Discourse, 31*(11), 5–8.

Akbar, N. (1981). Mental disorders among African-Americans. *Black Books Bulletin, 7*(2), 18–25.

Akbar, N. (1984). Africentric social sciences for human liberation. *Journal of Black Studies, 14*(4), 395–414.

Akbar, N. (1994). *Light from ancient Africa.* Tallahassee, FL: Mind Productions.

Akbar, N., Saafir, R., & Granberry, D. (1996). Community psychology and systems intervention. In D. D. Azibo (Ed.), *African psychology in historical perspective and related commentary*. Trenton, NJ: African Third World Press.

Allison, R. W., Crawford, I., Echemendia, R., Robinson, L., & Knepp, D. (1994). Human diversity and professional competence: Training in clinical and counseling psychology revisited. *American Psychologist, 49,* 792–796.

Allport, G. W. (1961). *Patterns and growth in personality*. New York: Holt, Rinehart, Winston.

Ani, M. (1980). *Let the circle be unbroken: The implications of African spirituality in the Diaspora.* New York: Nkonimfo Publications.

Ani, M. (1994). *Yurugu: An African-centered critique of European cultural thought and behavior.* Trenton, NJ: African Third World Press.

Appiah-Kubi, K. (1981). *Man cures, God heals: Religion and medical practice among the Akans of Ghana.* New York: Friendship Press.

Atkinson, D. R. (1983). Ethnic similarity in counseling psychology: A review of research. *The Counseling Psychologist, 22*, 79–92.

Atkinson, D. R. (1985). A meta-review of research on cross-cultural counseling and psychotherapy. *Journal of Multicultural Counseling and Development, 13*, 138–153.

Atkinson, D., Bui, U., & Mori, S. (2001). Multiculturally sensitive empirically supported treatments. In J. G. Ponterotto, J. M. Casas, L. A. Suzuki, & C. M. Alexander (Eds.), *Handbook of multicultural counseling* (2nd ed.). Thousand Oaks, CA: Sage.

Atkinson, D. R., Furlong, N. J., & Poston, W. C. (1986). Afro-American preferences for counselor characteristics. *Journal of Counseling Psychology, 33*, 326–330.

Atkinson, D. R., Morten, G., & Sue, D. W. (1979). *Counseling American minorities: A cross-cultural perspective.* Dubuque, IA: William C. Brown.

Atkinson, D. R., Morten, G., & Sue, D. W. (1989). *Counseling American minorities.* Dubuque, IA: William. C. Brown.

Atkinson, D., & Wampold, B. E. (1993). Mexican American initial preferences for counselor: Simple choice can be misleading. *Journal of Counseling Psychology, 40*(2), 245-248.

Atwell, I., & Azibo, D. A. (1991). Diagnosing personality disorders in Africans using the Azibo Nosology: Two case studies. *Journal of Black Psychology, 17*(2), 1–22.

Axelson, J. A. (1993). *Counseling and development in a multicultural society* (2nd ed.). Pacific Grove, CA: Brooks/Cole.

Ayoade, J.A.A. (1979). The concept of inner essence in Yoruba traditional medicine. *African Therapeutic Systems,* 49–55.

Azibo, D. (1989). *Advances in Black/African personality theory.* Unpublished manuscript.

Azibo, D. A. (1996). *African psychology in historical perspective and related commentary.* Trenton, NJ: African World Press.

Baldwin, J. (1990). *African personality from an Afrocentric framework.* Tallahassee: Florida A&M University Press.

Baldwin, J. A., & Bell, Y. R. (1990). The African Self Counsiousness Scale: An Afrocentric personality questionnaire. In T. Anderson (Ed.), *Black studies: Theory, research, and practice.* Pullman: Washington State University Press.

Banks, G., Berenson, B. G., & Carkhuff, R. R. (1967). The effects of counselor race and training upon counseling process with Negro clients in initial interview. *Journal of Clinical Psychology, 23*, 70–72.

Banks, W. M. (1980). The social context and empirical foundation of research on Black clients. In R. L. Jones (Ed.), *Black psychology.* New York: Harper & Row.

Barret, R. L., & Robinson, B. E. (1982). A descriptive study of teenage expectant fathers. *Family Relations, 31*(3), 349–352.

Barret, R. L., & Robinson, B. E. (1985). The adolescent father. In S. M. H. Hanson & F. W. Bozett (Eds.), *Dimensions of fatherhood* (pp. 353–369). Beverly Hills, CA: Sage.

Barrett, L. E. (1974). *Soul-force: African heritage in Afro-American religion.* Garden City, NY: Anchor.

Bascom, W. (1991). *Ifa divination: Communication between Gods and men in West Africa.* Bloomington: Indiana University Press.

Ben-Jochannan, Y., & Clarke, J. H. (1991). *New dimensions in African history.* Trenton, NJ: African Third World Press.

Bergson, H. (1946). *The creative mind: An introduction to metaphysics.* New York: Philosophical Library.

Biller, H. B. (1971). *Father, child and sex role.* Lexington, MA: D. C. Heath.

Biller, H. B. (1981). The father and sex role development. In M. Lamb (Ed.), *The role of the father in child development.* New York: John Wiley.

Block, C. (1980). Black Americans and the cross-cultural counseling experience. In A. J. Marsella & B. Pederson (Eds.), *Cross cultural counseling and psychotherapy.* New York: Pergamon.

Bohr, N. (1934). *Atomic physics and the description of nature.* Cambridge, UK: Cambridge University Press.

Borishade, A. (2000). Locating and operationalizing spirit biogenetics, and culture in the African psyche and sense of reality. *Psych Discourse, 31*(3–4), 4–11.

Boyd-Franklin, N. (1989). *Black families in therapy.* New York: Guilford.

Bray, J. J., Cragg, P. A., Macknight, A. D. C., & Mills, R. G. (1999). *Human physiology* (4th ed.). Malden, MA: Blackwell Science.

Brislin, R. W. (1981). *Cross-cultural encounters: Face to face interaction.* New York: Pergamon.

Brown, S. V. (1983). The commitment and concerns of Black adolescent parents. *Social Work Research and Abstracts, 19*(4), 27–34.

Bumpass, L. L., Rindfuss, R. R., & Janosik, R. B. (1984). Age and marital status at first births and the pace of subsequent fertility. *Demography, 15*, 75–76.

Busia, K. A. (1954). The Ashanti. In D. Forde (Ed.), *African worlds: Studies in the cosmological ideas and social values of African peoples.* London: Oxford University Press.

Casas, J. M. (1985). A reflection on the status of ethnic minority research. *The Counseling Psychologist, 13*, 581–598.

Cattell, R. (1965). *The scientific analysis of personality.* Baltimore: Penguin.

Cazenave, N. A. (1981). Black men in America: The quest for manhood. In H. P. McAdoo (Ed.), *Black families.* Beverly Hills, CA: Sage.

Chalmers, D. (1996). *The conscious mind: In search of a fundamental theory.* Oxford, UK: Oxford University Press

Chilman, C. (1983). *Adolescent sexuality in a changing American society.* New York: John Wiley.

Cimolic, P., Thompson, R. A., Waid, L. R. (1981). A comparison of Black and White students' preferences for help other than the university counselor. *Journal of College Student Personnel, 22*, 342–348.

Cole, N. (2000, December 20). *The Today Show.* New York: CBS.

Connor, M. E. (1986). Some parenting attitudes of young black fathers. In R. A. Lewis & R. E. Salt (Eds.), *Men in families.* Beverly Hills, CA: Sage.

Connor, M. E. (1987a). Black dads—Here they are! In J. Smollar & T. Ooms (Eds.), *Young unwed fathers: Research review, policy dilemmas and options.* Rockville, MD: Shared Resource.

Connor, M. E. (1987b). *Black male attitudes toward fathering: A follow up report.* Paper presented at the Western Psychological Association Annual Conference, San Francisco, CA.

Connor, M. E. (1988). Teenage fathers. In J. Taylor Gibbs (Ed.), *Young, Black and male in America: An endangered species.* Dover, MA: Auburn House.

Coon, D. (2001). *Introduction to psychology: Gateways to mind and behavior.* Belmont, CA: Wadsworth/Thompson.

Crick, F., & Koch, C. (1994). Why neuroscience may be able to explain consciousness. *Scientific American.*

Cross, W. E. (1971). The Negro to Black conversion experience: Toward the psychology of black liberation. *Black World, 209*, 13–27.

Cross, W. E. (1980). The Cross and Thomas Models of psychological nigrescence. In R. L. Jones (Ed.), *Black psychology* (2nd ed.). New York: Harper Row.

Cross, W. E. (1991). *Shades of Black: Diversity in African American identity.* Philadelphia: Temple University Press.

Cross, W. E. (2001). Encountering nigrescence. In J. G. Ponterotto, J. M. Casas, L. A. Suzuki, & C. M. Alexander (Eds.), *Handbook of multicultural counseling* (2nd ed.). Thousand Oaks, CA: Sage.

Cross, W. E., Parham, T. A., & Helms, J. E. (1998). Nigrescence revisited: Theory and research. In R. L. Jones (Ed.), *African American identity development.* Hampton, VA: Cobb & Henry.

Cross, W. E., & Vandiver, B. J. (2001). Nigrescence theory and management: Introducing the Cross Racial Identity Scale. In J. G. Ponterotto, J. M. Casas, L. A. Suzuki, & C. M. Alexander (Eds.), *Handbook of multicultural counseling* (2nd ed.). Thousand Oaks, CA: Sage.

Danquah, J. B. (1968). *The Akan doctrine of God: A fragment of Gold Coast ethics and religion* (2nd ed.). London: Cass.
Dennett, D. (1996). Facing backward on the problem of consciouness. *Journal of Consciouness Studies*, 3, 4-6.
Dillard, J. M. (1985). *Multicultural counseling: Toward ethnic and cultural relevance in human encounters.* Chicago: Nelson-Hall.
Diop, C. A. (1962). *The cultural unity of Negro Africa: The domains of patriarchy and matriarchy in classical antiquity.* Paris: Presence Africaine.
Diop, C. A. (1974). *The African origin of civilization: Myth or reality.* Westport, CT: Lawrence Hill.
Diop, C. A. (1989). *The cultural unity of black Africa.* London: Karnak House.
Dooyeweerd, H. (1953). *A new critique of theoretical thought.* Amsterdam: H. J. Paris.
Drummond, D. (1996). Tucson II conference proceedings. *Journal of Consciousness Studies, 3*(3).
Dukor, M. (1993, July). African concept of man. *Orunmilism, 2*, 27–34.
Einstein, A. (1960). *Relativity: The special and general theory.* New York: Crown.
Ephirim-Donkor, A. (1997). *African spirituality: On becoming ancestors.* Trenton, NJ: African Third World Press.
Eton, W. W., Regier, D. A., Locke, B. Z., & Taub, C. A. (1981). The NIMH epidemiological catchment area program for the National Institute of Mental Health. *Public Health Reports, 96*, 319–325.
Fairchild, H. (1970). *Dictionary of sociology and related sciences.* Totowa, NJ: Rowan & Allenheld.
Fanon, F. (1967). *Black skin, white masks.* New York: Grove.
Farrakhan, L. (1996, August). Address presented at the National Convention for the Association of Black Psychologists, Chicago, IL.
Feynman, R. P., Leighton, R. B., & Sands, M. (1965). Quantum behavior. In *The Feynman lectures on physics: Vol. 3. Quantum mechanics.* Menlo Park, CA: Addison-Wesley.
Finch, C. S. (1998). *The star of deep beginnings: The genesis of African science and technology.* Atlanta: Khenti.
Fisher, J. (1969). Negroes and Whites and rates of mental illness: Reconsideration of a myth. *Psychiatry, 32*, 428–446.
Fisher, R. B. (1998). *West African religious traditions: Focus on the Akan of Ghana.* New York: Orbis.
Franklin, A. J. (1971). To be young, gifted, and black with inappropriate professional training. *The Counseling Psychologist, 2*(4), 107-112.
French, A. P. (1968). *Special relativity.* New York: W. W. Norton.
Fu-Kiau, K. K. B. (1991). *Self-healing power and therapy: Old teachings from Africa.* New York: Vantage.
Fuller, N. (1969). *Textbook for victims of White supremacy.* Washington, DC: Library of Congress.
Furstenberg, F. F. (1976). *Unplanned parenthood—The social consequences of teenage child bearing.* New York: Free Press.
Gaines, A. (1982). Cultural definitions, behavior, and the person in American psychiatry. In A. J. Marsella & A. White (Eds.), *Cultural conceptions of mental health and therapy.* London: Reidel.
Garrett, J. T., & Garrett, M. W. (1998). The path of good medicine: Understanding and counseling Native Americans. In D. Atkinson, G. Morten, & D. W. Sue (Eds.), *Counseling American minorities.* Dubuque, IA: William C. Brown.
Gbadegesin, S. (1991). *African philosophy: Traditional Yoruba philosophy and contemporary African realities.* New York: P. Lang.
Gibbs, J. T. (1984). Black adolescents and youth: An endangered species. *American Journal of Orthopsychiatry, 54*(1), 6–21.

Glick, P. C. (1981). A demographic picture of black families. In H. P. McAdoo (Ed.), *Black families*. Beverly Hills, CA: Sage.

Gordon, S. (1986). What kids need to know. *Psychology Today*, 22–28.

Griaule, M., & Dieterlen, G. (1986). *The pale fox*. Chino Valley, AZ: The Continuum Foundation.

Grills, C. (1999). *African psychology*. Presentation at the annual meeting of the association of Black psychologists. Charleston, SC. August.

Grills, C. (in press). African psychology. In R. Jones (Ed.), *Black psychology* (4th ed.). Hampton, VA: Cobb & Henry.

Grills, C., & Rowe, D. (1998). African traditional medicine: Implications for African-centered approaches to healing. In R. L. Jones (Ed.), *African American mental health*. Hampton, VA: Cobb & Henry.

Gunnings, T. S., & Simpkin, G. (1972). A systematic approach to counseling disadvantaged youth. *Journal of Non-White Concerns, 1*, 4–8.

Gyekye, K. (1995). *An essay on African philosophical thought: The Akan conceptual scheme* (2nd ed.). Cambridge, UK: Cambridge University Press.

Hall, W. S., Cross, W. E., & Freedle, R. (1972). Stages in the development of Black awareness. In R. L. Jones (Ed.), *Black psychology*. New York: Harper & Row.

Halliday, D., Resnick, R., & Walker, J. (1997). *Fundamentals of physics* (5th ed.). New York: John Wiley.

Harrison, D. K. (1975). Race as a counselor-client variable in counseling and psychotherapy. *Counseling Psychologist, 1*, 124–133.

Helms, J. E., & Carter, R. T. (1990). Development of the White Racial Attitude Inventory. In J. E. Helms (Ed.), *Black and White racial identity: Theory, research, and practice* (pp. 67–80). Westport, CT: Greenwood.

Helms, J. E., & Parham, T. A. (1990). Racial identity attitude scale. In J. E. Helms (Ed.), *Black and White racial identity*. New York: Greenwood.

Hendricks, L. E. (1981). Black unwed adolescent fathers. In L. E. Gary (Ed.), *Black men*. Beverly Hills, CA: Sage.

Hendricks, L. E., & Montgomery, T. (1983). A limited population of unmarried adolescent fathers: A preliminary report of their views on fatherhood and the relationship with mothers of their children. *Adolescence, 18*(69), 201–210.

Hilliard, A. G. (1997). *SBA: The reawakening of the African mind*. Gainesville, FL: Makare Publishing.

Holloway, J. E. (Ed.). (1991). *Africanisms*. Bloomington: Indiana University Press.

Horton, R. (1993). African traditional thought and Western science. In R. R. Grinker and C. B. Steiner (Eds), *Patterns of thought in Africa and the West: Essays on magic, religion, and science* (pp. 327-339). New York: Cambridge University Press.

Hountondji, P. J. (1983). *African philosophy: Myth and reality* (H. Evans, Trans.). Bloomington: Indiana University Press.

Ibrahim, F. A., & Kahn, H. (1987). Assessment of world views. *Psychological Reports, 60*, 163–176.

Idowu, E. (1995). *Olodumare: God in Yoruba belief* (2nd ed.). Plainview, NY: Original Publications.

Irogebu, P. (1995). *Metaphysics: The Kpim of philosophy*. Owerie, Nigeria: International Universities Press.

Ivey, A. (1987). The multicultural practice of therapy: Ethics, empathy, and dialectics. *Journal of Social and Clinical Psychology, 5*, 195–204.

Ivey, A. E., Ivey, M. B., & Simek-Morgan, L. (1993). *Counseling and psychotherapy: A multicultural approach*. Boston: Allyn and Bacon.

Jackson, G. G., & Kirshner, S. A. (1973). Racial self-designation and preferences for a counselor. *Journal of Counseling Psychology, 20*, 560–564.

Jeff, M. F. X. (1994). Afrocentrism and African-American male youths. In R. Mincy (Ed.), *Nurturing young Black males*. Washington, DC: Urban Institute Press.

Jung, C. J. (1916). *The psychology of the unconscious* (B. H. Hinkle, Trans.). New York: Moffat, Yard.

Kamalu, C. (1998). *Person, divinity and nature: A modern view of the person and the cosmos in African thought.* London: Karnak House.

Kambon, K. (1992). *The African personality in America: An African-centered framework.* Tallahassee, FL: Nubian Nation Productions.

Kambon, K. K. K. (1999). *African/Black psychology in the American context: An African-centered approach.* Tallahassee, FL: Nubian Nation Publications.

Kardiner, A., & Ovesey, L. (1951). *The mark of oppression.* New York: Norton.

Karenga, M. (1990). *The book of coming forth by day.* Los Angeles: University of Sankore Press.

Kunjufu, J. (1986). *Countering the conspiracy to destroy Black boys.* (Vol. 3). Chicago: African American Images.

LaFromboise, T. D., & Rowe, W. (1983). Skills training for bicultural competence: Rationale and application. *Journal of Counseling Psychology, 30*, 589–595.

Lamb, M. (1986). *The father's role: Applied perspectives.* New York: Wiley Interscience.

Landrine, H. (1992). Clinical implications of cultural differences: The referential versus the indexical self. *Clinical Psychology Review, 12*, 401–415.

Lee, C. C. (1997). *Multicultural issues in counseling* (2nd ed.). Alexandria, VA: American Counseling Association.

Lee, C. C., & Richardson, B. L. (1991). *Multicultural issues in counseling: New approaches to diversity.* Alexandria, VA: American Association for Counseling & Development.

Lefton, L. A. (1997). *Psychology.* Boston: Allyn & Bacon.

Leong, F. T. L. (1986). Counseling and psychotherapy with Asian-Americans: Review of the literature. *Journal of Counseling Psychology, 33*, 196–206.

Lewis, O. (1968). *The children of Sanchez.* New York: Random House.

Liebow, E. (1967). *Tally's corner.* Boston: Little, Brown.

Lindskoog, D. P. (1998). *The idea of psychology: Reclaiming the discipline's identity.* Washington, DC: Howard University Press.

Little, K. (1963). The Mende in Sierra Leone. In D. Forde (Ed.), *African worlds. Studies in the cosmological ideas and social values of African peoples* (4th ed.). London/New York: Transaction Publishers.

Locke, D. C. (1992). *Increasing multicultural understanding.* Newbury Park, CA: Sage.

Lucas, J. (1996). *The religion of the Yorubas.* Brooklyn, NY: Athelia Henrietta Press.

Lynn, D. B. (1974). *The father: His role in child development.* Monterey, CA: Brooks/Cole.

Malson, C. (1984). *The flip side of black families headed by women: The economic status of black men.* Washington, DC: Center for Social Policy.

Mannix, D. P. (1962). *Black cargoes: A history of the Atlantic slave trade.* New York: Viking.

Marsella, A. J. (1985). Culture, self, and mental disorder. In A. J. Marsella, G. DeVos, & F. L. Hsu (Eds.), *Culture and self: Asian and Western perspectives.* New York: Tavistock.

Marsella A. J., & White, A. (Eds.). (1982). *Cultural conceptions of mental health and therapy.* London: Reidel.

Marsiglio, W., Amato, P., Day, R. D., & Lamb, M. E. (2000). Scholarship on fatherhood in the 1990s and beyond. *Journal of Marriage and the Family, 62*(4), 1173–1191.

Mbiti, J. S. (1990). *African religions and philosophy* (2nd ed.). Oxford, UK: Heinemann Educational.

Mbiti, J. S. (1991). *Introduction to African religion.* Oxford, UK: Heinemann Educational.

McGinn, C. (1991). *The problem of consciouness: Essays toward a resolution.* Cambridge, MA: Blackwell.

McLoyd, V. C., Cauce, A. M., Takeuchi, D., & Wilson, L. (2000). Marital processes and parental socialization in families of color: A decade of review. *Journal of Marriage and the Family 62*(4), 1070–1093.

Melfi, C. A., Croghan T. W., & Hanna, M. P. (1997). Access to treatment for depression in a Medicaid population. *Journal of Health Care for Poor & Underserved, 10*(2), 201–215.

Minkus, H. (1977). Causal theory in Akwapin Akan philosophy. In R. Wright (Ed.), *African philosophy: An introduction*. Washington, DC: University Press of America.

Myers, L. J. (1987). The deep structure of culture: Relevance of traditional African culture in contemporary life. *Journal of Black Studies, 18*(1), 72–85.

Myers, L. J. (1988). *Understanding the Afrocentric worldview: Introduction to an optimal psychology.* Dubuque, IA: Kendall/Hunt.

Nairne, J. S. (2000). *Psychology: The adaptive mind.* Belmont, CA: Wadsworth/Thompson.

Nobles, W. W. (1972). African philosophy: Foundation for a Black psychology. In R. L. Jones (Ed.), *Black psychology.* New York: Harper & Row.

Nobles, W. W. (1980). Extended self: Rethinking the so-called Negro self-concept. In R. L. Jones (Ed.), *Black psychology* (2nd ed.). New York: Harper & Row.

Nobles, W. W. (1986). *African psychology: Toward its reclamation, reascension, and revitalization.* Oakland, CA: Institute for the Advanced Study of Black Family Life and Culture.

Nobles, W. (1994). Healing the rupture and extending the splendor. *Psych Discourse 25*(9), 8–13.

Nobles, W. (1998). To be African or not to be: The question of identity or authenticity—some preliminary thoughts. In R. Jones (Ed.), *African American identity development,* (pp. 185–207). Hampton, VA: Cobb & Henry.

Nobles, W. W., King, L., & James, C. B. (1995). *Health promotion and disease prevention: Strategies in the African American community.* Focus group report submitted to the Congress of National Black Churches. Washington, DC: Association of Black Psychologists.

Noll, J. E. (1991). *Company of prophets.* St. Paul, MN: Llewellyn.

Obenga, T. (1992). *Ancient Egypt and Black Africa: A student's handbook for the study of ancient Egypt in philosophy, linguistics, and gender relations.* Chicago: U.S. Office and Distributors-Front Line.

Obenga, T. (1996). *Icons of maat.* Philadelphia: The Source Editions.

Obenga, T. (1997). Who am I? Interpretation in African historiography. In J. H. Curruthers & L. C. Harris (Eds.), *African world history project.* Los Angeles: Association for the Study of Classical African Civilizations.

Oguah, B. E. (1977). African and Western philosophy: A comparative study. In R. A. Wright (Ed.), *African philosophy: An introduction.* New York: University Press of America.

Ohlsen, M. M. (1983). *Introduction to counseling.* Istasca, IL: F. E. Peacock.

Opoku, K. A. (1978). *West African traditional religion.* Jurong, Singapore: FEP International Private Limited.

Padilla, A. M. (Ed.). (1980). *Acculturation: Theory, models, and some new findings.* Boulder, CO: Westview.

Padilla, A. M., & DeSnyder, N. S. (1985). Counseling Hispanics: Strategies for effective interaction. In P. B. Pedersen (Ed.), *Handbook of cross-cultural counseling and therapy* (pp. 157–164). Westport, CT: Greenwood.

Paniagua, F. A. (1994). *Assessing and treating culturally diverse clients.* Thousand Oaks, CA: Sage.

Paniagua, F. A. (2000). *Diagnosis in a multicultural context: A casebook for mental health professionals.* Thousand Oaks, CA: Sage.

Parham. T. A. (1989). Cycles of psychological nigrescence. *The Counseling Psychologist, 17*(2), 187–226.

Parham, T. A. (1993). *Psychological storms: The African American struggle for identity.* Chicago: African American Images.

Parham, T. A. (1999). African centered cultural competencies. In T. A. Parham, J. L. White, & A. Ajamu (Eds.), *The psychology of Blacks: An African-centered perspective.* Upper Saddle River, NJ: Prentice Hall.

Parham, T. A. (2001, February). *Clinical tools for cultural proficiency: Raising the bar of what passes for competence.* Paper presented at the Winter Roundtable Conference on Cross-Cultural Counseling, Columbia University, New York.

Parham, T. A., & Helms, J. E. (1981). Influences of Black students racial identity attitudes on preferences for counselor race. *Journal of Counseling Psychology, 28*(3), 250–256.

Parham, T. A., & Helms, J. E. (1985). Relation of racial identity to self-actualization and affective states of Black students. *Journal of Counseling Psychology, 32*(3), 431–440.

Parham, T. A., White, J. L., & Ajamu, A. (1999). *The psychology of Blacks: An African-centered perspective.* Upper Saddle River, NJ: Prentice Hall.

Parham, W. D. (2000). The meeting is adjourned: Dismantling the "old boys club" within the American Board of Professional Psychology. *The Diplomate, 20*(2), 18.

Parker, S., & Kleiner, R. J. (1966). *Mental illness in the urban Negro community.* New York: Free Press.

Pedersen, P. (1999). *Multiculturalism as a fourth force.* Philadelphia: Brunner/Mazel.

Peoples, V. Y., & Dell, D. M. (1975). Black and White student preferences for counselor roles. *Journal of Counseling Psychology, 22*, 529–534.

Pinckney, R. (1998). *Blue roots: African American folk magic of the Gullah people.* St. Paul, MN: Llewellyn.

Ponterotto, J. G. (1986). A content analysis of the Journal of Multicultural and Development. *Journal of Multicultural Counseling and Development, 14*, 98–107.

Ponterotto, J. G., Anderson, C. M., & Grieger, I. (1986). Black students attitudes toward counseling as a function of racial identity. *Journal of Multicultural Counseling and Development, 14*, 50–59.

Ponterotto, J. G., Casas, J. M., Suzuki, L. A., & Alexander, C. M. (1995). *Handbook of multicultural counseling.* Thousand Oaks, CA: Sage.

Price, R. (Ed.) (1979). *Maroon societies: Rebel slave communities in the Americas* (2nd ed.). Baltimore: John Hopkins University Press.

Rattray, R. S. (1923). *Ashanti.* Oxford, UK: Clarendon Press.

Redmond, M. A. (1985). Attitudes of adolescent males toward pregnancy and fatherhood. *Family Relations, 34*(3), 337–343.

Robbins, C., Kaplan, H. B., & Martin, S. S. (1985). Antecedents of pregnancy among unmarried adolescents. *Journal of Marriage and the Family, 47*(3), 567–585.

Robinson, B. E., Barret, R. L., & Skeem, T. (1983). Locus of control of unwed adolescent fathers versus adolescent non-fathers. *Perception and Motor Skills, 56*(2), 397–398.

Rosen, H. & Frank, J. D. (1962). Negroes in psychotherapy. *American Journal of Psychiatry, 119*, 456–460.

Rowe, D. (1995). The African psychology institute: A conceptual overview. *Psych Discourse, 26*(6), 15–16.

Ryckman, R. M. (1978). *Theories of personality.* New York: Van Nostrand.

Sanchez-Hucles, J. (2000). *The first sessions with African Americans.* San Francisco: Jossey-Bass.

Scanzoni, J. H. (1971). *The Black family in modern society.* Boston: Allyn and Bacon.

Schulz, D. A. (1969). Coming up Black. Englewood Cliffs, NJ: Prentice Hall.

Schwaller de Lubicz, R. A. (1998). *The temple of man: Apet of the south at Luxor.* Rochester, VT: Inner Traditions International.

Scott, A. (1995). *Stairway to the mind: The controversial new science of consciousness.* New York: Copernicus Books.

Skinner, B. F. (1974). *About behaviorism.* New York: Knopf.

Sklar, M. H. (1986). Employment and training for unwed fathers: An unmet and unrecognized need. Paper presented at Young Unwed Fatherhood Symposium, Washington, DC.

Smith, T. H. (1994). *Conjuring culture.* New York: Oxford University Press.

Snowden, L. (1999). African-American folks idiom. *Cultural Diversity and Ethnic Minority Psychology, 5*(4), 364–370.

St. Clair, H. R. (1951). Psychiatric interview experiences with Negroes. *American Journal of Psychiatry, 108,* 113–119.

Stark, E. (1986, October). Young, innocent and pregnant. *Psychology Today, 20,* 28–35.

Sue, D. W. (1981). *Counseling the culturally different: Theory and practice.* New York: John Wiley.

Sue, D. W., Arredondo, P., & McDavis, R. (1992). Multicultural counseling competencies and standards: A call to the profession. *Journal of Counseling and Development, 70,* 477–486.

Sue, D. W., & Sue, D. (1999). *Counseling the culturally different* (3rd ed.). New York: John Wiley.

Sue, D. W., Ivey, A., & Pedersen, P. B. (1996). *A theory of multicultural counseling and therapy.* Pacific Grove, CA: Brooks/Cole.

Sue, F. & Zane, N. (1987). The role of culture and cultural techniques in psychotherapy: A reformation. *American Psychologists, 42,* 37–45.

Sue, S. (1988). Psychotherapeutic services for ethnic minorities: Two decades of research findings. *American Psychologist, 43,* 301–308.

Sue, S., McKinney, H., Allen, D., & Hall, J. (1974). Delivery of community mental health services to Black and White clients. *Journal of Consulting and Clinical Psychology, 42,* 794-801.

Sullivan M. L. (1986). *Ethnographic research on young fathers and parenting.* New York: Vera Institute.

Sundermeier, T. (1998). *The individual and community in African traditional religions.* Piscataway, NJ: Transaction Publishers.

Taylor, J. V. (1963). *The primal vision: Christian presence amid African religion.* London: SCM Press.

Thomas, A. & Sillen, S. (1972). *Racism in psychiatry.* Secaucus, NJ: Citadel Press.

Thomas, C. (1971). *Boys no more.* Beverly Hills, CA: Glencoe.

Thompson, R. E. (1983). *Flash of the spirit.* New York: Vintage.

Trimble, J. E. (1990). Application of psychological knowledge for American Indians and Alaska natives. *Journal of Training and Practice in Professional Psychology, 4*(1), 45-63.

Turner, C. B., & Kramer, B. M. (1995). Connections between racism and mental health. In C. V. Willie, P. P. Rieker, B. M. Kramer, & B. S. Brown (Eds.), *Mental health, racism, and sexism.* Pittsburgh, PA: University of Pittsburgh Press.

Twumasi, P. A. (1975). Medical systems in Ghana: A study in medical sociology. Accra, Ghana: Ghana Publishing Corporation.

U.S. Department of Health and Human Services. (2001). *Mental health: A report of the Surgeon General* (Ch. 2). Rockville, MD: Author.

Utsey, S. O., Bolden, M. A., & Brown, A. L. (2001). A psychology of liberation for counseling African Americans confronting societal racism and oppression. In J. G. Ponterotto, J. M. Casas, L. A. Suzuki, & C. M. Alexander (Eds.), *Handbook of multicultural counseling* (2nd ed.). Thousand Oaks, CA: Sage.

Vontress, C. (1971). Racial differences: Impediments to rapport. *Journal of Counseling Psychology, 18,* 7–12.

Webster, D., & Fretz, B. R. (1978). Asian American, Black, and White college students' preferences for help-giving sources. *Journal of Counseling Psychology, 25*(2), 124–130.

Webster's ninth new collegiate dictionary. (1990). Springfield, MA: Merriam-Webster Publishers.

Welsing, F. C. (1991). *The Isis papers: The keys to the colors.* Chicago: Third World Press.

West, C. (1996, August). *Spirituality in Black psychology.* Paper presented at the annual meeting of the Association of Black Psychologists, Chicago, IL.

Westwood, M. J., & Ishyman, F. I. (1990). The communication process as a critical intervention for client change in cross cultural counseling. *Journal of Multicultural Counseling and Development, 18,* 163–171.

White, J. L. (1972). Toward a Black psychology. In R. L. Jones (Ed.), *Black psychology.* New York: Harper & Row.

White, J. L. (1984). *The psychology of Blacks.* New York: Prentice Hall.

White, J. L., & Parham, T. A. (1990). *The psychology of Blacks: An African-American perspective.* Upper Saddle River, NJ: Prentice Hall.

White, M. (1998). *Eternal dance: A musical anthology of Earth, wind, and fire.* Legacy Records.

Williams, R. (1972). Abuses and misuses of testing black children. In R. L. Jones (Ed.), *Black psychology.* New York: Harper & Row.

Williams, R. L. and Mitchell, H. (1980). The testing game. In R. L. Jones (Ed.), *Black psychology* (2nd ed.). New York: Harper & Row.

Wiredu, K. (1980). *Philosophy and an African culture.* Cambridge, MA: Cambridge University Press.

Wobogo, V. (1976). Diop's two cradle theory and the origin of white racism. *Black Books Bulletin, 4*(4), 20–29.

Wrenn, C. G. (1962). The culturally encapsulated counselor. *Harvard Educational Review, 32*(4), 444–449.

Wrenn, C. G. (1985). Afterword: The culturally encapsulated counselor revisited. In P. B. Pedersen (Ed.), *Handbook of cross-cultural counseling and therapy.* Westport, CT: Greenwood.

Wright, B. (1975). *The psychopathic racial personality.* Chicago: Institute of Positive Education.

Yang, K. S. (1997). Indigenising westernized Chinese psychology. In M. H. Bond (Ed.), *Working at the interface of cultures: Eighteen lies in social service* (pp. 62–76). New York: Routledge.

Zhang, A., & Snowden, L. (1999). Ethnic characteristics of mental disorders. *Cultural Diversity and Ethnic Minority Psychology, 5*(2), 134–146.

Index

About the Editor

Thomas A Parham, Ph.D., is Assistant Vice Chancellor for Counseling and Health Services and Director of the Counseling Center, as well as an adjunct faculty member at the University of California, Irvine. He is Past President of the National Association of Black Psychologists and of the Association for Multicultural Counseling and Development (a division of ACA). A current member of the American Counseling Association and the American Psychological Association, he is also a member of the Orange County Chapter of the 100 Black Men, where he has served as Chair of the Education Committee. He is the architect of the "Rites of Passage" program for the 100's "Passport to the Future" program and for the Los Angeles-based "College Bound" program.

For the past 20 years, Parham has focused his research efforts in the area of psychological nigrescence and has authored many articles in this area. Research in the area of racial identity development remains his primary focus. He is coauthor of the 2nd and 3rd editions of *The Psychology of Blacks: An African-Centered Perspective* and the author of *Psychological Storms: The African American Struggle for Identity*.

Among his many honors and awards are his selection as an American Psychological Association Minority Fellow in 1979 through 1982; the 1988 Research/Scholarship Award from the National Association of Black Psychologists; the 1989 Research Achievement Award from the American Psychological Association's Minority Fellowship Program; election to Fellow of Division 17 (Counseling Psychology) and Division 45 (Society for Psychological Study of Ethnic Minority Issues) of the American Psychological Association; and his election to Distinguished Psychologist by the Association of Black Psychologists in 1998.

About the Authors

Martin Ajei, MA, currently serves as Lecturer in the University of Ghana Philosophy Department. He received his master's degree in philosophy from the University of Ghana, Accra. His publications and research emphases includes the philosophy of consciousness, the Akan concept of self, communitarian social theory, Akan theories of knowledge, and the role of traditional cultural values and ethics in directing contemporary Ghanaian social, economic, and political development (the subject of his three most recent publications).

Michael Connor, PhD, is Professor of Psychology at California State University, Long Beach, and a licensed Clinical Psychologist who specializes in children and their families. His work with children in the early 1970s led to an interest in parents and parenting issues, particularly fathers. In 1975, he developed and commenced teaching a university-level course specifically focusing on fathers and fathering. In addition, he offers workshops and training sessions for fathers across the life span and from various socioeconomic circumstances. His primary objective is to develop, to enhance, and to improve relationships between fathers and their children. In 1994, he wrote a "best practices" model for the State of California, the "Role of Men Program," which attempts to improve birth outcomes and subsequent bonding through the inclusion of fathers from pregnancy through the first year of the child's life.

Cheryl Grills, PhD, Professor of Psychology and Coordinator of the American Cultures Program at Loyola Marymount University, is a graduate of Yale University and UCLA. She is CEO of the Imoyase Group, Inc., a community based, multiethnic research and program evaluation organization. Her research interests, publications, and current projects include developing and testing an African-centered model of treatment engagement with African American substance abusers, research on traditional medicine in West Africa, African concepts of consciousness and models of the self, and program evaluation with community based organizations engaged in social action, community change, and prevention. She is a licensed psychologist in California, and consults nationally on a number of prevention and treatment issues particularly regarding matters of cultural and social competence, multiculturalism, and Africentric interventions.

Ezemenari Obasi, BS, is the son of Joy, who is the daughter of Arveal, who is the daughter of Arveal, who is the daughter of Elizabeth, who is the daughter of an enslaved African from the Bretuo abusua of Ghana. He received a bachelor's degree in physics at the University of California, Irvine, and is a doctoral student at Ohio State University in counseling psychology.

William D. Parham, PhD, ABPP, is Associate Director of Clinical and COPE Services at the Student Psychological Services office at UCLA, where he also serves as the chief psychologist for the Department of Intercollegiate Athletics. He also maintains a part-time psychological and consultation practice in which he provides sport and performance consultation services to athletes, coaches, trainers, and administrators at the collegiate, amateur, professional, and Olympic levels. He has worked with performance artists in drama, theatre, and music.

Parham also consults with Children's Hospital of Orange County in the Department of Health Psychology, where he participates as a member of the diabetes treatment team. In that capacity, he started and continues to offer a support group specifically targeting parents of newly diagnosed type I diabetic children. He was awarded the Diplomate in Counseling Psychology from the American Board of Professional Psychology. He is an active member of several professional and civic organizations, holding leadership positions and serving on various committees and task forces. A Fellow of the Academy of Counseling and immediate Past President of the American Board of Counseling Psychology, his other past and current professional activities include member, Examination Committee, the Association of State Provincial Psychology Boards; Oral Examination Commissioner and Case Reviewer, Board of Psychology, State of California; Board Member, Pediatric Adolescent, Diabetes, Research and Education Foundation, affiliation with Children's Hospital of Orange County; consultant, listed in the Sport Psychology Registry of the United States Olympic Committee; sport psychologist for the United States women's volleyball team during the 1996 Olympics; and currently consulting with the United States Figure Skating Association.